The Consumer's Book
of
Hints and Tips

Richard Trubo

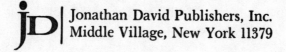 Jonathan David Publishers, Inc.
Middle Village, New York 11379

To my mother
—a very enlightened
and informed consumer

———◆··◆———

**The Consumer's Book
of
Hints and Tips**

Copyright © 1978
by
Richard Trubo

No part of this book may be reproduced in any manner
without the written permission of the publisher. Address all
inquiries to:

Jonathan David Publishers, Inc.
68-22 Eliot Avenue
Middle Village, New York 11379

Library of Congress Cataloging in Publication Data

Trubo, Richard.
The consumer book of hints and tips.

Bibliography: p.
Includes index.
1. Finance, Personal. 2. Consumer education.
I. Title.
HG179.T78   332'.024   76-26125
ISBN 0-8246-0212-9

Printed in the United States of America

Table of Contents

Preface

Introduction: Preparing a Budget...................... 1

Chapter One: Food..................................... 10

Chapter Two: Health Care............................. 30

Chapter Three: Clothing.............................. 48

Chapter Four: Housing................................ 63

Chapter Five: Furnishings and Appliances............. 90

Chapter Six: Household Economics.....................:113

Chapter Seven: Automobiles...........................131

Chapter Eight: Banking and Investing 154

Chapter Nine: Credit and Loans......................180

Chapter Ten: Insurance..............................199

Chapter Eleven: Taxes...............................227

Chapter Twelve: Legal Matters 249

Chapter Thirteen: Travel and Recreation for less Expense. 269

Chapter Fourteen: Retirement 291

Appendices......................... 307

Index 311

Preface

More than 300 years ago the poet George Herbert wrote: "The buyer needs a hundred eyes, the seller not one." Herbert's words are still valid. Although the consumer now has a louder and more influential *voice*, he or she is more often than not still blind.

The marketplace is in some ways as hazardous as it was before Ralph Nader first took on the corporate lions. The consumer continues to be the victim of deception and fraud, and although the average person doesn't always know how to combat it, he has, at least, become aware of the predicament.

The consumer's plight lately has become increasingly aggravated by the spiraling inflation that has sent retail prices skyward. The shopper has to contend with all kinds of rip-offs, and fish for a bargain in a sea of exorbitant prices.

But there remains hope, at least for the enlightened consumer. Inflation can be fought and unscrupulous dealings can be challenged—and the average consumer's greatest weapon is his own awareness.

The Consumer's Book of Hints and Tips is intended to increase the reader's awareness by equipping him with a vast array of information that will allow him to become a shrewd and careful consumer. It is filled with money-saving tips on buying the necessities and the luxuries—food, health care, clothing, furniture, appliances, automobiles, and leisure accessories. There are also tips on how to bank, budget, invest, insure, and cope with repairmen and attorneys. In short, the book will help anyone get more for his money without falling prey to fraud or deception.

The hints and tips will be presented in a very uncomplicated, easy-to-read manner. The main purpose of this book is to motivate—to motivate the consumer to protect his interests and to awaken his friends and neighbors to the realities of the consumer's world.

INTRODUCTION

Preparing a Budget

The mere word "budget" repels many people, because it suggests scrimping and penny-pinching. However, budgeting does not mean unreasonable thrift; it is actually nothing more than a plan for sensible spending, a systematic way of using funds to the best advantage.

Of course, some consumers have no need for a budget. They are able to handle their day-to-day finances quite efficiently. Their expenses never seem to exceed their income, their bills are always paid on time, and they even have money to spare.

Unfortunately, these people are exceptions. Most of us need help in stretching our incomes as far as possible. And although a budget can't magically make every dollar turn into two, it can show us where our money is being spent and the areas in which those expenditures can be reduced.

Budget-making need not be an overwhelming chore. True, it is time-consuming, but when one considers that one earns between $350,000 and $1 million in one's lifetime, it may be helpful to know that a system has been devised to ensure that this money is spent wisely. Most consumers find that once they become accustomed to working with a budget, it becomes an indispensible planning tool. Money management becomes a habit—and a good one.

DETERMINING ASSETS AND LIABILITIES

Overall Financial Standing

The first step in planning a family budget is to analyze the family's financial situation. Examining the family's assets and liabilities will give a clear impression of both net worth and obligations. When listing personal assets, include: cash in checking and savings accounts, the current market value of all stocks and bonds, the cash value of life insurance policies and pension plans, money loaned to others, the market value of all real estate, the trade-in value of any automobiles, and the market value of all home furnishings (furniture, appliances) and possessions (clothing, jewelry, sports, hobby equipment). Personal

1

liabilities will include items like the home mortgage, money still owed on cars, and other unpaid debts and bills.

Here is one family's comparison of its assets and liabilities:

ASSETS

House	$38,500
China, crystal, antiques, household goods	6,900
Savings	5,134
Automobiles	5,925
Cash value of life insurance	1,114
51 shares of stock	920
Total assets	$58,493

LIABILITIES

Mortgage	$28,000
Balance due on car	1,240
Credit card debts	717
Total liabilities	$29,957
NET WORTH	$28,536

DEFINING GOALS

Long-Term and Short-Term

To plan a budget properly, goals must be clearly defined. On a large piece of paper, write down the goals you have set for yourself and family. Determine short-term and long-term aims—purchasing a new car next year, paying for a new automatic washing machine in two years, buying a home in five years, financing a child's college education in 15 years, retiring in 30 years. Then estimate as realistically as possible the cost of meeting these goals and the amount of money that will have to be set aside.

Spacing Out Purchases

Try to space out anticipated big purchases. For example, if you plan on buying your son a motorcycle this year, your daughter may have to wait until next year for the stereo she so desperately wants. Large expenses can't all be handled at once.

Flexibility

When planning long-range goals, remain flexible. Make allowances for changes in income, size of family, and other events that are often difficult to foresee. Review the goals at least once a year. What has been accomplished over the past year? Do any changes in direction need to be made?

Regular Savings

Meeting long-range goals requires a great deal of discipline. Get into the habit of regularly placing predetermined amounts of money into a savings account. Cash for a down payment on a dream house or for a child's college education will not be available unless a savings program has been established. Deposit something into that savings account every week, even if only $5 or $10. As the family becomes more proficient at reducing weekly expenditures, increase the amount of the savings deposits.

Make yourself a chart to help you plan for your long-range goals:

Goal	Cost	Target date	Years to Save	Amount to Save Each: Year	Month
New car	$6,000	8/1/1980	1977, 1978 1979, part 1980	$1,710	$142
Hawaiian vacation	$900	7/1/1979	1977, 1978 part 1979	$360	$30
Movie camera	$225	12/25/1978	1977, 1978	$117	$9

ESTIMATING INCOME

Income Sources

The next step in preparing a budget is to estimate the family's spendable income for the forthcoming year—including take-home salaries, bonuses, tips, savings account interest, stock dividends, gifts, and money from all other sources. If yearly income varies—that is, if you're a salesman who earns a different amount of money each year—determine the minimum yearly earnings and work with that figure. Basing expenditures on a figure that is too high could lead to disaster. As the year progresses, if the family income is greater than anticipated, adjust the budget accordingly:

Income Sources	Amount
Wages	
Husband	
Wife	
Interest	
Dividends	
Gifts	
Other	
TOTAL	

Salary Increases

Salary increases often seem greater than they really are; we sometimes forget how much will be deducted in taxes. Once it has been determined what the salary increase will amount to *after taxes,* figure that into the budget. These extra funds should be spent as thoughtfully as the rest of the income.

COMPUTING LIVING EXPENSES

Fixed Expenses

Next, compute the family's fixed living expenses—including the cost of housing, automobile payments and maintenance, insurance, taxes, union dues, repayment of loans, and utilities. Some of these figures may be difficult to calculate so be willing to informally chart expenses for a few weeks. Review old checkbook records and credit card receipts to see what expenses were in past months and years.

MONTHLY FIXED EXPENSES

Rent/Mortgage Payment
Gas & Electricity
Fuel & Water
Telephone
Life Insurance
Fire/Theft Insurance
Health Insurance
Installment debt
Taxes not
   already deducted
Union, Club dues
Transportation to
   work, school
Other

                                    TOTAL

Everyday Expenses

Estimate the family's everyday expenses for food, health care, clothing, furniture, gifts, entertainment, recreation, vacations, charitable donations, miscellaneous expenditures (haircuts, family allowances, newspapers, etc.). Keep track of these figures for several weeks to come up with a reasonable estimate of what the expenses will most likely be for the entire year.

FLEXIBLE EXPENSES

	Week 1	Week 2	Week 3	Week 4	Monthly Total
Food					
Household supplies					
Toilet articles					
Clothing					
Laundry, dry cleaning					
Newspapers, magazines, books					
Car maintenance					
Entertainment					
Transportation					
Recreation					
Gifts					
Donations					
Other					
TOTAL					

Unpaid Bills

Make a separate list of all unpaid bills. These might include loans from friends or finance companies, plus department store debts. Make provisions in the budget to pay them off as soon as the money becomes available.

Emergency Funds

A practical budget will allow for emergencies. Aside from death and taxes, about the only certainty these days is the inevitability of unplanned events. There's no way to predict when it might be necessary to make a long-distance trip because of a family illness, or when the family income might be temporarily halted.

TYPICAL SPENDING PATTERNS

A Typical Spending Plan

There are no rigid rules to follow in deciding how much income to spend on particular items. After all, each family has its own unique needs and aspirations. It is interesting nevertheless to see how a well-planned budget might work. The United States Bureau of Labor Statistics has provided the following information on how a typical American family of four spends its annual income of $15,675. How do your family's expenses compare?

	Annual cost	Percent of budget
Housing (including furnishings, utilities)	$3,919	25.0
Food	3,057	19.5
Income taxes	2,743	17.5
Clothing and personal care	1,646	10.5
Transportation	1,254	8.0
Medical care (including insurance)	627	4.0
Other	2,429	15.5
TOTAL BUDGET	$15,675	100%

ANALYZING THE RESULTS

Expenses vs. Income

Ideally, a family's expenses should be at least slightly less than its income. This will allow for saving some money after all bills have been paid.

Reducing Expenses

If family expenditures consistently exceed family income, make a hard evaluation of where cuts can be made. Can a few dollars a week be saved by shopping more carefully in the supermarket? Can money be saved by bringing lunches from home rather than eating out? Can a little less be spent on new clothes? Are there any smokers in the family who might, by ridding themselves of the habit, reduce expenses by more than $500 a year?

Priorities

If funds are insufficient to buy everything you'd like in a short time, decide on some realistic priorities. If buying a house is extremely important, consider cutting back on vacation plans. If purchasing new living room furniture is necessary, then go to the movies less frequently. When setting up priorities, make them reasonable—that is, don't assume that dining out, and other such pleasures, can be eliminated.

Analyzing Debts

If the family's anticipated expenses include paying many past-due bills, analyze the reasons for having accumulated these debts. Have too many credit purchases of luxury items been made? If so, refrain from buying on credit until all debts are paid.

Unnecessary Purchases

Many families spend money on unneeded items in order to create an "image" for their neighbors. The result is money down the drain. That gas-guzzling Lincoln really isn't necessary when a Mercury Monarch can transport the family from place to place just as well. The expensive living room furniture that seems enticing is probably no more comfortable than reasonably-priced furnishings. In short, make sure that the family lives within its means.

Impulse Buying

One way to make cutbacks in expenditures is to reduce or eliminate impulse buying. Each time your teenage son is in the vicinity of a record store, is it really necessary that he buy an album? Can you learn how to trim your children's hair so as to reduce or eliminate the money spent on barbering? Always plan purchases carefully and try not to deviate without thinking about it.

Utilizing Talents

Cut back further on day-to-day expenses by capitalizing on family talents—whether it be making clothes, growing vegetables, or refinishing furniture. Also, take advantage of the many recreational activities that are available at no cost, such as free concerts, free museums, and camping.

Trimming from the Bottom

One technique for reducing expenses is to take a stack of blank 3x5 cards, and list each planned annual expense on a separate card. Be as specific as possible. For those items that are not absolute necessities, include a cheaper alternative. For instance:

Eating out once a week
Cost: $730 a year

Way of trimming expense:
eat out every other week

On another stack of cards, list those expenses that it would be desirable to include this year—a new wardrobe of clothes, a trip to the mountains, etc.—and estimate the dollar amount of each. Then take all the cards, and place them in order of priority, with those expenses most essential at the top of the pile. After that, add up the costs on all the cards. If they total $21,500, and your annual income is $19,000, then begin throwing out the cards at the bottom until $2,500 of expenses have been removed. Or adjust your expenses by selecting some of the cheaper options on each card—like dining out only half as much, or doing some car repairs at home rather than hiring a mechanic to do them all.

CHARTING EXPENSES

Daily Expenditures

Until family spending habits are under control, chart daily expenditures. Buy a looseleaf notebook, and use a separate page for each budget category (food, transportation, clothing, etc.). At the top of each page, write the amount of money that you think should be spent on that category during the month. As the month progresses, keep track of *actual* expenses (not necessarily to the exact penny, but relatively close estimates). If month after month, more money is spent than had originally been appropriated for that category, either adjust the allocation there, or find ways to cut back expenses.

FOOD
January 1978
Anticipated Expense $_____

Actual Costs:

Date   Expense

Keeping Track

When keeping a record of expenditures, jot them down as they occur; do not wait until the end of the day or week to enter them into the looseleaf notebook. Saving up all entries for late in the day makes budgeting more of a chore than it needs to be. Keep a small pad in pocket or purse or scribble down the approximate amount of purchases as they are made. It will only take a few minutes to transfer them to the looseleaf notebook.

Developing Patterns

For at least a few months, keep this running record of family spending. Patterns will soon become apparent, as will areas of potential cutbacks.

INVOLVING THE ENTIRE FAMILY

Expanding Experiences

Every family member should get some experience in all aspects of family buying. The teenage kids should do the grocery shopping once in a while—after the shopping list has been prepared—so they realize the cost of filling up a couple of bags of groceries. Everyone should participate now and then in the bill-paying and check-writing sessions to become aware of how quickly a healthy checking account balance can be depleted. Once the entire family recognizes the difficulty of making ends meet, there will be increased understanding and fewer quarrels about money.

CHAPTER ONE

Food

The average American consumes about $100,000 worth of food in his or her lifetime. That's a large figure, particularly considering that the Department of Agriculture estimates that 20 percent of us have diets that can be considered no better than poor.

We spend a lot of money on food, but a high percentage of that money goes to buy food lacking in nutritional value. Americans are consuming 21 percent fewer dairy products, 23 percent fewer vegetables, and 25 percent fewer fruits than before World War II. By contrast, 300 percent more soft drinks are being devoured, and 70 percent more desserts.

Healthy foods are, of course, available in abundance. But when most shoppers go to the market to spend part of their $3,500-a-year family food budget, they fail to consider food value.

How does one spend his food dollar wisely? It certainly isn't easy to be a disciplined shopper. Most supermarkets stock between 8,000 and 10,000 items, and they try to encourage the consumer to purchase products he had no intention of ever buying.

Packaging, of course, is one of the big persuaders in the supermarket today. For every $20 spent on food itself, another $2 is spent on packaging. For some items, in fact, the package actually costs as much as the food inside! People easily swayed by attractive designs or catchy phrases are pushovers for many of the clever packages on the market shelves.

There is another unusual phenomenon occurring in the contemporary grocery store. When some people see two products that are actually identical in quality, they often buy the more expensive of the two, using the erroneous premise that higher price means better quality. These people simply can't accept the fact that cheaper food can be as nutritious as the more expensive variety—that margarine is as nourishing as butter, or that grade B eggs are as nourishing as grades A or AA.

Baby food is an industry all its own. It comprises a $450 million a year enterprise, with more than 400 varieties of products on the shelves. Frankly, not all of them are good for babies. Too many of them contain excess salt, sugar, and food starch.

To eat well, some families have turned to home gardening and canning. Launching a vegetable garden takes time and perseverance, but an estimated six million Americans took to the outdoors in 1976 to grow their own food.

It's certain that food prices will continue to rise overall in the coming years. The world demand for food is increasing, and the cost of producing food is growing because of stricter standards in food inspection, the use of additives, and improved labeling. However, it is still possible to keep a food budget within reasonable limits, despite the continuing inflation.

PRE-MARKETING STRATEGY

Preparing a List

The wise consumer will always prepare a list before embarking on a shopping trip. The list should take into account the family's food needs and wants, as well as the size of the budget. Use the supermarket ads as a guide for the list, building menus for the week around sale items.

The Average Shopper

The average American shopper spends $6.06 out of every $20 at the supermarket for non-food items—like beer, candy, soft drinks, and paper goods. The wise consumer should channel as much of his *food* dollar as possible into food.

Here's how the typical shopper spends a $20 bill at the supermarket, according to the United States Department of Agriculture:

FOOD

Fresh meat, provisions	$3.81
Produce	2.17
Dairy products	1.28
Baked goods, snacks	1.18
Coffee, tea	.53
Fresh poultry	.50
Canned vegetables	.30
Cereals, rice	.25
Canned meat, poultry	.22
Dried fruits, vegetables, milk	.22
Canned fruits	.19
Canned juices	.19
Sugar	.16
Fresh fish	.14
Canned seafood	.14
Canned soups	.13

(continued)

FOOD *(continued)*

Baby foods (including cereals) .... .08
Macaroni, spaghetti, noodles...................... .08
Jams, jellies, preserves .... .07
Canned milk...................................... .05
Puddings .... .04
All other edibles 1.17

TOTAL $13.94

NON-FOOD

Beer... $ .93
Tobacco products................................ .80
Health, beauty aids (non-Rx) .... .77
Soaps, laundry detergents......................... .45
Soft drinks...................................... .44
Paper goods...................................... .33
Pet foods .... .26
Candy .... .21
Housewares .... .19
Wine, distilled spirits .... .14
Prescriptions.................................... .07
Other household products .... .47
Other non-classified merchandise................ 1.00

TOTAL $6.06

Impulse Buying

The shopping list helps eliminate impulse buying, which is most often wasteful buying. One study has shown that impulse buying increases food bills as much as 67 percent. Children are responsible for a considerable amount of impulse buying. So whenever possible, avoid bringing them along on shopping trips.

Because supermarkets are arranged to encourage the consumer to buy more than he had planned, shopping lists are sometimes difficult to adhere to. Impulse buying is particularly common during a long wait at the checkout line. The products displayed near the cash register are intentionally tempting. But if they are faithful to a shopping list, consumers will save money by not buying unneeded items.

Hungry Shoppers

Never shop for food on an empty stomach. Psychologists testify that hungry shoppers buy more. So shop after breakfast or lunch, or when a snack has removed hunger pangs.

Shop Quickly!

Shop as quickly as possible. Studies indicate that 50 cents is spent for every minute in a store after the first half-hour.

Checkout Errors

As the cashier totals up the grocery bill, watch carefully to see that the proper prices are being rung up. Mistakes are made more frequently than most consumers realize. If an error is made, call it to the attention of the cashier immediately.

Frozen Goods

When the groceries are being bagged, ask that all frozen foods be placed in insulated packages to avoid spoilage. If the boxboy won't do it for you, do it yourself.

WHERE TO SHOP

Compare Prices

Compare the prices at various neighborhood markets. Some stores sell products for substantially less than others. The Office of Consumer Affairs in New Orleans recently checked the prices of 55 popular items at 71 different markets in the city. It found that the 55 items cost $25.88 in the least expensive store, and $33.81 in the most expensive—a difference of nearly 31 percent. So a family spending $3,000 a year on food might save about $900 by shopping regularly in the cheapest rather than the costliest market.

Specialty Shops

All food shopping need not be restricted to supermarkets. Milk, eggs, and butter, for example, are often obtainable more cheaply from a dairy. Even if prices are identical, quality may be better in specialty stores. You may wish to shop in bakeries or candy shops for a similar reason—quality.

Butcher Shops

Some shoppers prefer buying meats from butcher shops, even if prices are slightly higher. They frequent butcher shops for the personal service, and better quality meat and trimming. Incidentally, butchers often give customers bones and trimmings, which can be used for making soups, at no charge.

GENERAL SHOPPING TIPS

Prices

Economy or Regular?

Compare the prices of the various sizes of items to determine whether the "economy" size is really the best buy. Purchase the larger cans or containers if they will be used—they are usually better buys. But remember, even if the large size is a bargain, it's not worth buying if it cannot be put to use.

Unit-Pricing

Careful shoppers like to patronize markets that feature *unit-pricing*. Under the unit-pricing system, a store not only posts the prices of its products, but also the cost per ounce, or per pound, or per square inch, etc. Thus, items packaged in various-sized containers can be price-compared easily.

As an example, let's assume a 150-square-foot package of Brand A paper towels costs 49 cents, and a 115-square-foot package of Brand B paper towels costs 39 cents. Which is the best buy? The unit-pricing label on the shelf will solve the mystery, revealing that the price per 100 square feet of Brand A is 33 cents, while for Brand B, it is 36 cents. You immediately know that Brand A is the better buy.

Universal Product Code System

The Universal Product Code System is making its way into the supermarkets. Notice that most items are now imprinted with a series of lines and numbers to be used when computers are installed at checkout stands. The checker simply passes the item over a scanner—rather than punch the price on the cash register—and the item is automatically recorded on the register receipt. The UPC system speeds up the checkout process and eliminates mistakes (The scanner cannot misread the code). Some shoppers, however, object to the absence of a price on every item; prices will still be posted on the shelf where each item is displayed.

Buying Sale Items

Buy What You Need

A sale is only a sale when one needs the items being offered. If a product is being sold for 60 cents apiece, or two for $1.15, and only one is needed—then buy only one.

"Rain Checks"

If a store has run out of an advertised special, ask the manager for a "rain check." Almost all stores will issue one, allowing the holder to purchase the product at the sale price when it is back in stock.

Driving for a Special

It may cost more to drive to a distant supermarket for a single special than to purchase the item at a higher price in a nearby store. The cost of gas may exceed the 25 to 35 cents that will be saved at the distant store.

Coupons

Those cents-off coupons in newspapers and magazines are being used by millions of consumers these days as a means of combating spiraling food costs. A dedicated coupon collector may save between $2 and $3 a week on the family grocery bill.

Coupons are usually published in the Wednesday night and Thursday morning editions of newspapers. Clip them out the same day they appear, and if a single paper has several coupons for staple items, buy an extra paper or two and save the coupons for future use. Remember to keep tabs on the expiration date of each coupon.

Avoid buying an unneeded product merely because a coupon will allow purchase at a reduced cost. Too many consumers treat the products on which discounts are offered as desirable because of the discount! So before clipping out a coupon, make sure it's for an item that will be used.

Deciphering Labels

Read the Labels

Get into the habit of reading labels on all packaged foods. Manufacturers must list the ingredients in descending order, according to net weight. Thus, an item which lists water as its *first* ingredient cannot possibly be very nutritious or economical, since it contains more water than anything else.

Freshness Dating

Freshness dating is another code to check. The stamped date on dairy products and baked goods indicates the last day the item is to be *sold* (its "pull date"). The date stamped on meats indicates when the item was *packed*.

The Contents

The way a label identifies a product tells the consumer a lot about its contents. For instance, according to government regulations:

—An item labeled "ham with water added" is composed of 10 percent or less water; "imitation ham" contains more than 10 percent water.

—"Beef with gravy" contains at least 50 percent beef; "gravy with beef" contains 35 percent beef.

—"Orange juice" is 100 percent real orange juice; "orange juice drink blend" contains 70 to 95 percent real orange juice; "orange juice drink" contains from 35 to 70 percent orange juice; orange drink has between 10 and 35 percent orange juice; "orange-flavored drink" contains less than 10 percent real orange juice.

—Chicken "burgers" must consist of 100 percent chicken; chicken "patties" may contain cereals and fillers.

—"Chili con carne" must contain at least 40 percent meat; "chili con carne with beans" need only contain 25 percent meat.

—A package of cheese that is simply labeled "cheese" can legally contain no more than 41 percent water. A "cheese food" is limited to 43 percent water. A "cheese spread" may contain up to 59 percent water. An "imitation cheese spread" may contain 60 percent water or more.

House Brands

Buy House Brands

The typical major supermarket has its own house brand on about one out of every 10 items—including milk, eggs, canned and frozen vegetables and fruits, bread, margarine, butter, coffee, ice cream, paper products, and dish and laundry detergents. National companies like General Foods, Heinz, Banquet, Del Monte, Hunt-Wesson, Kraft, and Kimberly-Clark all manufacture house brands for supermarket chains.

Buy the store brands rather than national brands. They are almost always of equal quality (and are often packaged at the same factory), but invariably cheaper. Save between 10 and 15 percent by substituting store-brand items for better-known brands. When *Money* magazine bought 31 common grocery items using brands names, the bill was $21.18; but when house brands were substituted, the tab dropped to $18.26—a 14 percent saving.

Coupons

Don't use a coupon for a national brand item before checking the price of the house brand. Even with the coupon, the national brand is often still more expensive.

"Loss Leaders"

Many stores sell nationally-advertised brands of detergents as "loss leaders" in order to attract customers. So before buying the house brand of detergent, check prices carefully; the national brand may actually cost less than the house brand.

MEATS

Beef

Government Inspection

The beef sold in markets has been analyzed for quality by government inspectors. One of four possible "grades" is assigned to the beef: *Prime* (exceptionally tender, the highest priced, but rarely found in supermarkets because of short supply); *choice* (the best grade found in most markets); *good* (favorable quality at a reasonable price, but leaner and less tender); and *standard* (a satisfactory, lean grade). Experts say that the lower grades of beef have as much food value as the higher grades.

Don't be afraid to buy the less tender cuts of meat because of less desirable taste. They are cheaper, and when cooked properly, are just as delicious. The tougher cuts normally require long, moist cooking—most often, stewing or braising—rather than broiling or roasting.

Fat

When selecting beef in the supermarket, examine its fat: it should be white, firm, and no more than one-half inch thick. According to experts, *white* fat indicates that the beef was corn-fed. If the fat is *yellow*, the animal was grass-fed, which is less preferable. If there are many striations within the fat, the feed was probably changed several times, causing the meat to be of lower quality.

Improper Labeling

Check that the labeling of beef is correct. Improper labeling—either accidental or intentional—is not uncommon. Look carefully at a T-bone steak. If it doesn't have some fillet, it's actually rib steak and should be priced 15 to 20 cents less. Porterhouse steak should have a very liberal share of fillet; if it doesn't, it's probably T-bone.

Fancy Names

Don't be fooled by fancy names. A "breakfast steak" is, in reality, chuck steak—but at a higher price. The same is true for "Spencer steak," which is actually boneless rib steak.

Boned Chuck Steak

When buying chuck steak, select the bone-in variety, which is a better buy. When chuck steak is boned, the price is usually two or three more cents per pound.

Refrigerating

When meat has been bought, but will not be cooked immediately, place it in the refrigerator unopened. It may be kept for no more than two days (roasts can be kept up to four days). If it will not be used for more than two days, freeze it. Meat can be frozen in its original wrapper for up to two weeks. When freezing for more than two weeks, overwrap the original package with a special covering designed for freezer use.

Long-Term Freezing

Prepare for summer outdoor barbecuing in April or May, when beef prices are somewhat cheaper than in the hotter months. Buy in quantity, and freeze most of it at a temperature not exceeding zero degrees until summer arrives. Frozen steaks will retain quality for up to a year.

Limit Portions

Doctors warn that red meat is high in both cholesterol and calories, so don't overload menus with it. Cutting down on meat intake will not only reduce food bills, but may be good for your health. According to experts, single servings of meat need not exceed seven or eight ounces, and even smaller servings are often adequate.

Hamburgers and Hot Dogs

Fat Content

Whether hamburger is labeled "lean," "leaner," or "extra lean," the fat content is not much different. Try the least expensive hamburger grades first, and gradually move up in quality until you find one that meets your taste. According to Consumers Union, although price difference from grade to grade varies as much as 40 cents per pound in the same market, the difference in fat, water, and protein content is "indistinguishable."

Protein and Chemicals

Hot dogs, which were once high in protein and low in fat, now contain less than half the protein found in equal portions of beef, pork, lamb, fish, or poultry. In addition, such chemicals as sodium nitrate and nitrite are now routinely used in most hot dogs. Research shows that these chemicals, when combined with other ingredients from a typical diet, are cancer-causing. Therefore buy hot dogs manufactured without nitrates or nitrites— such as the Shiloh Farms Brand produced by the Maple Crest Sausage Co.

Buy Frankfurters

Hot dogs labeled "frankfurters" are a better value than those called "all-beef" or "all-meat." Frankfurters are not only cheaper, but their protein value is higher because of the addition of cereals and nonfat powdered milk. The "all-meat" hot dogs are not all-meat at all; they contain as much as 30 percent added fat. The same is true for "all-beef" hot dogs.

Other Types of Meat

Veal

Veal is a relatively expensive meat. But when bought as veal cutlets or veal scallopini, there is little waste. The best veal has a grayish-pink color, and comes from young calves (6 to 10 weeks) that have been milk-fed. If the veal is red, the animal has been raised on something other than milk.

Lamb

Lamb chops (taken from the loin) are also a relatively costly dish, but other types of lamb—such as leg of lamb—are more reasonably priced. Supermarkets often have specials on leg of lamb, which can be used to make shepherd's pie or lamb curry.

Ham

Uncanned hams are a better buy than canned hams. In the canning process, fillers and gels are added, increasing the weight but not the food value of the ham. Among the canned hams, imported brands are often better buys than domestic ones; they contain fewer additives and more meat.

Bacon

The cost of the protein in bacon is the highest of all meats. In fact, from a nutritional point of view, bacon is more accurately classified as a fat rather than a protein food. Limit bacon spending; more protein per dollar can be obtained from other types of meat.

Luncheon Meats

Luncheon meats also have low protein value. Most have considerable amounts of fat and water added. Of the luncheon meats, purchase those in chunk form, not sliced. Sliced luncheon meats cost nearly 50 percent more per pound than their chunk counterparts.

The nutritious value of this meat is questionable at best. For instance, when *Consumer Reports* (March 1976) analyzed bologna, it concluded that with bologna averaging $1.68 a pound, the cost per pound of protein would be $14.28; by comparison, hamburger at 89 cents per pound would provide the same amount of protein for $4.63. (*Consumer Reports* analyzed 35 different brands of bologna for overall quality, but only gave its top rating to four of them: A & P Beef Bologna, Grand Union Beef Bologna, Schickhaus Beef Bologna, and Schickhaus Bologna.)

POULTRY

Protein Value

A serving of chicken contains as much protein as the equivalent of sirloin steak. The chicken, however, is much cheaper—yet another example that expensive foods are not necessarily better than cheaper ones.

Large vs. Small

When buying chicken or turkey, select large birds if the price per pound is equal to that of a small one. A large bird has more meat per bone than a smaller one.

Whole vs. Pre-cut

Buying poultry whole is less expensive than buying it pre-cut. Two or three whole chickens are sometimes sold in a single bag at considerable savings. Freeze what will not be used immediately.

Age

Ask the butcher the age of various poultry. The younger birds (6 to 20 weeks old) are usually more tender, and should be used for broiling, frying, roasting, or barbecuing. Older birds (more than 20 weeks) should be used for baking, stewing, salads, and soups.

FISH

Protein Value

Fish, as good a source of protein as meat, contains less fat. Those who live or work near a source of supply of fresh fish should buy directly from the fishermen who sell their catch on the waterfront. There's no way to buy fresher fish, and the price is usually lower then in the market.

Selecting Fresh Fish

Gill fish should have clear bulging eyes, red gills, firm and elastic flesh, and no strong unpleasant smell. Shell seafood should have a tightly-shut shell.

Canned Seafood

Savings on canned tuna are possible by buying light tuna rather than white, and flaked or grated rather than chunk.

DAIRY PRODUCTS

Milk

Cost

Home milk delivery adds from two to five cents to the price of a quart. Another one to three cents can be saved per quart by buying milk in half-gallon containers. Milk will keep fresh in a refrigerator for at least a week.

Nonfat

The cheapest form of milk available is nonfat dry milk. It contains most of the nutritional value of whole milk (minus the fat), and sells for less because shipping and handling costs are reduced once the fat and water have been extracted. There are about 110 calories in ten ounces of nonfat dry milk. By comparison, there are 200 calories in ten ounces of whole milk. Those who dislike the taste of dry milk might consider putting it in soups, stews, omelets, desserts, and other dishes.

Vitamins

Some nonfat dry milk lacks both vitamins A and D. Before purchasing dry milk, check the contents.

Eggs

Weight

Eggs are normally sold by weight. A dozen small eggs weigh about 18 ounces; a dozen medium eggs weigh about 21 ounces; large, about 24 ounces; extra large, about 27 ounces; and jumbo, about 30 ounces.

Grades

Eggs rated grades B or C are as nutritious as grades AA or A. Grade B or C eggs have yolks that are slightly flatter, whites that are slightly thinner, and flavor that is slightly less pleasant. For the best taste, buy grade A eggs for boiling, frying, and poaching, but grade B will suffice for scrambling, making omelets, and most other uses.

Buying Guidelines

Apply the following rule of thumb when purchasing eggs: if there's more than a seven- or eight-cent difference between one size and the next smaller size in the same grade, the smaller size is the better buy. When the price difference is under seven or eight cents, the larger size is the better buy.

Egg Consumption

Eggs should always be refrigerated, and ideally should be consumed within about a week of purchase. After a week, the whites of eggs could become thin, and the membrane of the yolk might deteriorate and burst when the shell is broken.

Butter, Margarine, Cheese

Margarine

The cost of margarine is about two-thirds that of butter. Whipped margarine costs more than the stick variety: the consumer pays for the whipping process and the air that was added to make it more spreadable.

Butter

The individual who considers the taste of margarine unpleasant can still save by buying U.S. Grade A butter for use on the table, instead of top-grade AA. U.S. Grade B can be used for cooking.

Bulk Cheese

Sliced and grated cheese costs more per ounce than bulk cheese. So buy cheese in bulk form, and slice and grate it at home.

Hard vs. Soft Cheeses

Because hard cheeses have less moisture than soft cheeses, they generally tend to be more nutritious. However, one of the best protein buys is still cottage cheese.

VEGETABLES AND FRUITS

Consider the Use

Buy vegetables with their intended use in mind. For instance, when shopping for tomatoes to use in a stew, there's no need to buy whole fresh tomatoes, but rather cheaper, canned tomato chunks. Pineapple for a fruit salad can be purchased cheaper sliced in cans. Many types of produce rated U.S. Grade B can be bought for use in the cooking pot, while Grade A produce should be bought to place on the table.

Selecting Fresh Vegetables

When buying fresh vegetables, look for signs of decreasing freshness. Avoid potatoes with a greenish color and artichokes with scaly surfaces. Keep away from peas with tarnished or limp pods and broccoli with tips that have spread out.Tomatoes should not have yellow or green discoloration around the stem. Don't buy lettuce with leaves browning around the edges.

Fruits

During peak seasons, buy fresh fruits instead of canned: they taste better, and are more nutritious and cheaper. Apples peak between the months of September and March; grapes peak from August through October; Anjou pears and grapefruits, October through May; cantaloupe, watermelon, and peaches, June through August; oranges, December through May; pineapples, February through June; strawberries, April through June; and plums, July through September.

BREAD

Weight vs. Size

When buying bread, be concerned more about weight than size. Some large loaves are puffed with air, and without checking the weight on the package, one might end up buying more air than bread. Also look for the word "enriched" on the package, which indicates that the bread has extra nutritional value.

Avoiding Special Types

It's more economical to purchase the standard whole wheat, rye, and white breads than special breads—such as "egg bread" or "rolls." "Egg bread" costs 50 percent more than regular enriched white bread. Rolls cost over 100 percent more than white bread.

Bargain Breads

Many supermarkets carry their own house brand of breads, which usually costs about 10 cents less per loaf than the nationally-advertised brands. Day-old bread can also be bought at reduced prices, with very little loss of freshness.

Storing

Bread will keep its freshness longest when stored at room temperature. However, if the weather is hot and humid, the chances of mold developing will be reduced by keeping the bread refrigerated. By freezing bread, its quality can be preserved for two to three months.

CEREALS

Nutritional Value

Not all breakfast cereals are equal in nutritional value. In fact, some provide little or no nutrition at all. In a February 1975 study of 44 brands of cereal, *Consumer Reports* concluded that, by far, the most nutritious cereals on the market were Maypo 30-Second Oatmeal, Cheerios, and Special "K." All other cereals surveyed ranked significantly lower in nutritional value.

Highly-Refined Cereals

Do not buy highly-refined cereals loaded with artificial colorings and flavorings. Their main ingredient is usually sugar, which is undesirable in such large quantities.

One-Serving Packages

When buying cereals, avoid those sold in one-serving packages. They cost three times as much as the same cereals bought in large packages.

CONVENIENCE FOODS

Fresh vs. Processed

Fresh foods are almost always more nutritious than processed and packaged foods. About the only advantage of processed food is its convenience, and even that is sometimes questionable. (Is it worth 40 cents to buy seasoned breadcrumbs to make baked chicken, when fresh breadcrumbs can be made in a blender in a few seconds?) Many of the so-called "convenience" foods can be made at home with very little effort, and without chemical additives.

TV Dinners

Frozen TV dinners are convenient and fun to eat once in a while, but they are expensive and comparatively low in nutritional value. They cost at least twice as much as home-prepared meals! The portions are usually small and unbalanced—that is, they often contain more gravy than roast beef, and more cranberry sauce than turkey. Other convenience items also have large price mark-ups—frozen pies cost 100 percent more than their homemade counterparts; and premixed pancakes cost 20 to 40 percent more.

Frozen Orange Juice

Frozen orange juice concentrate is one of the few convenience foods that offers good nutrition and is attractively priced. It is usually the cheapest form of orange juice, and is as nutritious as fresh juice. Squeezing one's own orange juice costs nearly three times as much as buying the frozen variety. Concentrate is also easier to store.

When *Consumer Reports* evaluated frozen concentrate orange juice in its August 1976 issue, it gave its highest rating to two brands: Ralph's and Donald Duck. Ranking close behind were five other brands: Top Frost, Tropicana, Minute Maid, Pantry Pride, and Snow Crop. Twenty other brands were judged to be of lower quality than these.

Cheaper Convenience Foods

Several other convenience foods cost less than if they were prepared from scratch. These include frozen green peas, corn, lima beans, and spinach; instant coffee (not freeze dried); and brownie and chocolate cake mixes.

Frozen Goods

When shopping for frozen foods, never buy an item that was on display above the freezer line. If the product is covered with frost, avoid it. Only buy those items that are stored at zero degrees or below, and that show no signs of having been thawed out and refrozen.

OTHER FOOD TIPS

Soups

When shopping for soups, buy the condensed rather than the prewatered variety. The water alone can end up costing $1.00 to $1.30 a gallon.

Canned Goods

When buying canned goods, look for cans that are undented and undamaged. The possibility exists that the food in a damaged can is spoiled. Also, *never* buy a can with a leak or a bulge.

Soft and Fruit Drinks

One of the worst "nutritional" buys on the market is soft drinks. So-called "fruits drinks" are almost as bad, consisting mostly of water and sugar.

Coffee

Skyrocketing coffee prices in the 1970's have stimulated many coffee-lovers to economize in a variety of ways. Because beans cost less than comparable vacuum-packed ground coffee, some people are grinding their own, using a $15 grinder that pays for itself in about a year.

For individuals who are sticking with vacuum-packed coffee, many are stocking up during sales. Sealed cans will keep for many months. Once opened, full flavor will be retained for less than two weeks if kept in the refrigerator, but up to a month when stored in the freezer.

BABY FOODS

Commercial vs. Homemade

Commercially-prepared baby foods contain water and seasonings, which add to the cost. Homemade baby foods are cheaper—and more nutritious. Using an electric blender and a strainer, it is easy to prepare foods for baby like corn and green beans.

Label-Reading

Read the ingredients carefully before buying baby food. Avoid those items that list water first, and try to do without those that contain sugar, salt, or starches.

In mid-1977, neither Heinz nor Beech-Nut baby foods had any salt added to them. By comparison, Gerber added salt to its products. All three of these major producers still added modified starches, sugar, and other sweeteners to many of their foods.

Juices

Most doctors agree that babies can drink the same juices as the rest of the family after they are a few weeks old. There's no need to buy special baby juices that are sold for about double the cost of regular juices.

Dating Codes

When buying baby formula, examine the dating code on the package. The formula should be no older than 18 months, at which time it will start losing its nutritional value.

Booklet

An excellent booklet on the proper diet for a baby is *White Paper on Infant Feeding Practices*. It costs $1, and is available from the Center for Science in the Public Interest, 1779 Church Street, N.W., Washington, D.C. 20036.

FOOD CO-OPS

Collective Savings

Many families are forming or joining food co-ops in their

neighborhoods as a means of beating the high cost of food. By pooling the food needs of 10 to 30 families, the co-op is able to accumulate a large enough order to buy directly from a wholesaler. Its members save from 25 to 50 percent off their normal food bills. Co-ops usually place their orders by phone, and pick the food up the following morning. (Wholesale grocers are listed in the Yellow Pages.)

Sharing the Workload
The families that belong to successful co-ops share the workload of placing orders, collecting money, and picking up and distributing the food. Each family spends about three to four hours per month working for the co-op.

Overhead Expenses
To cover the expenses of gasoline and incidentals, food co-ops usually charge members slightly more than the cost of the food itself.

Free Brochure
For complete information on creating a food co-op, write to the Cooperative League of the U.S.A., 1828 L Street, N.W., Suite 1100, Washington, D.C. 20036.

VEGETABLE GARDENS

Is It Worthwhile?
Even a small vegetable garden will yield more produce than the average American family can eat in a season. A packet of seeds doesn't cost much more than a quarter.

Considering the Seasons
Plant according to the growing season. In the summer, plant vegetables such as rhubarb, cucumbers, and lettuce. In cooler months, choose peas, beets, and cabbage. Those who are permanently settled in their homes may want to plant some long-term foods, including fruit trees, asparagus plants, and berry bushes.

Location
Most vegetables need full sunshine for rapid growth, so select a sunny area—an area that receives at least seven hours per day of direct sunlight—as the garden site. Avoid planting near trees, not only to avoid shade, but also because the tree roots will compete with vegetables.

Planting Depth
The biggest mistake made by most home gardeners is to

plant seeds either too deep or too shallow. As a general rule, plant seeds at a depth four times their diameter.

Direction of Planting

When planting rows, run them north to south. If they must run east to west because of the property layout, plant the taller vegetables—corn, for example—on the north side so as not to shade the smaller ones.

Watering

Keep vegetables well watered. If they are allowed to completely dry out, they may never recover. Soak them thoroughly once a week (tomatoes can go two to three weeks between heavy waterings).

"Adopt-a-Lot"

Apartment dwellers might consider participating in their city's "adopt-a-lot" program. Under this plan, individuals lease a portion of a vacant lot from the city—sometimes at no cost, but often for a very small fee (to cover the watering bills). The participants grow whatever vegetables or fruits they desire and the harvest is theirs to keep and eat.

EATING OUT

Choosing Restaurants

Everyone enjoys dining in restaurants from time to time. In fact, 20 percent of the average American's food dollar is spent eating out. But if restaurants are not carefully selected, dining away from home can be a real budget-wrecker. As a general rule, avoid restaurants with a large, specialized staff, each of whom must be tipped separately—that is, a separate tip for the doorman, the hat check girl, the maitre d', the headwaiter, the wine captain, and the car attendant. One's money is better spent on the food itself.

Restaurant Locations

Suburban restaurants are often more reasonably priced than those of equal quality in midtown. In addition to paying for food, customers also help pay a restaurant's operating costs when eating out. A restaurant with minimal rent should be able to sell a meal for less than what its counterpart in the most expensive area of town can. Try the restaurants in the outlying communities and see how they compare.

Short-Menu Restaurants

Restaurants featuring a limited and simple menu can often provide quality food at a lower price than an establishment preparing a very large number of menu items. A restaurant specializing in only a few dishes has much less waste in the kitchen, because it must not purchase food for many items that may or may not be ordered by customers over the ensuing day or two.

Reducing Liquor Bills

If you enjoy a pre-dinner drink, why not have it at home before leaving for the restaurant? At many restaurants, liquor has the highest markup of any item being offered—about 100 percent or higher. If you feel you must have drinks *with* dinner in order to really enjoy yourself, try limiting yourself to a single drink per person.

Also, some restaurants—particularly those that do not yet have a liquor license—will let customers bring their own bottle of wine with them onto their premises. Finding such a restaurant can cut considerably into the overall dinner price.

CHAPTER 2

Health Care

Good health is our most precious possession, but maintaining it has become outrageously complex and expensive. Medical costs are the fastest-rising expense in the family budget. Every year of the past decade, the price of health care has increased more than the overall cost of living.

Americans collectively visit physicians more than a billion times annually. In the process, they spend more than $100 billion on medical care—nearly $500 for every man, woman, and child. The largest increase in medical bills has occurred in hospitals, where the average cost of a single day of care was $120 in 1977. One out of every seven Americans can expect to be hospitalized during an average year—or about 35 million people.

Simultaneously, more than $8 billion a year is spent on drugs, about evenly split between prescription and nonprescription. Doctors write a staggering 2.4 billion prescriptions annually, and the drug industry is the most profitable enterprise in the United States. The Boston Consumers' Council found a pharmacy in South Boston charging $8 for a supply of antibiotics that a nearby drug store was selling for $2.60. The American Medical Association, in a survey in Chicago, found that the same drug can vary in price by as much as 1,200 percent from store to store!

Certainly the competency of doctors is another one of the nation's greatest concerns. Is there a chance that surgeons, for example, may act in their own self-interest and recommend costly surgery that may not be necessary at all? Several years ago in New York City, several unions hired a panel of surgeons to provide a second opinion on cases in which surgery had been recommended for union members. Over a three-year period, 28 percent of the recommended operations—or a total of 594 surgeries—were deemed unnecessary by the panel. The program, which cost $200,000 to run, had saved over $1.5 million in hospital costs, and an inestimable amount of human pain and suffering.

Nursing homes have also been the subject of concern in recent years. With more than one million elderly Americans as their residents, nursing homes are big business—to the tune of $8 billion a year. However, government investigations have concluded that over half of the nation's 23,000 nursing homes are "substandard." A report by the Senate Subcommittee on Long-Term Care concluded that "long-term care for older Americans stands today as the most troubled, and troublesome, component of our entire health care system."

A patients' "bill of rights" is definitely necessary. One has already been created, and in fact has been adopted by the American Hospital Association. In New York State, a copy of this bill of rights is given to each patient upon being admitted to a hospital. According to this document, a patient has to be clearly told what his ailment is and what treatment is being recommended for him. Except in isolated cases, a patient can refuse this treatment. All costs must be explained to him as well.

As John Alexander McMahon, president of the American Hospital Association, has said, "People today no longer regard health care as a privilege, but a right."

DOCTORS AND CLINICS

Choosing a Doctor

When

The best time to select a doctor is before an emergency arises. Waiting for an emergency to start looking for a physician may mean ending up with an excessively expensive and/or incompetent one.

Some people use the hospital emergency room as a substitute family doctor. These innocents would be surprised to learn that emergency room care is often three times more expensive than private medical attention. Take the time to find a family doctor now.

Who

To obtain names of reputable doctors, contact the local city or county medical society or a nearby accredited hospital. The medical society will provide background on any of its member physicians, including the medical school attended, place of residency training, years of experience as a practicioner, and hospital affiliations.

Although membership in the American Medical Association was once thought to be a necessary credential for any proficient doctor, that is no longer the case. The AMA's conservative policies have chased many physicians away from its membership rolls. In fact, less than half of all licensed doctors in the country now belong to the AMA. So, lack of membership in the Association is certainly no negative reflection upon a physician's competence. A better clue to a physician's skills is certification by the American Board of Medical Specialties. A general practitioner should belong to the American Academy of General Practice, indicating that he keeps up to date by taking a minimum of 50 hours of continuing education a year.

Interviews

Before making a selection, make appointments for interviews with several doctors. There is rarely any charge for these meetings, which are usually about 10 minutes in length, sufficient to get a sense of the doctor's personality, philosophy, and manner. Ask him about his policy regarding middle-of-the-night or weekend emergencies. What does he charge for office visits? Does he insist on a fee for filling out insurance forms? Is a particular time of the day set aside for telephone consultations? How long does one normally have to wait for a "routine" office appointment, and how long for an "urgent" one?

Dealing with Doctors

Judging Competence

If a doctor does not take an adequate medical history, if he rushes his patients in and out of his office without a complete diagnosis, or if he doesn't sufficiently explain why certain tests have been recommended, consider him incompetent or indifferent. A good physician should also thoroughly explain the risks of various tests, and the possible side effects of any prescribed drugs.

Avoiding Test Duplication

When it is necessary to change doctors, have the new physician request that the former one send over your entire medical record. This medical history will be helpful to the new doctor in making diagnoses, and will help to avoid expensive duplication of tests or immunizations.

Physical Examinations

One of the best methods of limiting medical expenses is to have each family member undergo regular medical examinations. Some studies have indicated that nearly 60 percent of all hospitalizations could be avoided if ailments were diagnosed and treated early. Tests for high blood pressure and, for women, breast and pelvic examinations and Pap smears, should be conducted at least once a year.

The young and the healthy may only need a complete physical every two to five years. (Individuals with specific complaints, or those whose family histories or occupations indicate they may be susceptible to illness should be checked more often.) For people over 65, an examination at least every two years is preferred. Although the annual physical exam is considered passé by many doctors, avoiding them completely may jeopardize one's health.

Telephone Advice

Reduce doctor bills by using the telephone. A personal physician who knows his patient's medical history will usually give free advice over the phone.

Office vs. Home Visits

If it is necessary to see the doctor in person, visit his office and avoid paying the additional $10 to $20 charge for a house call. Besides being more expensive, a house call is less efficient because the doctor does not have adequate diagnostic equipment at his disposal. Very often, a doctor who makes a house call will ask the patient to come to his office the next day anyway, and the patient will be charged for both a house call and an office visit.

Complaints

When it is suspected that a doctor is guilty of overcharging, discuss the matter with him or his billing secretary immediately. If this does not resolve the matter, send a letter to the doctor, succinctly explaining your side of the story, and asking for an explanation. If satisfaction is still not forthcoming, submit a formal complaint to the local medical society. Every society has a grievance committee, which will contact the doctor and attempt to settle the matter. If the committee is unable to resolve the dispute, contact an attorney.

Low-Cost Care

Clinics

Those who cannot afford the care of a private physician can get treatment at minimal or no cost from a clinic or hospital run by a government agency or a university medical center. Local health departments or social services departments are the best source of information about eligibility requirements. The care at these facilities is usually competent, although a patient can expect to wait a long time to receive the attention of a physician.

Medicaid

Medicaid is a joint federal-state program designed to provide medical insurance for poor families. The welfare system in each state administers Medicaid, although federal money pays for part of the program. Generally, the program provides free hospitalization, doctors' services, laboratory tests, X-rays, nursing home care, drugs, and ambulance services. To find out what benefits are available in your state and who is eligible for them, contact the state welfare department.

Inexpensive Treatment

Those who have a personal physician should nevertheless avail themselves of the various treatment and screening programs offered at minimal cost in most communities. The United States Public Health Service offers immunizations against such diseases as tetanus, polio, and smallpox (usually at $1 per injection) in cities throughout the nation. Most local health departments provide tuberculin "scratch" tests, chest X-rays, blood pressure readings, and sickle-cell anemia tests for a nominal fee. The American Cancer Society sponsors Pap tests for women to detect cervical cancer, and the American Heart Association conducts screening programs for high blood pressure.

HOSPITALS

Rating the Hospital

Accreditation

Do not voluntarily enter a hospital that has not been accredited by the Joint Commission on Accreditation of Hospitals (JCAH). This accreditation ensures that the standards for minimum professional care are being met by the facility. Nearly 75 percent of all general hospitals in the United States are accredited. Most prominently display their accreditation certificate; if it is not displayed, ask the administrator if the facility is accredited, or write to JCAH, 875 North Michigan Avenue, Chicago, Illinois 60611.

Teaching Hospitals

Hospitals that have teaching facilities, and that conduct vigorous research programs, rank highest in providing good medical care. They attract the area's top doctors, and have extensive facilities to carry out complex medical procedures efficiently.

Cutting the Costs

Outpatient Tests

Hospital bills can be reduced by requesting that routine tests be conducted prior to admission. If the hospital is willing to administer these tests in its outpatient clinic, the number of days of inpatient hospitalization—and thus the cost—will be reduced. However, first check your health insurance policy, and make sure that outpatient services are covered.

Admission Days

If possible, don't check into a hospital on the weekend, particularly Friday evening or Saturday. Because hospitals are not fully staffed over the weekend, most complex tests won't be done until Monday anyway. Except in an emergency, check in between Sunday evening and Friday morning—and eliminate unnecessary expenditures.

Private Rooms

It is advisable *not* to stay in a private hospital room. Not only is a private more expensive than a semiprivate room, but hospital insurance rarely covers its entire cost. Some doctors hike their fees for private-room patients, feeling that if they can afford private rooms, they can also pay inflated doctor bills. Further, there is a certain peace of mind that comes with sharing a room and knowing that someone is nearby should an emergency occur.

Nursing Care

In instances when a doctor permits you as a patient to leave the hospital a day or two early if you agree to bring a private nurse into your home—do it! A nurse will cost half of what a hospital charges for just being there. Inquire of the doctor the degree of nursing care that will be needed. If a licensed vocational nurse (LVN) will suffice, don't hire a more expensive registered nurse (RN).

Ambulatory Facilities

When a family member faces a minor operation—simple ear and eye surgery, children's hernias, certain urological or gynecological procedures—save 25 to 50 percent by having the procedure done in an "ambulatory surgery" clinic rather than a hospital. These same-day clinics perform about 40 simple operations, have proved to be safe, and are relatively inexpensive. A tubal ligation to prevent pregnancy at a clinic costs less than half of what a nearby hospital charges for the same operation when the patient stays overnight.

The Bill

Carefully examine a hospital bill before paying it. The charges should be itemized; if they aren't, ask for an itemization.

Make sure that each of the services listed on the bill have been received. Is there a charge for a recovery room when one hasn't been used? Is the drug bill much higher than had been anticipated? Mistakes in hospital charges are not uncommon.

Unnecessary Surgery

A Second Opinion

Many unnecessary surgeries are performed in the United States. Dr. Lawrence P. Williams has estimated that "two million operations [out of 14 million] are performed without justification every year." In agreement are a Ralph Nader task force study, and a study by the Columbia University School of Public Health and Administrative Medicine. To be safe, if a doctor recommends that surgery be performed, seek out the opinion of another doctor who is independent of the first. Tell the second doctor that if surgery is necessary, it will be performed by someone other than him; this will remove financial considerations from his decision.

The total cost of a consultation with another physician is about $20 to $25, unless the second doctor insists that new X-rays or tests be taken. (In most cases, he'll be willing to use the tests conducted by the first physician as a basis for his decision, avoiding duplicate charges.)

Questionable Operations

The most common types of operations that are performed unnecessarily are those to cure tonsillitis, vaginal bleeding (for which a hysterectomy is suggested), hemorrhoids, peptic ulcer, knee cartilage problems, sinus disorders, varicose veins, and an overactive thyroid.

DONATING BLOOD

Should You Donate?

To protect yourself against the time when you or a family member might need a blood transfusion, it's wise to donate blood on a regular basis. Blood normally costs from $25 to $60 a pint. But those who contribute blood through a Red Cross program can receive free at least as many pints of blood as they have donated. If an individual's donation has been made in association with a union or church group, and that organization has met its designated donation quota, the donor and his family are usually eligible to receive as much blood as needed—whether it be one pint or 1,000 pints!

How Often?

The Red Cross stipulates that an individual cannot donate

blood more frequently than every eight weeks, and no more than five times a year. A donor must weigh at least 110 pounds, and be between the ages of 17 and 65.

Blood Replacements

An individual scheduled for surgery that will involve transfusions should request friends and relatives to donate blood in his name. Most hospitals will consider these donations as blood replacements, and won't charge the patient for the blood he receives as long as each pint is matched by a donation.

DRUGS

Prescription Drugs

Comparison Shopping

Price shopping for prescription drugs is easy in states that require druggists to post prices for the most commonly prescribed drugs. This posting is mandatory in California, New York, Texas, Michigan, Minnesota, Washington, Vermont, and New Hampshire, as well as in the city of Boston. Drugs that are not among the most popular will not be posted—ask the druggist for the price.

Generic vs. Brand Names

Save additional money on prescription drugs by asking the prescribing doctor to specify generic, or chemical, drug names rather than brand names. Generic drugs are usually cheaper. (The generic drug is identical in composition to the brand name drug, but is simply not branded.) For example, when ampicillin is sold under Bristol-Myers' brand name, Polycillin, it costs about 16 percent more than an equal amount of generic ampicillin. Many doctors write prescriptions for brand-name medications because they are more familiar with them. So always ask the doctor specifically for a generic prescription. Incidentally, in some states, even if doctors write brand-name prescriptions, pharmacists are permitted to substitute the cheaper generic equivalents.

Generic Savings

The differences in price between generic and brand name drugs can be immense. In 1974, the Council on Economic Priorities, a non-profit research organization, discovered these variations in the prices of antibiotics:

Brand Name	Generic Name	Brand Price	Lowest Generic Price
Terramycin	oxytetracycline	$18.43	$1.90
Pentids	penicillin G	8.36	1.20
V-cillin K	penicillin V	8.32	1.85

Buying in Quantity

When a particular drug will be used for a long period of time, it is possible to buy it in large quantities (100 or even 500 tablets) at a reduced price. Ask the doctor for his opinion, and unless the drug deteriorates dramatically over time, he'll probably write a prescription which will allow purchase in bulk. The pharmacist will advise how the drug should be stored to preserve its potency.

Drug Fraud

Consumer groups have discovered that pharmacists occasionally put fewer pills in the bottle than were prescribed. If a consumer pays for 50 pills, he wants 50 pills, not 49—so count the contents of all bottles.

Samples

Some drug costs can be eliminated completely by asking the doctor for free "samples" of the drugs he prescribes. Every doctor receives dozens of drug samples each week from pharmaceutical company salesmen who visit his office, and most doctors distribute these samples at no cost to their patients. Those with minimal drug needs ought not to be reticent about asking their doctors for samples.

Mail-Order Drugs

Considerable drug savings can be enjoyed through mail-order purchase. One of the better known mail-order organizations is the American Association of Retired Persons (AARP), which serves anyone age 55 or over. (AARP) sponsors a nonprofit mail-order pharmacy service. The association's address in 1909 K Street, N.W., Washington, D.C. 20049.

Alcohol and Drugs

Never drink alcohol while under medication. Alcohol is especially unsafe when consumed with tranquilizers or sleeping pills. If a doctor hasn't approved consumption of alcohol while taking medication, refrain from doing so.

Over-the-Counter Drugs

Limiting Use

No drug—not even an over-the-counter (OTC), nonprescription drug—should be used for a prolonged period of time without first checking with a doctor. Some OTC drugs are strong, and may cause unwanted side effects. In its booklet *First Facts About Drugs,* the FDA states: "An OTC drug may relieve your symptoms, but that's all it does. You think you are getting better while the disease is getting worse. Do not use an OTC drug steadily except at your doctor's order."

Drug Interactions

The FDA also discourages people from taking more than one over-the-counter drug at any one time. The ingredients in these drugs may react negatively with one another, doing one's body more harm than good.

Deceitful Ads

A doctor, not television advertisements, should serve as a guide to various nonprescription medicines. When an ad is deceitful, the Food and Drug Administration will only take action *after* it has been aired. There is no truth to the commonly-held belief that ads for health-related products are checked for accuracy by the government prior to broadcast.

Aspirin

Aspirin, which was first marketed in the nineteenth century, is commonly found in almost every American medicine cabinet. Most doctors (as well as the FDA and the FTC) agree that simple aspirin is the best all-around pain killer and fever reducer on the market, probably just as effective as higher-priced analgesic compounds that combine aspirin with other pain killers. Still, in recent years, 80 cents of every dollar spent on nonprescription pain relievers is spent on aspirin's more expensive competitors. Anacin tablets, for instance, contain aspirin as well as a small amount of caffeine, and cost more than three times as much as plain aspirin. Yet the usefulness of this caffeine as a pain killer or a stimulant is doubtful, leading the American Pharmaceutical Association to comment that such combinations "are of greater economic significance to the manufacturer than of increased therapeutic benefit to the patient."

Other Pain Relievers

Several OTC drugs combine aspirin and sodium bicarbonate (Alka-Seltzer is probably the best known). Although these products may be used successfully as an occasional pain reliever, Consumers Union has cautioned that an excessive amount of sodium bicarbonate can cause bladder and kidney disorders. CU discourages the regular use of these medicines.

Children's Medicine

Many doctors suggest that sweet-tasting children's medicine, such as children's aspirin, not be bought. Unfortunately, some children (with parents' encouragement) have been led to believe that these drugs are candy, not medicine. When parents are not looking, youngsters have swallowed the entire contents of an aspirin bottle, with catastrophic results.

HEARING DEFICIENCIES

Consult a Doctor

Hearing loss is an ailment that should be diagnosed by a physician (preferably an ear specialist), not a hearing-aid salesman. Nevertheless, a task force of the United States Department of Health, Education and Welfare has estimated that 70 percent of those seeking treatment for hearing problems go first to a hearing-aid dealer. Don't make that mistake; salesmen have no way of detecting such serious problems as tumors, infections, perforated eardrums, and allergy-related ailments.

Buying a Hearing Aid

If an ear specialist (an *otologist* or *otolaryngologist*) determines that a hearing aid is needed, ask him to recommend a certified clinical audiologist, who will assist in selecting the device. Before buying a hearing aid, ask for a 30-day trial period. It can usually be rented for that period, and the rental fee is applied to the purchase price.

Choosing the Device

The most expensive hearing aid is not necessarily the best for an individual's needs. Lower-priced devices may be adequate, so ask about them as well. Never choose the device solely on the basis of cost or even appearance; an inconspicuous hearing aid is worthless if it doesn't amplify sound well. Also read the warranty or guarantee completely, and make sure its provisions are clearly understood.

DENTAL CARE

Tooth and Gum Problems

Teeth and gums are probably the most neglected parts of the entire body. The importance of periodic dental checkups cannot be overemphasized. About 20 percent of all Americans have lost their upper teeth by their mid-30s, and have had to have expensive bridgework. Serious gum disease can usually be cured if it is treated by a dentist in its early stages.

Selecting a Dentist

Choose a dentist carefully. Herbert S. Denenberg, former Pennsylvania Insurance Commissioner, has charged that at least 15 percent of the nation's 120,000 dentists are "incompetent, dishonest, or both." According to Denenberg, about 56 million teeth are extracted each year, six million unnecessarily. Many, he says, could have been saved through alternative treatment.

The procedure for finding a good dentist is similar to that for locating a good doctor. Start by asking the local dental society for its recommendations. Also contact local accredited hospitals and dental schools, and ask for the names of the dentists associated with them. Or ask the family physician to recommend a dentist.

Visiting the Dentist

Before deciding upon a particular dentist, visit his office. What is his fee per visit or per filling? Will he make arrangements for extended payments when major work is performed? Once under his care, don't hestitate to ask about fees charged for unusual treatment.

Competent Care

Be aware of the various indicators of good dental procedures: (1) a competent dentist will place a lead apron on patients when taking X-rays, (2) he will polish fillings, and (3) he will take a complete medical and dental history, actively soliciting information as to whether the patient suffers from certain ailments— diabetes, hemophilia, drug allergies—that may affect the type of dental care administered.

If a dentist seems more eager to pull a tooth than to save it, the patient would be wise to consult another dentist. A competent dentist will carefully explore every possible means of treatment, and make the decision about treatment *with* the patient, not *for* him.

Clinics

As an alternative source of care, most dental school clinics offer many inexpensive or free services to the general public. Although the work is done by students, it is checked very carefully by their professors, who are practicing dentists. Emergency dental service is often available around-the-clock at some university schools. Because the clinics do not provide services for profit, it is unlikely that *unnecessary* dental work will be recommended.

EYE CARE

Regular Examinations

Every family member should have a checkup by an

ophthalmologist every two to four years. Although this may seem like an expensive luxury, particularly if one's family is fortunate enough to have good vision, early detection of eye problems prevents serious disorders from developing.

Eyeglasses Discounts

Discounts on prescription eyeglasses can be obtained at cut-rate optical chain stores, which have mushroomed across the country in recent years. New lenses that cost $75 at conventional optical retailers might cost half that much at a chain store with a large volume. Because all outlets buy their lenses from the same major producers, lens quality is not likely to vary.

Contact Lenses

Despite their high cost, contact lenses are worn by about six million Americans. Although they are primarily bought for cosmetic reasons, contacts sometimes offer better vision, particularly in the peripheral-vision area where glasses provide no assistance.

Two Types of Lenses

Two types of contact lenses are on the market: *hard lenses,* made of a firm plastic; and *soft lenses,* made of a pliable, water-absorbing plastic. Although soft lenses are more expensive, they are also more comfortable. An optometrist who surveyed his own patients found that three years after their initial fitting, 87 percent of the soft lens patients were still wearing them, compared with only 33 percent of the hard lens patients.

Fitting Contacts

The first step in being fitted for contact lenses is to have a complete eye examination performed by an ophthalmologist (a medical doctor) or optometrist (a state-licensed eye specialist). Most people can wear contacts, but those with eye diseases should avoid them. Ask a doctor for his advice.

Insurance

Contact lenses are insurable for a nominal fee, usually from $15 to $25 a year. The insurance can be purchased in the doctor's office or from an insurance dealer.

CHILDBIRTH EXPENSES

Choosing an Obstetrician

When selecting an obstetrician, inquire as to his fees. Most charge a flat fee that covers all prenatal care, the delivery, hospital visits, and a postpartum checkup about six to eight weeks after delivery. In addition to this fee, ask the doctor about an additional charge in the event that a Caesarian section is needed. Discuss his billing procedures—monthly installments, a single bill in the ninth month, or a bill after giving birth.

Prices vary considerably from one obstetrician to another. If the fee quoted seems unreasonable, be willing to "shop around" for an obstetrician with more moderate rates. The local medical society knows the average charge for pregnancy care and childbirth (as well as any other medical procedure) in the community, so it can provide a basis for comparison.

Maternity Clinics

Maternity clinics in some cities accept not only the poor, but anyone who desires care. These clinics, usually affiliated with a teaching hospital, charge their patients on an ability-to-pay basis. Although some women dislike the impersonal nature of the care that many clinics provide, the money saved is considerable.

Home Delivery

Some women completely eliminate hospital childbirth costs by delivering their babies in their own homes. They are usually assisted by a nurse-midwife, although some obstetricians are now willing to come to the home. When planning for home delivery, be sure to select a highly competent midwife. Also, arrange in advance for quick admission to a nearby hospital should complications develop.

HEALTH MAINTENANCE ORGANIZATIONS

Preventive Care

Health maintenance organizations (HMO's) are a relatively new health care phenomenon. About eight million Americans now receive medical care from HMO's. Simply explained, an HMO is a prepayment plan in which subscribers pay an annual set fee to a group of physicians. In return, families receive complete medical care—including hospitalization, emergency care, physicians's services, and preventive treatment.

At most health maintenance organizations, such as Kaiser-Permanente (the nation's largest HMO), patients are encouraged to have regular checkups. HMO's operate on the theory that early treatment will, in the long run, save money. HMO patients are rarely reluctant to seek frequent medical treatment because care has been paid for in advance. Because of their emphasis on preventive treatment, HMO's have been able to reduce the amount of hospitalization their members require. And since hospitalization is the costliest aspect of medical care, HMO's have been able to pass along these savings to subscribers.

HMO Option

By law, all employers with at least 25 employees must provide their employees with the option of joining an HMO instead of the company's normal health insurance plan. Make sure your employer offers this opportunity.

Staff Physicians

Ideally, HMO physicians should be employed full-time by the organization. If they also maintain private practices, conflicts over where the physician channels most of his time and energy may arise. The HMO should run its own hospitals and clinics. Those that do have more power to control costs and quality of care than those that must deal with outside facilities.

Additional Considerations

Before joining a particular HMO, two additional factors should be considered:

—What is the doctor-patient ratio? It should be limited to about 1 to 1,000. As the ratio increases, the quality of individual care is likely to diminish.

—Is the HMO nonprofit? Although HMO's designed to make money can operate effectively, nonprofit organizations are less apt to cut corners to increase profits.

CHIROPRACTORS

Doctor-Chiropractor Association

Although the American Medical Association officially opposes chiropractic, some medical doctors work in conjunction with chiropractors. A 1975 survey by *Medical Economics* magazine revealed that more than 20 percent of 1,000 physicians questioned stated that they receive referrals from chiropractors. Almost five percent of the doctors said they have sent their patients to chiropractors. When seeking treatment from a chiropractor, ask him if he ever refers patients to medical doctors; if he never does, and if he vehemently belittles the entire medical profession, do not enlist his services.

Improved Status

Chiropractors are gaining an improved status in the United States: they are now licensed in all 50 states. Almost all insurance companies now provide policies covering chiropractic care. Workman's compensation laws in most states accept chiropractic treatment in paying claims. And Congress has included chiropractic services in the Medicare program.

KICKING THE CIGARETTE HABIT

Turning Off

Those who sincerely want to quit smoking can choose from many clinics and programs. The American Cancer Society sponsors clinics in many cities, limits class size to 18 people, and charges a $5 or $10 registration fee for eight two-hour classes. The American Health Foundation conducts stop-smoking sessions of its own. The Seventh-Day Adventists run sessions of their "Five-Day Plan to Stop Smoking" for groups as large as 100.

Aside from these nonprofit clinics (which usually charge a nominal fee), there are many private organizations that charge anywhere from $75 to $450 for treatment. SmokEnders is the largest commercial program, charging $125 to $175 (depending on location), and boasts more than 60,000 graduates. The Schick Centers for the Control of Smoking use electrical shocks to create an aversion to smoking. Even acupuncture has been tried by some to halt the smoking habit. But not all of the techniques have been very successful. On the average, only 30 percent of the stop-smoking students are still not smoking 12 months after the therapy has ended.

Suggestions for Quitting

The American Cancer Society provides these suggestions to help one quit smoking:

—List the reasons for and against smoking.

—Chart your smoking habits for two weeks, noting how many cigarettes you smoke, and when you smoke them.

—Eliminate one cigarette from your normal routine, and see how well you cope.

—Decide upon a day to quit for good.

—Quit on the pre-selected day. Keep busy on that day— exercise, take walks, go to the movies, or visit friends. If you have the urge to smoke, chew gum instead, or eat raisins or sip water.

One of the best guides to this subject is *You Can Quit Smoking in 14 Days,* by Walter S. Ross (Reader's Digest Press).

"Safer" Cigarettes

Smokers who cannot or do not want to quit would be wise to at least switch to cigarettes that are low in tar and nicotine (such brands as Doral, Merit, Carlton 70's, Vantage, and Now). According to government physicians, the chemical compounds in tar may cause cancer of the lungs and other organs. Nicotine is believed to have harmful effects on the heart and bloodstream. Any reduction in the amount of these substances taken into the body is favorable.

NURSING HOMES

Quality of Care

A study by the Senate Subcommittee on Long-Term Care, published in December 1974, concluded that more than half of the nation's 23,000 nursing homes are substandard. It is, therefore, imperative that when choosing a nursing home for a relative or friend, the choice should be made carefully.

To begin the selection process, contact the local health department, medical society, or Social Security office, any of which will have available a list of nursing homes in the area. Also ask the family doctor for recommendations. Any nursing home being considered should be state-licensed. Ideally, it should also have a certificate from the Joint Commission of Accreditation of Hospitals.

Visiting Homes

Visit all nursing homes under consideration. To avoid the possibility of special preparations having been made in anticipation of the arrival of a guest, make inspections unannounced. A good time to vist the facility is when lunch is being served. Observe the quality of food served to the residents, and ask them how they like it. Inquire about the variety of menus, and provisions for special diets. Also ask if food is available at other than mealtimes.

During the visit, inspect the bedrooms. Are they large, clean, and well lit? Are there toilet facilities in each room? Can patients decorate their rooms as they choose? Are special provisions made for the disabled, such as handrails in the hallways and near the toilets?

Medical Care

A *good* nursing home will have a complete physical therapy program, with therapists qualified to administer care. Doctors will supervise all medical care, and a physician should be on-call around the clock. Patients will be able to see their personal physicians if they choose. In addition, the nursing home will have an arrangement with a nearby hospital for quick admission of nursing home patients who become ill.

The Staff

A nursing home should be staffed with warm, friendly people who like to work with the elderly, and who encourage them to care for themselves as much as possible.

Visiting Hours

Nursing home visiting hours should be generous and convenient for both visitors and residents. The staff should encourage visits by outsiders.

Recreation

A nursing home with an outdoor patio area furnished with tables and chairs provides a welcome change of scenery for residents. A recreation room equipped with games and craft materials is another attractive nursing home feature.

Fees

Ask the nursing home administrator for an itemized list of fees. Some homes charge extra for therapy, or for such special care as feeding patients in bed. Others charge extra for laundry, care of hair and nails, and for wheelchairs and walkers. Find out whether the basic charges are covered by the patient's Medicaid or Medicare benefits.

CHAPTER 3

Clothing

The average American—man, woman, or child—spends about $350 a year on clothing. That's a stiff yearly bill, particularly for a family of four, which finds itself paying an average of $1,400 annually for clothing.

With prices so high, most people cannot afford to be extravagant in their clothing purchases. For them, it is very important to select apparel wisely and carefully.

The clothing industry has changed in many ways in recent years. Selecting the proper material for a suit or selecting clothing confuses even the experts these days. There are now over 700 man-made fibers on the market, and differentiating between them requires an encyclopedic mind. With so much to choose from, careful planning of purchases is extremely important. Separating good-quality garments from bad, and bargains from rip-offs, requires careful thought.

The wise shopper must be practical. If he allows himself to be excessively swayed by current fads or fashion, he'll probably end up with a closet full of outdated clothes. (Remember the Nehru jacket of the 1960's, which became obsolete almost overnight?)

True, some fashion trends seem more lasting. Dress shirts of all hues have replaced the white shirt, and seem destined to stay around. Ties are brighter, too, for both casual and dress wear.

Shoes are one of the most important items in everyone's wardrobe. The typical seven-year-old takes 30,000 steps a day—a total of 10 miles of walking. Many adults walk even more. Yet an outrageous number of people are poorly fitted for shoes and have serious problems because of it. In 1976, Americans paid 30 million visits to podiatrists (foot doctors), and spent more than $150 million on foot care powders, lotions, and other products.

There is no doubt, that clothes are among the most prized possessions of some consumers. Saks Fifth Avenue, in fact, once advertised its clothes as investments ("Build a portfolio of the tweeds that are classic"). Clothes may not appreciate in value like gold or silver, but some people certainly feel like a million with stylish, well-chosen clothes upon their backs.

BASIC SHOPPING TIPS

Planning Clothes Purchases

Inventory

Before venturing out to shop for new clothes, look through the closet and inventory the wardrobe. Which items are wearable, which need to be repaired, and which should be donated to the Salvation Army or other charitable groups? All the clothes you need may already be there, and the planned shopping excursion can be canceled.

A Complementing Wardrobe

Careful planning avoids impulse buying. Too often, when people buy clothes without forethought, they spend more than they should on garments that do not blend with the rest of their wardrobe. As a result, they eventually end up having to buy new accessories to complement their hasty purchases.

Buying clothes to match what you already own is both simple and economical. If, for instance, you have two favorite blouses—a green one and a blue one—plan to buy a pair of slacks with both colors in it. You will in effect be stretching both your wardrobe and your budget.

Pressure-Free Shopping

When you know far in advance about a special occasion for which you'll need clothes, plan to shop early. Most people spend more money than they'd like when they shop under pressure.

General Clothes-Buying Advice

A Second Opinion

Shop for clothes with someone whose opinion you respect. When trying to decide if a garment is complimentary, a second opinion is helpful. And the salesman's judgment is too often affected by the size of his commission on various items.

Trying On Clothes

Never purchase a costly piece of clothing without first trying it on. A garment may look great on a hanger, but terrible on a person. If the dressing rooms are crowded, or time is short, come back another day. When trying on an item, walk out of the dressing room and examine it in a different light. Stand in front of a three-way mirror and look at its fit on all sides.

Alterations

When asking about the price of a garment, find out whether

it will be altered free. Also, try to find out from friends if the tailor at that shop is competent. A bad tailor can ruin what was once a good suit. If the tailor has a poor reputation, have the garment altered elsewhere.

Body Size

Select clothes according to your own body size. If you're short, garments with vertical stripes or lines will make you look taller. If you're tall and don't want to emphasize your height, avoid clothing with vertical stripes.

Flattering Necklines

Women should wear necklines that flatter their faces and necks. If your face is thin, rounded collars are best for you. A full face and a short neck look best with a V-neckline.

Off-Season Sales

By watching for sales, one can purchase an entire wardrobe at discount prices. Buy during the off-season, and store the garments until the appropriate season. Buy a swimsuit during the fall sales, and pack it away until the next summer. Other basic items—hats, scarves, boots, coats—can be bought at the end of one season, with little risk of their being out of style by the next year.

Clearance Sales

Besides specialized clothing sales at various times of the year, some stores sponsor clearance sales on much or most of their entire merchandise at a few key times—usually just after Easter, just after the Fourth of July, and again after Christmas. There are usually excellent bargains available during these sales, so check newspaper ads carefully at these times.

Factory Outlets

Year-round bargains—discounts as high as 30 to 50 percent—can be found at factory outlets many of which are run by clothing manufacturers. The first such store was Loehmann's, which opened in Brooklyn in 1920 and now has expanded to 34 stores in 13 states. Factory outlets are located in most major American cities. Although labels may have been removed, the salesmen can usually identify the manufacturer of a given garment. Suits, dresses, slacks, shirts, ties, and shoes are available at these stores.

Locations of all factory outlets in the United States are listed in *S.O.S. Directory*, published by S.O.S. (Save on Shopping). The guide ($7.95) can be purchased from S.O.S., P.O. Box 10482, Jacksonville, Florida 32207.

Mail-Order Buying

A very tall or very short person may have difficulty finding a local store that caters to his clothing needs. If such is your predicament, ask a department store manager to recommend a mail-order house specializing in the type of clothes you need. For example, Jos. A. Bank Clothiers Inc., 714 East Pratt Street, Baltimore, Maryland 21202, sells suits for short men by mail order. Suit jacket sizes begin at 35 short, and pants waist sizes at 28 inches. Because a mail-order suit cannot be tried on before purchase, be sure it can be returned if it is an improper fit. Some mail-order houses will agree to this arrangement.

Exchange Policies

Most reputable clothing stores have liberal exchange policies. Make an effort to shop in stores that offer the choice of exchanging apparel, receiving full credit or obtaining a cash refund.

Evaluating the Item

Once you've bought a piece of clothing, take it home and examine it even more closely than you did in the store. If a defect is found, or if you simply decide that the color or style just isn't right, take it back immediately—before the receipt is lost or any labels are removed from the garment.

"Out of Business" Policies

Be particularly cautious when buying clothes at a store that's going out of business. Once the store closes, there will be no opportunity to exchange faulty merchandise.

Analyzing Workmanship

The following are signs of good clothing workmanship:
—The seams should be at least one inch wide to permit letting out and to allow for strain.
—Lapels should lie properly.
—Plaids, prints, and other patterns should match where they join, particularly at the sides, the back center, and the armhole seams.
—Machine-stitching along the hem and the collar should be even and close together.
—The undercollars should be totally concealed from view.
—Buttons should be sewn on very securely.
—Squeeze the material; if it has resilience (which it should), it will immediately return to its original shape when let go.

Cleaning Instructions

On almost all items of clothing, the manufacturer is required to attach a permanent label that includes recommendations for cleaning the garment. The only pieces of clothing exempt from this requirement are those on which the label might detract from the overall appearance of the item—such as shoes and gloves. Items that are (1) completely washable and (2) sell for less than $3 are other exceptions. Generally, look for a label and heed its suggestions; by so doing, you'll extend the life of your wardrobe.

Fading

Inspect clothing labels for indications of whether the fabric will fade either in the sunlight or during normal laundering. Clothing made of natural fibers, such as wool or cotton, shouldn't be bought without a guarantee against fading. Most synthetic fibers should be colorfast as well.

An item that's labeled "sunfast" will have a much stronger color permanence than one labeled "sun resistant." With the latter designation, some fading from sun exposure can be expected.

Shrinkage

When checking clothing labels, note the shrinkage rate of the garment. The less shrinkage, the better. (Ideally, it should not exceed two percent.) If the shrinkage rate is substantial, buy a size larger than you normally would.

If a garment is labeled "pre-shrunk," don't presume that it won't shrink anymore. In reality, most items that carry this description can be expected to shrink another two to three percent. If the label reads "Sanforized," the shrinkage may only be about one percent.

Saving Labels

Use an empty cigar box or a similar container to keep all garment tags that specify recommended cleaning techniques. They'll be in a convenient place when they have to be referred to. It is wise to take the appropriate tag to the dry cleaners when the item needs cleaning.

MEN'S CLOTHES

Bargain Prices

Depending on the item, bargains in men's clothes are available at various times of the year. Men's winter suits are marked down in January and February; summer suits are marked down in August. Coats are discounted in both January and August. Men's shirts are traditionally placed on sale in January, February, and July.

Selecting a Men's Suit

Wool Suits

A men's suit made of wool or a wool blend is always a good buy. Wool lasts longer and tailors better than most other fabrics. Although double-knit polyester suits are cheaper, they often bag at the knees and their lapels frequently curl. Despite the popular misconception, a wool suit is practical for the traveler; it usually loses its wrinkles when hung up.

Worsted Suits

Even though wool suits are usually good buys, worsted suits may be even better. True, worsted suits are more expensive than wools, but they are also more durable. Worsteds (sharkskin, serge, gabardine, challis) have a smooth finish, and they are highly resistant to soiling and staining. When shopping for a worsted, inspect a yarn from the inside edge of the trouser cuff. Does the yarn consist of two strands twisted together (a two-ply grade), or just one strand? The two-ply is preferable.

Evaluating the Fit

When judging the fit of a man's suit, try it on and then (1) place a belt in the trousers, (2) insert a wallet and other items into the pockets, and (3) look for wrinkles or stretching. Vertical wrinkles are a sign of excess width; horizontal wrinkles are a sign of excess length. If the wrinkles are diagonal, tailoring is needed in the shoulders, underarms, or sleeves.

Vested Suits

Shopping for a suit with a vest? Try on a few, and be sure to sit down while wearing each of them. A vested suit should be comfortable when the wearer is seated; unfortunately, many are not.

Slacks

Never buy a pair of men's or women's slacks that are a smaller size than needed, with the intention of letting them *out* to gain a perfect fit. If you can't find your exact size, buy the pants a bit bigger than needed, and have them taken *in*.

On a good pair of slacks, there will be generous seam allowances (particularly at the back), and the fly will lie flat and smoothly overlap the zipper.

In its 1976 annual, *Consumers' Research Magazine* gave its highest men's washable slacks recommendations to Farah-Hi-Straight ($13), Haggar ($14), Jaymar ($25), Majestic ($19.95), and Reston ($19.95).

Dress Shirts

A good quality dress shirt should be made of a durable fabric. The fabric design should match at the collar, pocket and front pleat. The stitches should be even and close (20-23 per inch).

Consumers' Research Magazine (March 1977) gave its highest rating for men's durable press shirts to Manhattan's "The Natural" ($12), the Sero Natural Classic Oxford ($17.50), and Ward's Finest ($8.99-$10.99).

Purchasing Men's Shoes

Advantages of Leather

Probably more than most items of clothing, shoes should be thought of as an investment. Cheap shoes will not last long; more expensive shoes, made with real leather, will give long wear and a comfortable fit. Leather has small pores that allow the shoe to "breathe"; synthetics, which have replaced leather in many shoes, don't have this breathing capacity (This tip, in addition to many of the following ones, apply to women's shoes as well as men's.)

Rubber Soles

Leather shoes are available with rubber soles. These shoes are less expensive, and simpler and cheaper to repair.

Extra Pairs

Men's shoes are less likely to fall out of style than any other type of attire. So when shoes are on sale at an unbeatable price, buy one or two extra pairs.

Proper Fitting

A properly-fitted shoe should extend from one-half to three-quarters of an inch beyond the tip of the longest toe. The front of the shoe should be shaped to match the shape of the wearer's toes. The ball of the foot should sit in the widest part of the shoe.

Don't let a salesman try to convince you that an uncomfortable shoe will feel "just fine" after a breaking-in period. Shoes that fit properly don't require a breaking-in period.

If you're concerned about obtaining the best possible fit (which you should be), shop for shoes about midday. Experts say that feet tend to swell up slightly during the day, often by as much as five percent, so purchasing shoes in the afternoon rather than the morning makes sense.

"Damaged" Shoes

Shoes that are slightly "damaged" can often be bought at about a 50 percent discount from factories and factory outlets. These imperfect shoes usually have no more wrong with them than a nick, which is sometimes not even noticeable without close examination. Ask the salesman what the damage is if it's not obvious; if you can live with it, the savings can be significant.

Other Men's Garments

All-Purpose Raincoats

One of the best buys in men's garments is a versatile raincoat with a detachable lining. When the lining is in, the coat provides protection from the most frigid weather. On' warmer days, the lining can be removed, allowing the garment to be used as a topcoat.

Most raincoats lose some of their water repellency after dry cleaning or laundering. Most dry cleaners can re-waterproof a coat, and this should be done at least once a year. Shrinkage is minimal in most raincoats.

Ties

When shopping for ties, keep in mind that not only do knit ties resist wrinkles better than woven ones, they maintain their shape better. Polyester, wool, and silk ties are more resistant to wrinkles than rayon. A hand-stitched tie will probably hold its shape better than a machine-stitched one.

WOMEN'S CLOTHES

When to Buy

Many stores traditionally have sales on women's dresses in January, June, and November, although specials are likely to be offered any time a store is overstocked. Sales on women's coats are usually held in April, October, and December, and bargains in women's sportswear are likely to be found in January, February, May, and September, and possibly as late as October. Lingerie is often placed on sale immediately after Christmas, and continuing through January.

For Special Occasions

When buying for a special occasion, choose apparel that can be worn at other times as well. This includes a wedding gown, which can be bought in a style that—once minor alterations have been made—can be worn long after the church bells have stopped ringing.

Buying Dresses

Quality

A good dress will have a deep hem (a two-inch minimum). There will be about 15 stitches to an inch on the seam, and the seams will be uniform and not puckered. The fastenings will be sturdy, and the plackets at least 10 inches long (as much for convenience as anything).

Sizes

Keep in mind that sizes for ready-to wear dresses are not standardized. Use the labels as a general guideline to size, but be sure to try on garments before buying.

Dressing to Buy

When shopping for a fancy dress, make sure to dress up—with heels, hose, and so on. Only then can you get an accurate picture of what you'll look like when that new dress is worn.

Blouses and Sweaters

Blouse Quality

Look for the following characteristics when shopping for a blouse:

—Low-priced washable polyester knits and cottons should be considered; they hold their shape and size well after laundering.

—Collars or lapels should lie flat, and the collar points should be smoothly finished.

—Horizontal buttonholes are preferable to vertical ones because they do not tend to gape as readily.

Sweater Quality

—Waist and cuff bands should resume their shape quickly after being stretched. Cuffs should be knitted onto the sleeves rather than just sewn.

—Full-fashioned sweaters are likely to keep their original shape, since this shape is actually knitted into the garment by increasing and decreasing the stitches at various points. These sweaters can easily be spotted by looking at the armholes; a row of knitted-in dots will be visible, and will turn and run parallel to the seam.

CHILDREN'S CLOTHES

Fast Growth

When buying clothes for babies, keep in mind their fast growth rate. Babies typically double their birth weight at five months, and triple it in a year. Therefore, it's foolish to buy many clothes in the "newborn" size (up to 15 pounds).

Keeping Down Cost

Don't buy expensive children's clothes that guarantee longer wear. Your youngster will probably outgrow these expensive clothes before they're worn out. Exception: if younger children will inherit the clothes as hand-me-downs.

Wise Shopping

Because children often grow at such an erratic pace, it's unwise to buy clothes on special, say in the spring, hoping they'll still fit during the back-to-school season in September. So the best route is simply to take your time and shop carefully for the best bargains that can be found—no matter what the time of the year. For instance, do back-to-school shopping when the department store displays are first put up in August; don't wait until after Labor Day when the stores are jammed. When stores are crowded and the atmosphere is hectic, wise choices of garments will be more difficult to make.

Features to Look For

—Pants pockets should lie flat so they won't become entangled in tricycle handlebars or swing sets.

—Seams should be particularly soft to avoid irritating the sensitive skin of children.

—Hems of pants and dresses should be well-stitched to keep the youngster from catching his or her heel.

Children's Shoes

Footwear Needs

Until a baby begins to walk, he has no need for shoes. But once he begins taking those first few steps, many pediatricians say the best type of shoes have high tops (which are hard for the child to kick off). Baby footwear should also have firm soles (to fully protect the feet).

Walking Barefoot

Once a baby is walking, many pediatricians recommend that he be allowed to go barefoot in the house. This is believed to help prevent flat feet. Shoes should be worn outdoors.

Proper Fit

For the times when shoes are needed, properly-fitted ones are essential for children. According to the American Medical Association, half of all young children have foot defects, with the figure rising to 80 percent by high school age. To avoid such problems in your family, buy your child a pair of shoes that fits perfectly. If the shoe store you patronize doesn't stock a size that fits your youngster exactly, find another store.

Check the length, width, and height of the instep to ensure that the new shoe does not restrict or cramp the foot and toes. There should also be ample toe height at the tips of the shoes.

Until a child reaches adulthood, his feet and shoes should be checked for size every few months. When he outgrows a pair of shoes, discard them, even if they're not yet worn out. Unlike other types of apparel, shoes should never serve as hand-me-downs. Shoes that fit one child will probably never fit another one properly.

The following chart indicates how frequently a child's shoe size should be checked:

Age	Check Shoe Size Each
1 to 6 years	1 to 2 months
6 to 10 years	2 to 3 months
10 to 12 years	3 to 4 months
12 to 15 years	4 to 5 months
15 to 20 years	6 months

Heels

Despite what current fashions dictate, children's shoes should not have heels thicker than one-quarter to one-half inch, at least up to age six. A child older than that should still not wear heels more than one-inch thick.

CARING FOR CLOTHES

Life Extenders

Airing Out Apparel

If an individual wears any piece of clothing—suit, dress, shirt, blouse, shoes—for several consecutive days, its life-span is going to be shortened. All garments need time to air out between wearings. Shirts, for example, need time to return to their natural shape. Shoe leather needs a chance to dry out from the absorption of a full day's worth of foot perspiration.

Garment Bag Storage

Clothes that are rarely worn should be hung up in a garment bag to better protect them from the elements.

Removing "Stays"

The removable plastic stays in the collar of men's shirts can be left in the shirts when they are laundered without risking any damage to the garment. However, they do slide in and out easily, and there is always the chance of their falling out in the washing machine or dryer.

Avoid Overdrying

Don't overdry garments in the clothes dryer. Probably the greatest single cause of shrinking and wrinkling of fabrics is overdrying. It shortens the life of clothing, and consequently increases clothing expenses.

Caring for Shoes

Rain Protection

The life of shoes can be extended by wearing rain boots or rubbers over them during wet weather. When caught in the rain without protection for the shoes, remove them as soon as you get indoors. Wipe away as much moisture as possible immediately. Place the shoes in their shoe trees and allow them to dry out at room temperature. Do not put them next to a heater. (The heat will make the leather brittle, causing it to crack.) Once the shoes are dry, polish them with a good paste wax polish. Use wax polish instead of a liquid variety; very often, liquid polish will cause cracking in the surface of the shoe, and will not allow the pores of the leather to "breathe."

Shoe Repairs

To keep shoes in good shape, visit the cobbler long before the soles are worn away. Ideally, new soles should be applied before the inner soles have been completely worn. New heels should be put on even more often: a heel that's even partially worn can cause severe stress on the leg and back muscles.

Cost

Although the cost of shoe repairs is going up, it isn't rising as fast as the price of new shoes. In fact, having a pair of shoes mended is 50 to 70 percent cheaper than purchasing a new pair. Good footwear can be resoled or reheeled many times before finally being relegated to the trash can.

The Life of a Garment

How Long Will Clothes Last?

Even with excellent care, clothes won't last forever. According to the National Institute of Dry Cleaning, the average life span of a man's winter suit is four years; a summer suit is three years. Other typical life expectancies include: men's shirts, two years; men's cotton and synthetic slacks, two; shoes, three; sweaters, three; pajamas, two; dresses, two to three; blouses, two to three; skirts, two; women's slacks, two; slips, two; underwear, one; and swimsuits, two.

Coping with Dirt and Stains

Launder Quickly

Soiled clothing should be laundered as soon as possible. Dirt can actually wear down a fabric, as can perspiration. So don't delay washing soiled garments, unless you are willing to run the risk of permanent damage.

Cleaning with Water

Some stains can be removed simply with water. A bit of liquid detergent can be added to hasten the cleaning process, but be sure that all detergent is fully rinsed out afterwards to prevent a ring from appearing. Those stains most easily cleaned with water are those caused by soft drinks, wine, milk, ice cream, catsup, washable ink (excluding ballpoint), and most solid food stains.

Dry Cleaning Fluids

Some stains can be removed at home by using a commercially available dry cleaning fluid (or powder). Rub the cleaner on the stain with the fingertips. Once the stain is gone, put additional cleaner on a piece of cheesecloth and wipe the spot again—this time from the edges to the center, to inhibit the formation of a ring. This dry cleaning technique should be attempted on stains caused by mascara, ballpoint ink, printing ink, and cooking oil or grease. Some stains (lipstick, salad dressing) need both cleaning fluid and water for removal.

Spray-On Shield

Potential harm to clothing by perspiration can be eliminated by applying a spray-on shield. When properly used, the spray will effectively safeguard the fabric.

Fabric Protectors

Many other types of fabric protectors are available to guard against various stains. A product such as Scotchgard, for example, can be applied to raincoats and neckties for protection against food and water spots. Scotchgard prevents liquids from being absorbed by the material, and they can be wiped away rather easily.

Self-Service Dry Cleaning

Self-service dry cleaning machines are an economical way to keep many of one's clothes in good condition. They work particularly well for wool sweaters and children's clothes (as well as drapes, bedspreads, and blankets), but are not quite as advisable for very expensive garments, such as tailored suits or evening gowns.

Most self-service dry cleaning machines have an eight-pound capacity. Garments of different colors can be dry cleaned together with no worry as long as the colors are fast.

Clothes cleaned in a dry cleaning machine will sometimes give off a strong chemical odor, which will linger for several minutes. These fumes can be dangerous; as a safety precaution, leave the car windows open when driving home with the clothes.

Professional Cleaning Problems

If a professional cleaner has ruined an expensive garment, request that he reimburse you for the item. If he refuses, contact the Better Business Bureau. The BBB will usually send off a stern letter, which sometimes will convince the firm to pay you right away. However, if this does not settle the squabble, the BBB may decide to send the garment to the International Fabricare Institute, which will analyze it and determine whether the cleaner, the manufacturer, or you are to blame for the problem. If the fault lies with the manufacturer, complain to the store that sold you the item. (According to the Institute, the dry cleaner is to blame in 20 percent of all cases, and the customer and the manufacturer are each responsible 40 percent of the time.)

SUNGLASSES

Avoid Eye Damage

Sunglasses are becoming a commonplace piece of apparel— as much for style as to protect the eyes from glare and brightness. However, select sunglasses for more than their appearance; inferior lens material can cause eye fatigue and injury. Only buy sunglasses that block ultraviolet sun rays and that are made of impact-resistant glass or plastic.

Visual Distortion

Sunglasses should be free from visual distortion. To examine a pair of glasses, hold them about 18 inches from your face, positioned as though you were going to slide them in place over your eyes. Stand in front of a window pane or a painting with clear horizontal and vertical lines. While looking at the lines through the lenses, move the glasses up and down and sideways; if the lines curve or bend, the lenses are distorting.

Tints

Sunglasses are available in a variety of tints, although optometrists generally recommend only those that are neutral gray, green, or brown. These provide a minimum amount of color distortion and the best protection from brightness. Avoid lenses that are tinted blue, violet, red, pink, and orange—they are sold because some people find them flattering, not because they provide protection from the sun.

Photochromic Lenses

Many optometrists discourage the use of photochromic lenses, which are prescription sunglasses with lenses that change from clear to dark and back again as the wearer moves from indoors to outdoors. According to some eye specialists, the lenses don't adapt equally well to all light levels. Some lenses never darken enough for complete protection from glare.

CHAPTER 4

Housing

Every American family eventually has to confront such difficult questions as: Are we ready to buy a house—or should we continue to rent? If we decide to buy, how much can we afford? What kind of house do we want? Should it be new or old, and where should it be located? What's actually involved in the buying and selling of a house? And what's the best way to move from one home or apartment to another?

Housing is the single greatest expense of nearly every American family. Yet millions of people buy homes and rent apartments without the knowledge needed to intelligently make the important decisions that can involve many thousands of dollars.

The housing market is particularly confusing because it is constantly changing. About all that is certain about homes and apartments is that prices are rising. The prices of homes are going up by the day. Current mortgage interest rates of nine and ten percent would have been unthinkable a generation ago (they averaged 4.5 percent in 1950), but today consumers accept them resignedly, almost grateful that the rates are not even higher.

Probably few subjects confuse the general public as much as mortgages and the fine print that accompanies them. By assuming a *mortgage*, an individual is in effect agreeing to pay for a house out of his future income, rather than having to save up the entire purchase price in advance. Most people could never afford to buy a house if such loans were not available.

Then there are the bewildering—and often unanticipated—*closing costs*, which are all the fees involved in transferring ownership of a new home, and in processing a loan. They can range anywhere from 2 to 10 percent of the loan—thus, from $600 to $3,000 on a $30,000 mortgage. The closing costs include fees for:

—The *title search*. During this procedure, the ownership of the property is verified to ensure that the transaction is legal, and a search is made to ascertain whether the property has any liens against it.

—The *title insurance*, which the lender often requires the

buyer to obtain, and which protects against any altercations over ownership that may arise after the house has been sold.

   —*Legal services* provided by the lender's attorney, which the borrower must pay for.

   —*Loan origination costs,* which are the fees the lender charges for putting into motion the procedures for arranging a mortgage.

   —*State and local transfer taxes.*

   —*Deed registration costs.*

   Despite the rising price tag on houses, it is still usually wiser to buy rather than rent. The greatest advantage to buying a house is that *equity* is accumulated with each mortgage payment. This equity (the value built up in property over the years) equals the amount of principal paid, minus all debts against the property. By contrast, all a tenant is left with after making rent payments is a stack of receipts. The homeowner can also take advantage of enormous tax breaks that a renter cannot—specifically, deducting mortgage interest.

   Homeownership also offers an individual his best chance to amass a sizable amount of capital. It is one of the better hedges against inflation, since house prices typically rise at a rate equal to or faster than the overall inflation rate.

   In addition to mortgage payments, owning a home involves other costs for which one should be prepared. Generally, it costs an additional four to five percent of a house's value per year to keep it operating—over and above the mortgage payments. This four to five percent figure includes property taxes, fire and theft insurance, general upkeep, and utilities (water, electricity, gas, telephone).

   Although the financial advantages of owning a home outweigh the disadvantages, some people are still more suited to renting than buying. Many enjoy the feeling of mobility that renting affords—the knowledge that it is easy to move to a new locale once a lease expires. A renter does not have to deliver a large down payment, leaving his money free to be used for other purposes. Also, upon signing a lease, a tenant knows precisely what his cost of housing will be for a specified period of time— there are no unforeseen or hidden expenses, such as replacing a water heater or repairing a roof. Renting is also advisable for those interested in becoming acquainted with a neighborhood before deciding where to settle permanently.

   Some experts also recommend rental for those who plan on remaining in a particular location for less than three years. Value does not actually begin to build up rapidly in owned property until about the fourth year. If a house is sold much before then, not enough equity has accumulated in the house to offset the initial buying costs. A home is almost always an excellent long-term investment, but its short-term benefits are not nearly as impressive.

HOMEOWNING

Shopping for a Home

Taking Time

Shop for a house leisurely. Look for one that fits the family's desires, needs, and budget—even if it takes months to find. The average new-house buyer has looked at 10 different houses over a three-month period before finding the one he wants. The older-house buyer shops an average of two months and examines five different houses. Plan on spending as much time as it takes to locate the right house for you.

The Classifieds

Scan the classified ads in local newspapers for homes listed "For sale by owner." Buying a house through a real estate broker may be more costly than dealing directly with the homeowner. The broker receives a commission (six to eight percent of the price of the house), and although his fee is paid by the seller, it is usually added on to the purchase price. If the homeowner wants $47,000 for his home, he will have to sell it for $50,000 in order to pay the broker a six percent commission.

Listing Cards

When using a broker to help locate a home, read his listing cards carefully. Take particular note of the date each house was listed. A buyer has a much better chance of negotiating a lower price on a house that has been for sale for quite a while.

Ignoring Pressure

Don't feel pressured into making an immediate decision about a house because two or three other people have also expressed interest in buying it. Because hasty decisions often breed regret, if you feel any hesitation at all, give yourself more thinking time. Better to lose the house to another buyer than risk the chance of buying a home and later regretting it.

Common Objections

The most common complaints of home buyers, according to the United States Housing and Home Finance Agency, are (1) small bedrooms, (2) tiny kitchens, (3) awkward layouts, (4) insufficient closet space, and (5) unsatisfactory laundry facilities.

If the house under consideration is faulty in any of these ways, keep looking. What may seem like minor shortcomings to you now may become serious liabilities when you eventually try to sell the house.

Neighborhood

When evaluating a particular house, examine the neighborhood carefully. Nearby houses should be at least equal in value to the house under consideration. The homes should be well maintained, and their grounds kept up. Also check the proximity of schools, shopping, and hospitals, and the availability of public transportation. Consider the smog and traffic noise. Is there an airport nearby? Are fire and police protection adequate?

Distance from Work

An important factor to consider when buying a home is its proximity to the family's chief source of employment. To get "more house for the money," many families move to newly-developed suburbs, which often means a long commute to and from work each day. Spending an hour or two a day on the freeway often produces great physical and mental strain, and is not worth the additional living space homes in distant suburbs offer. That time on the freeway could be spent with the family, which seems like a much better use of those hours. Also keep in mind that at 65 cents (or more) a gallon, one can save $13 a month by eliminating just one gallon of gas from a daily round-trip commute.

Future Problems

Before buying a particular home, check with city planners about the possibility of future projects that might affect the house. Is a change in zoning imminent that would allow high-rise apartments to be constructed next door? Contact the state highway planning department, and inquire as to whether a freeway will be built through or near the property. A freeway at the end of the block can ruin the property value of a house in the middle of the block.

New Houses

Better Investment

Newer homes are usually better investments than older ones, even though the latter may be larger and have bigger pieces of land. Smaller cash down payments are usually required for new houses, and mortgages of a longer duration are more easily obtainable. New houses are also more likely to have many modern conveniences, such as built-in appliances and central air conditioning.

Frills

When buying a new home in a development from a model, find out exactly which features will come with it, and which are "frills" only displayed in the model home. If construction of all houses in the development has not been completed, it may be possible to arrange for the addition or deletion of specific features from a unit.

Trouble-Free

New houses do not have many problems often associated with older ones. New homes tend to be "tighter" than older ones, and thus suffer less heat loss. The major and costly repairs and remodeling which sometimes accompany an older house are not necessary in a new one.

Warranties

Warranties on new houses were often mediocre at best until mid-1974, when the National Association of Home Builders developed a warranty program that is administered by its own Home Owners Warranty Registration Council. The warranty stipulates that faulty workmanship and materials are guaranteed for one year following purchase; flaws in the heating, cooling, electrical, and plumbing systems are covered for the first two years; and major construction defects are guaranteed for 10 years. This protection is available to home buyers for a one-time fee based on the price of the house (for example, $90 for a $45,000 home). It is a worthwhile investment.

Using the Warranty

Those who carry the Home Owners Warranty must simply notify the builder in writing when a problem occurs in the house. If he refuses to correct the flaw, the owner files a formal complaint with the local HOW council, and the dispute may then move to arbitration. If the arbitrator decides in the home-owner's favor, and the builder still refuses to make the necessary repairs, the builder faces potential dismissal from the HOW program, in which case the council itself will pay to have the problem corrected.

Old Houses

Workmanship

The workmanship and materials that went into the building

of an old house are usually superior to those of a new home. Larger rooms are more frequently found in older homes, as are such features as basements, attics, and walk-in closets.

Digging for Information

When considering an older home, talk with the present owner, and ask what his property taxes and utility bills are. Inquire about the improvements he has made in recent years, and his reasons for selling. Don't be concerned about being "too nosy"; take advantage of every opportunity to find out whether the particular house is suited to your needs. (The real estate broker's listing form for the house probably includes the previous year's property taxes and heating costs.)

Bargaining

The chances of bargaining with the owner of an older home are better than the chances of bargaining over a new one. In fact, often the price of new homes is nonnegotiable. So if a new house and an old house carry identical asking prices, expect to pay less for the old house through bargaining.

Taking Over the Mortgage

Purchasing an older home is particularly attractive when the buyer is able to assume the existing mortgage, which will very likely carry with it a lower interest rate than that currently being offered by banks. When this can be arranged, make certain that the contract explicitly states the buyer's right to assume the mortgage without a change in interest rates. Remember, however, that an older mortgage might require a larger down payment than normal. But in return, monthly payments will be lower, and equity will build faster on the seasoned mortgage than on a new one.

How Old a House?

Although age is not necessarily synonymous with faltering quality, keep in mind that in many houses, mechanical equipment often needs replacing beginning at age ten to fifteen years. Problems frequently develop with everything from heating systems to sewage lines. Generalizations are difficult to make regarding age, because many old homes are highly sought after and are particularly valuable. But still, in most cases, a newer house (less than ten years old) may be a better buy. The landscaping of a five-to-ten-year-old house will be developed, the problems of a brand new home will have already been resolved, and the house will not yet be in need of major repairs.

Inspecting the House

A thorough inspection of a house under construction should be conducted. There are several points to be examined in particular:

—Check for sagging structure. Are the exterior walls square?

—Be sure there are enough electric outlets and sufficient amperage. The wiring should not be exposed or worn.

—The heating system should be in good condition.

—The walls should be well-insulated. Ask if the attic and the space between the interior and exterior walls has been filled with insulating material, and if so, what material was used.

—Ask for the name of the plumber who last serviced the house. Get his opinion on the condition of the plumbing system.

—Check the size and type of hot-water heater to determine if it will be adequate for your family's needs.

—How old is the roofing material? Will it have to be replaced soon?

—Check for signs of water penetration around the foundation walls of the basement. A basement that appears dry upon superficial inspection in summer may have telltale signs of flooding from the previous winter.

—Termite infestation should be looked for carefully. Any sign of termite damage should be referred to the attention of an expert.

Professional Inspection

A more reliable safeguard against buying a home needing major repairs is to have it inspected by an expert. The fee for this inspection will be about $100, but the investment will be worthwhile. An inspector has the skill to detect flaws in construction, and problems and potential problems in the house's heating system, electrical wiring, roofing, plumbing, and paint. He will provide an estimate of what it would cost to make all necessary repairs, which is a strong bargaining tool when negotiating with the present owner. (Home inspectors are listed in the Yellow Pages under "Building Inspection Service.")

Warranties

Various warranty programs for older homes are available, and they differ in coverage and effectiveness. All are more expensive than the HOW plan for new homes, and have shorter protection periods. One of the most popular, the Home Protection Program, is sponsored by the National Association of Realtors. It is, in effect, an insurance policy that warrants used homes for three additional years. An inspector initially checks the house and determines what is insurable. The new owner can protect himself against flaws or failures in those items that have been approved (from the electrical and plumbing systems to structural defects in the floors and ceilings). The cost is about one-half of one percent of the selling price of the house—for example, $250 a year on a $50,000 home, with a $100 deductible.

Building a Home

Expensive

Although hiring an architect to design a custom-built house sounds exciting, such a venture can be expensive. With today's construction prices so high, a custom-built home will cost at least 20 percent more than equivalent existing living quarters. In addition, because of the unforeseen events that may occur during construction, banks are more hesitant to lend money for building a new home.

An Alternative

Before deciding whether to build a home, spend several months checking existing houses on the market. If one is available that meets most of your specifications, and if it is reasonably priced, consider purchasing it and adding on extra rooms, or making any desired changes. Of course, check to see if legal barriers exist to building onto the present structure. Will building authorities grant the necessary permits? Is the house situated on a large enough plot to allow for the addition of an extra room?

The Land

When building a new house from scratch, the first step is, of course, to buy land on which to build. The land should be zoned for the type of residence desired. Check to make certain that nearby property is not zoned for commercial use, which could eventually decrease the land value. Hire a lawyer to oversee your purchase of the land, and to make sure that the title is valid before launching into the house-building stage.

The Architect

An architect hired to design a home normally receives as his fee a percentage of the building costs, which ranges from 8 to 18 percent, and is usually paid in installments. Although the fee may seem high, it will be offset somewhat by the money his expertise may save. For instance, he will be able to deal with contractors with more skill than a novice. As the construction proceeds, a good architect will make certain that the plans are precisely followed.

The Contractor

The job of a contractor is to bring a house from the planning stage to reality. He takes the specifications created by an architect, and plans and executes construction. Arrangements for paying contractors vary. Some contractors charge flat rates, and bear responsibility if the costs of construction eventually exceed their estimates; others demand a "cost-plus" contract, in which the client pays for all materials and labor, plus a fee to the contractor (10 to 20 percent of the building costs).

Obtaining a Mortgage

Interest Rates

Those interested in buying homes should not be deterred by current high mortgage interest rates. The rapid rise in prices of homes—an average of 10 percent per year since 1969—will more than offset any savings that might be gained should mortgage rates drop in the coming months or years. And, of course, there is no guarantee that mortgage rates will ever decrease.

Tax Savings

Current interest rates also seem a bit less awesome when one considers that interest payments are tax-decuctible. The cost of a nine percent mortgage to an individual in the 32 percent tax bracket is actually 6.12 percent when tax advantages are taken into account. The following chart indicates the "net" interest rates for various tax brackets and interest charges:

Tax Bracket	Interest Rate				
	8.5%	9.0%	9.5%	10.0%	10.5%
22%	6.63%	7.02%	7.41%	7.80%	8.19%
28	6.12	6.48	6.84	7.20	7.56
32	5.78	6.12	6.46	6.80	7.14
39	5.19	5.49	5.80	6.10	6.41
42	4.93	5.22	5.51	5.80	6.09
48	4.42	4.68	4.94	5.20	5.46

Shopping for a Mortgage

It's a good idea to shop for a mortgage before actually signing the papers to purchase a house. Check with banks, savings and loan associations, and mortgage companies. Discussions with these lenders help individuals ascertain what price homes they can afford, how large a down payment they can make, and what mortgage interest rates and repayment terms they can expect.

Meeting the Lender

Be prepared when meeting a lender. Bring a history of your employment and income, and an estimate of future income. Also prepare a statement of your personal net worth, including a list of all assets: the market value of all your property and possessions (including appliances, furniture, tools); total savings; the value of automobiles; the cash-surrender value of life insurance; and the value of securities. Subtract from these assets the liabilities you have accumulated (outstanding loans and other debts).

Two Parts

Monthly mortgage payments include two parts: payment on the loan, and the interest on the unpaid balance. Over the years, monthly payments remain constant, but how those payments are divided between the two parts changes proportionately. With each reduction in the total balance, the interest gets less and less. Thus, a larger segment of each successive payment goes toward reducing the principal of the loan. In the early years of a mortgage, most of each payment goes for interest; in the later years, most of it pays off the principal itself.

Term and Down Payment

The term of a mortgage can vary from 15 to 30 years. Although monthly payments may be less if the mortgage is spread out over an extended period, the total interest will be greater. Nevertheless, make as small a down payment as possible, and try to negotiate as long-term a mortgage as possible. Under such conditions, it will be mostly the bank's money that is being used to buy the house. And with inflation continuing to escalate, the value of the monthly payments will actually decrease over the years.

Rate Differences

Within a given community, most major lending institutions offer home mortgages at very similar rates. Compare mortgage rates carefully nevertheless, since just a fraction of a percentage point can make an enormous difference in the amount of money a home will cost. For example, the monthly mortgage payment on a 25-year loan of $30,000 at 9.5 percent is $262.20. But that same loan at 8.5 percent is $241.80—a savings of over $20 a month, and $7,344 over the 25-year period.

Calculating Payments

Use the following chart to gauge what your monthly mortgage payments (principal plus interest only) would be at various interest rates and time periods. The chart indicates the monthly payment for every $1,000 borrowed. So a $30,000 loan for 20 years at nine percent interest would require a $270 per month payment (30x9.00=$270).

Interest Rate	20 years	25 years	30 years
7.75%	$8.21	$7.56	$7.17
8.00	8.37	7.72	7.34
8.25	8.53	7.89	7.52
8.50	8.68	8.06	7.69
8.75	8.84	8.23	7.87
9.00	9.00	8.40	8.05
9.25	9.16	8.57	8.23
9.50	9.33	8.74	8.41
9.75	9.49	8.92	8.60
10.00	9.66	9.09	8.78
10.25	9.82	9.27	8.97
10.50	9.99	9.45	9.15

Price Limitations

It is unwise ever to buy a house that is beyond one's means—that is, if the monthly costs for the mortgage, taxes, insurance, utilities, and upkeep would be financially binding. Overextension could lead to problems—including possible foreclosure. Experts say that a house should not cost more than 2.5 times one's annual income, and that monthly costs should not exceed one percent of the sales price. So if one's annual gross income is $20,000, he can afford a house costing $50,000. This, however, is only a guide. Individuals with sizable savings accounts who can make larger-than-average down payments may safely be able to buy a higher-priced house. Those who expect large salary increases in the near future may also consider buying a more expensive house.

Escrow Accounts

Although they remain controversial, "escrow accounts" are becoming commonplace nowadays, and are required by many lenders. Under such a system, monthly payments include not only principal and interest, but property taxes and property insurance as well. The lender holds this money in an escrow account, often at no interest, and then pays the homeowner's tax and insurance bills as they are received. Because the escrow system is a form of forced budgeting, it has positive aspects. For one thing, the homeowner never has to worry about not paying his property taxes and insurance on time. However, he should logically receive some interest on the money that the bank may hold for several months until the bills come due. A growing number of states, but a relatively small number, now require that interest be paid to homeowners on their funds in escrow accounts.

Life Insurance

Although a life insurance policy on the chief source of family income is rarely required, the lender may recommend it. It is usually a low-cost decreasing term policy, in which the amount of coverage lessens as the unpaid part of the loan decreases. If the insured dies, the mortgage is automatically paid for in full by the insurance policy.

Foreclosure

Should the homeowner fall behind on his mortgage payments, the lender has the right to foreclose (he can sell the home to recover his money). But foreclosures occur very rarely. Most lenders are willing to work out a payment schedule with the homeowner instead of foreclosing. Should a homeowner encounter problems in meeting his monthly payments, he would be wise to let the lender know immediately. Ignoring the situation will not make the problem disappear. In most states, foreclosure proceedings can legally begin 90 days after the first late-payment notice is sent. But most loan officers will pass up that option if the homeowner explains what his problem is, and they work out some plan to eventually pay back the overdue money.

Variable Interest Mortgages

Fluctuations

In some parts of the country, lending institutions are beginning to offer "variable interest" or "variable rate" mortgages. Under these plans, if interest rates rise during the term of a loan, the homeowner is required to pay the higher interest rate. Conversely, if interest rates decrease, the homeowner pays the lower rate. Because of their unpredictable nature, variable interest mortgages should be avoided if possible.

Ceilings

Those unable to obtain a loan other than a variable interest mortgage loan should be sure that a ceiling is included in the contract, ensuring that the interest rate will never rise above a certain level—for example, 2.5 percent higher than the original interest rate. Under this kind of arrangement, no corresponding limit is usually placed on rate decreases. Also obtain a guarantee that the interest rate will increase no more than one-half of one percent in any six-month period.

Amount of Variability

What would an increase (or decrease) in a variable interest mortgage rate amount to in dollars? If a homeowner is financing a $30,000, 30-year loan, and his rate of interest rises from 8.5 percent to 11 percent over five years, his monthly payment would increase from $231 to $283. A rate decrease from 8.5 percent to 6 percent would reduce those payments from $231 to $183. Some banks that offer variable interest mortgages allow homeowners to increase or decrease the terms of their loans to keep monthly payments constant—that is, extend the mortgage from 25 to 30 years, or decrease it from 25 to 20, to compensate for fluctuations in interest rates.

FHA and VA Mortgages

FHA Loans

Besides the conventional home loan, another excellent source of financing is the Federal Housing Administration (FHA) mortgage. This kind of loan, from a bank or other traditional lending institution, is insured by the Federal Housing Administration. Although the guidelines for these loans change periodically, the 1977 provisions give a clear idea of how they are arranged. In 1977, an FHA guarantee allowed an individual to borrow 97 percent of the initial $25,000 of the appraised value and closing costs of a house. He could then borrow 90 percent of the next $10,000, and 80 percent of the remainder up to a $45,000 maximum. Interest was set at a limit of nine percent (plus a one-half of one percent fee for insurance). The loans usually ran for terms as long as 30 years. One of the major disadvantages to FHA loans is the imposed ceiling (in this case, $45,000), which is not high enough to finance many homes today. FHA rules prohibit using a second loan to finance the balance of the home's sale price.

FHA Loan Availability

FHA loans are often difficult to obtain; many lenders don't want to bother with them because of the excessive amount of paperwork and the relatively low interest rates involved. FHA loans are more often available at mortgage companies than at banks or savings and loans.

VA Mortgages

Veterans Administration (VA) mortgages are another alternative to conventional home loans. Like FHA loans, VA mortgages (also called GI mortgages) usually offer comparatively low interest rates. No down payment is required, and terms extend to 30 years. There is no limit to the size of the loans, but the guarantees apply to only the first $17,500 (in 1977). VA loans are available to veterans of the United States Armed Forces and other service personnel, and are primarily used to finance older homes. Veterans who have previously taken out VA or GI loans are only eligible for a second loan if the first loan has been paid off.

Dealing with the Legal Matters

The Need for an Attorney

Since the acquisition of a home is usually the largest purchase one makes in his lifetime, it's foolish to try to handle this major transaction without retaining an attorney. Don't depend on the lawyer representing the mortgagor to protect your own interests as well; that is not what he has been hired to do. In most communities, an attorney's fee is about one percent of the sale price of the house.

Closing Costs

Try to find out in advance what the closing costs of the home purchase will amount to. Unfortunately, under a federal law enacted in 1976, mortgage lenders are not required to disclose these fees until one day before closing—and then only if the mortgagee so asks, and only if the lender has prepared the fees in advance. Until this new law went into effect, lenders were required to disclose closing costs at least 12 days before closing. It is wise to ask the lender for a complete rundown of closing costs; some will cooperate and prepare the information in advance as a courtesy, despite the fact that they are no longer legally required to do so. One's lawyer will also work to obtain closing costs in advance.

Paying Off the Mortgage

Many mortgage contracts include a clause that penalizes the mortgagee for paying off the balance of the mortgage before it is due. This provision, quite legal, is nothing to be concerned about; it rarely makes sense to pay off the mortgage ahead of time.

True, some people feel great emotional relief when this large debt is eliminated, and for them, the comfortable feeling may outweigh other factors. But from an economic point of view, paying off a mortgage in advance is foolish. The homeowner could invest that money elsewhere—in corporate bonds, for example—and earn more money than he could save in interest by paying the mortgage in full before its due date. The money could also be placed in a savings account, where it would be available for emergencies. Further, assuming that interest rates remain high, a house with an eight percent mortgage would be more marketable if the new buyer has the opportunity to take over a relatively low mortgage.

The Final Inspection

The day prior to taking legal title to a new house, conduct a personal and thorough inspection tour. Check all built-in appliances, faucets, doors, and windows. If something is wrong, request that it be altered immediately. There may be no later opportunity to do so.

Documents

When taking possession of a house, the buyer and his lawyer should demand the following papers:(1) certificate of occupancy, (2) warranties from all manufacturers for all appliances and equipment in the home, and (3) health department certificates clearing the sewer and plumbing installations.

CONDOMINIUM LIVING

Advantages

Condominiums are a relatively recent phenomenon, but they have become extremely popular throughout the nation. With a condominium, one buys his living quarters much as he would a regular house. He also purchases interest in the complex's community property—from greenbelts and swimming pools to gymnasiums and garages. One of the major advantages of buying a condominium is that the purchase can often be made with a down payment of 10 percent, compared with the 20 percent average down payment required for most conventional houses. The condominium owner also reaps all the tax deductions and equity buildup of the regular homeowner. Many of the tips in the preceding section on homeownership apply to condominium ownership as well.

Disadvantages

Among the major drawbacks to condominiums is that even

though the living quarters are sold to and owned by individuals, ownership of the grounds and recreational facilities is shared by all residents of the condominium. Consequently, an individual owner has relatively little influence in how the grounds and facilities are maintained. If they are cared for poorly, the property value of the entire complex could drop.

Maintenance Fees

Condominium owners pay a monthly "maintenance fee," which covers the costs of maintaining the community property. The fee varies from complex to complex, but for a $50,000 condominium, it may range as high as $50 to $100 a month, which is often more than the typical conventional homeowner pays for similar maintenance of his own house.

Condominium Rip-Offs

Some unscrupulous builders have infiltrated the condominium marketplace, so be careful. The most frequent complaint is that buyers are promised features or services that never materialize. For instance, swimming pools or gymnasiums are presented as part of the entire package, but they are never built. Buyers also frequently complain that promised occupancy dates are not met, and that maintenance fees are understated. Often the total number of units in the complex is overestimated, thus forcing each condominium owner to bear a larger share of the common costs. Be sure all promises are put in writing, in case legal action has to be taken later.

The Builder

Before buying a condominium, find out as much as possible about the builder. Check with local banks, real estate boards, and tenants in his other developments. Also contact the Community Association Institute, 1200 18th Street, N.W., Washington, D.C. 20036. If doubts about his reliability surface, don't invest in the development.

Escrow Account

When placing a deposit on a condominium, don't allow it to become part of other funds of the developer. Instead, ask that it be placed in an escrow account in your name. All bank statements relative to this account should be sent to you.

Resale Potential

Before investing in a condominium, consider what its resale value may be several years from now. For resale purposes, the best location for a condominium is in an area where property values are rising, and where there is a combination of apartments and relatively expensive single-family homes.

Evaluate who the neighbors are. They must be financially reliable, or it could affect everyone in the condominium complex. If they default on their payments when maintenance costs rise, everyone else may have to share the burden.

Also make certain that a condominium owner will be free to sell his unit whenever he wishes and to whomever he wishes. In some complexes, the developer has a right of first refusal, or some other control over the right of re-sale. Avoid such restrictions.

MOBILE HOMES

Less-Expensive Housing

Mobile home living is generally less expensive than other types of housing. That conclusion is reached in a 1973 study published in the *Washington and Lee Review*. The study compared the 10-year cost of a $6,500 mobile home, a $19,000 condominium, and a $150-a-month apartment—taking into account the costs of renting or buying, insurance, taxes, and maintenance. The money spent for the mobile home turned out to be $4,000 less than the money expended for the apartment, and $5,000 less than that for the condominium. Although the average costs of the three kinds of housing have increased significantly since the study was made, mobile home living remains the cheapest.

Two Types

There are two basic types of mobile homes—the *single-wide* and the *double-wide*. The single-wide is composed of one section, and is usually 45 to 65 feet long, and 12 to 14 feet wide. It contains five rooms, plus a bath, and will fit the needs of those who don't require large amounts of space. The average price of a single-wide home is $10,000 to $12,000.

Double-wide mobile homes are manufactured in two sections—like two halves of a house. They are transported on flatbed trucks, and are attached when they reach their permanent or semipermanent site. The homes have as many as four bedrooms, a kitchen, a living room, a den, and two and one-half baths. Each half of this double-wide home is 10 to 14 feet wide and 40 to 70 feet long. This home averages $16,000 to $18,000 in cost, although some range as high as $40,000 and up.

Building Codes

Local building codes that apply to conventional homes

usually do not apply to mobile homes. But in mid-1976, a building code specifically for mobile homes went into effect. The national code assures mobile home buyers that the units they purchase have met minimum standards of construction, design, and safety. Included are requirements that the materials used for walls and ceilings resist the spread of flames, and that an approved smoke detector be installed in each bedroom area. Before buying a mobile home, look for a certification label indicating that it has been inspected and that it meets the code's standards.

Points to Check

When shopping for a mobile home, check the following points in each unit: Is the floor strong, or are there soft spots? Is there adequate storage space? Are electrical outlets conveniently located? Is the quality of the furniture good? Is the home well insulated? Do the windows move freely, and are storm windows and screens provided?

Check the weight of a mobile home; as a rule, the heavier a home, the better.

Negotiating the Deal

Request a copy of the manufacturer's written warranty, which is typically good for one year. Also ask the dealer for a copy of the *Official Mobile Market Report*, which compares the current retail prices of major mobile homes. See how the price of the model being considered compares to similar homes.

The buyer who has furniture should request a discount for furnishing the unit on his own, rather than using the seller's furniture.

Sales Tax

In many states, mobile homes are considered motor vehicles, not real estate. Accordingly, sales tax is charged when they are purchased, and annual registration and license fees must be paid. As with property taxes, however, registration costs are usually tax-deductible on both state and federal tax returns. Mobile homes are normally financed as automobiles rather than as regular houses, and at higher interest rates (12 percent to 14 percent).

Depreciation

One of the major drawbacks to purchasing a mobile home is its tendency to depreciate in value. Whereas a regular house almost always appreciates—it is worth more when it is sold than when it was bought—the opposite is usually true of mobile homes. Those mobile homes least likely to depreciate are the double-wide models that are located in well-kept parks in metropolitan centers.

Parks

Because the site on which a mobile home is placed is important, select a mobile home park carefully. The better parks now charge between $50 and $125 a month for spaces about 30 to 40 feet wide and 80 to 110 feet long. Some parks don't allow children; if you are a parent, be prepared to pay an extra $5 per child per month in the parks that permit youngsters. A similar $5 fee is charged for pets. To find the mobile home parks in your area, look in *Woodall's Mobile Home & Park Directory,* which lists and describes the nation's 22,000 mobile home parks. Visit several parks, comparing facilities and services. Is the park located near shopping centers and schools? Are nearby streets paved, and is the landscaping attractive?

Moving

Moving a mobile home from one site to another usually requires the assistance of professionals. There are many companies across the country that specialize in transporting modern mobile homes. For moves across state lines, they usually charge about $1.50 per mile for a single-wide model, and $3.50 per mile for a double-wide model.

APARTMENT RENTALS

Finding an Apartment

Apartment-hunting services exist in many communities. But beware! These agencies charge a flat fee (usually about $25), and provide a list of apartments for rent in the area. Sometimes many of the listed "available" apartments aren't for rent at all. Others are in such poor condition as to be unrentable. These services offer no guarantee that suitable living quarters will be found.

Analyzing an Apartment

When shopping for an apartment, take into consideration many of the following points: What kind of security has been provided for the building and its tenants? What appliances come with the apartment? Are the appliances in working order? How much furniture will have to be bought? Is there space enough to accommodate the furniture you already own? Will some of it have to be sold or put in storage? Are the walls soundproof? Are there storm windows? Is there air conditioning? A fireplace? Adequate ventilation? A convenient floor plan?

Also, is there an adjacent garage or carport that can be used at no additional charge? Is laundry equipment available? Does the manager live on the premises, and is he easily accessible to the tenants?

Free Rent?

In order to attract tenants, some apartment owners offer a free month's rent on a one-year lease. That savings is usually spread out over the 12-month period. Thus, if one rents a $240-a-month apartment, the rent will be reduced by $20 each month to cover the rent concession. No one can argue that the saving isn't attractive, but when the lease expires, the rent will probably be raised based on the real monthly rent ($240) rather than on what has actually been paid ($220). If the increase is 15 percent, in this case the rent will rise from $220 to $276—which could be a substantial strain of one's budget.

Federal Rent Assistance

Individuals unable to afford the rent demanded for the size apartment they require may be eligible for federal rent assistance. One qualifies for aid under the Section 8 program of the Department of Housing and Urban Development if his income is no more than 80 percent of the median income in the area and at least 25 percent of his income is now being spent on rent. When a qualified individual moves to a larger and more expensive apartment, he is eligible to receive federal funds that will pay for the increase in rent. As an example, let's assume that the median annual income in a given community is $12,000, and that Mr. X's income is $9,600. Further, let's assume that Mr. X now pays $200 a month for rent, or $2,400 a year, which is 25 percent of his income. If Mr. X moves to a larger apartment that rents for $275, HUD would pay the landlord the $75 difference between Mr. X's new and old rents. (Because the rent assistance program is designed to encourage the construction of new apartments, assistance is only available to those moving into *new* apartment buildings. For additional information, contact the local office of HUD.)

Leases

Before signing a lease, read it carefully, looking specifically to see that the following stipulations are included:

—The time period of the lease, with starting and termination dates clearly stated.

—The amount of rent to be paid, and monthly due date.

—A clear description of the property being rented.

—The terms under which a security deposit will eventually be returned.

—A description of who is responsible for necessary repairs and maintenance, including how frequently the landlord will paint the apartment.

—Services (electricity, gas) and appliances (stove, refrigerator, air conditioner) to be provided by the landlord.

—Rules regarding use of the apartment (Are pets acceptable? Can an outside television antenna be installed? Do tenants have free access to the swimming pool or recreation room?).

—Right of the tenant to sublease the apartment.

—Right of the tenant to legally cancel the lease before its expiration date if his employer transfers him to another location.

Unacceptable Lease Clauses

There are certain lease clauses that should be considered unacceptable. Ask that they be deleted before signing the lease. Some of the more common undesirable provisions include:

—The right of the landlord to cancel the lease and hold the tenant liable for rent due for the balance of the lease if the tenant should ever be late in paying rent by even one day.

—The right of the landlord to arbitrarily evict the tenant if he should decide that he dislikes the tenant's behavior or feels that his mere presence is somehow harming his property.

—The right of the landlord to enter the apartment when the tenant is not present (at times other than emergencies).

—The stipulation that the tenant and his immediate family shall be the only tenants of the apartment, thus making it impossible for the tenant to have overnight guests.

—The right of the landlord to raise the rent under certain conditions before the lease expires—for example, if the landlord's taxes or energy bills increase.

Landlords

After a tenant has occupied his apartment, if the landlord becomes uncooperative and refuses to honor legitimate requests, the tenant would be wise to join with other tenants to carry out an organized action. Serve the landlord with a petition, demanding that he provide the requested services. If the landlord remains unresponsive, file formal complaints with appropriate local agencies, such as the health department. If necessary, contact the tenants' rights group in the community to further pressure the landlord to comply with the law. Before withholding rent, check with a lawyer to ascertain the tenants' rights, and to see whether such action might make the tenants subject to eviction. Withheld rent can sometimes be legally placed in an escrow account, where it is held until all justified requests have been met.

SELLING A HOUSE

Springtime Sales

Is there a best time of the year to try to sell a house? Most brokers say the peak buying season is the spring. A house purchased in the spring can be made ready for occupancy by its new owners in the summer, thus not disrupting their children's schooling. Autumn is usually the next-best time to sell.

Preparing for Sale

Put the house in order before placing it on the market. Paint or paper any walls that really need it (use neutral-colored paint that won't clash with a potential buyer's furniture—or taste). Clean the carpets, straighten up the closets and the attic, fix leaky faucets, and make any other minor repairs. These small improvements usually bring the seller a higher price for the house, although it is harder to recover investments made for major improvements. So avoid making such significant enhancements as installing new carpeting or central air conditioning. (Minor repairs that cost a total of $100 or $200 can often bring an additional $1,000 in the sale price!)

The Price

How does one decide upon an appropriate selling price? One way is to ask several brokers to appraise the house, having them take into account the neighborhood and current price trends. Be aware, though, that some brokers will quote what seems to be an outrageously high price in hopes of obtaining an exclusive listing.

Another means of determining the selling price for a home is to personally examine similar houses that are for sale, and price yours competitively. Or hire a professional appraiser (for $75 to $200), who will analyze the house and neighborhood, quote a price, and offer his reasons for deciding upon that figure. Appraisers can be located through the Yellow Pages, usually listed under "Real Estate Appraisers."

Once an appropriate *selling* price has been decided upon, add five percent to determine the *asking* price. This will allow some room for bargaining.

The Real Estate Broker

By selling a house without the aid of a real estate broker, a homeowner will save the broker's fee, which usually ranges from six to eight percent of the selling price. Before deciding to do so, however, weigh the many factors involved. For instance, through their extensive advertising, brokers are better able to attract buyers. They can show the house when the owner is not home; they will keep away people not serious about buying; and they will often help the buyer locate mortgage money. Incidentally, never grant a broker permission to handle a very salable house without first negotiating with several brokers for a reduction in their commissions.

Exclusive Listing

A broker will normally ask for an exclusive listing of a house, which usually binds the homeowner to paying him a commission even if the homeowner finds a buyer on his own. Under such circumstances, try to choose the best broker in the community (ask a local banker for suggestions), and limit his exclusivity to three months—although some will try to win six-month listings.

Open Listing

An open-listing contract is the preferred arrangement. Under this system, the seller can work with as many brokers at one time as he wishes; the broker who finds a buyer receives the entire commission. If the homeowner finds the buyer himself, no commission is paid.

With another alternative, the multiple listing, the house is listed with a single agent, who then shares it with other brokers. This original agent splits the commission with whichever broker finds a buyer.

The broker should be asked to advise the seller in advance when a prospective buyer is being brought over to look at the house. When a prospective customer is expected, the house should be tidy. Once the broker arrives with the client, the homeowner should be as unobtrusive as possible. The broker will show the individual around; the homeowner should only offer comments when asked. The broker is more experienced at "saying the right things."

Guaranteed Sale

Some real estate brokers buy houses outright, or guarantee sale within a particular time period (often 90 days). However, unless a job transfer or other circumstances require that a house be sold immediately, such transactions are not advisable for home-owners. These brokers normally only guarantee the seller 80 percent, or possibly 85 percent, of the market value of the home—less than could probably be obtained by selling it in the normal manner. If it is absolutely necessary to make such an arrangement, obtain bids from three or four brokers regarding their guarantees.

Selling It Yourself

When acting as your own agent, use the brokers' technique of placing classified ads in local newspapers and in company newsletters. Also post notices on supermarket bulletin boards. Put a "For Sale" sign on the front lawn, with the phone number clearly visible.

Selling a house on your own will entail having to handle many of the other tasks normally handled by a broker. Before looking for a buyer, try to locate a source for financing. Talk to the loan officers at various banks. Hire an attorney to handle all legal matters, including the purchase agreement, the deed, and the transfer papers.

THE ART OF MOVING

Early Planning

Moving can be either an exciting or a traumatic experience, depending on how well one is prepared. Begin planning as early as possible. When moving during the summer months—the peak periods for moving companies—book well in advance (at least 30 and preferably 45 days ahead of time). If possible, avoid the busy periods; try to schedule the move between mid-October and mid-May, when rates are cheaper. Also, try not to move early or late in the month, when rental leases usually expire and the moving business increases.

Estimates

Get estimates from at least three moving companies as to what they will charge for the move. Each will come to the house to make the estimate; be certain to point out *all* the items to be transported—not just the major pieces of furniture. Don't forget the bicycles, power tools, and the dozens of smaller possessions. Inform them of special situations that may affect the price of moving—for example, stairs that the movers will have to climb at the new home. Be suspicious if one estimate is considerably lower than the others—the difference in price will be made up somewhere.

Performance Record

Every year, all interstate moving companies are required by law to file a report of their performance record, which is then published by the Interstate Commerce Commission. The moving companies submit such information as how often shipments were picked up or delivered late, what percentage of shipments had damage claims, and how frequently shipments were underestimated. All interstate movers are required to provide copies of their performance records to potential customers. Although these reports may be helpful in comparing the efficiency of moving companies, they are no more than the company's report about itself. There is always a possibility that some have submitted evaluations that make their performances appear more impressive than they really are.

Fees

For local moves, moving companies usually base their fees on the number of hours worked. Long distance moves that cross state lines are under the regulation of the Interstate Commerce Commission, and charges are usually based on weight and distance. Incidentally, if movers have to make more than one stop, extra charges will be added. So gather all possessions in one place for pickup.

Weight

When moves are charged by the weight of the items being moved, it is important to the customer that the reported weight figures are accurate. By Interstate Commerce Commission regulations, the mover must inform the customer in advance where the van will be weighed. Once the move is completed, the mover must give the customer the official tickets that show what the van weighed both *before* and *after* the goods were loaded. At the point of destination, the customer can demand that the loaded van be weighed again, and the mover must pay for this second weighing if the load turns out to be more than 100 pounds under the weight claimed.

Change of Address Notification

Shortly before moving, the following parties should be notified of change of address: the local post office branch, the magazines to which one subscribes, insurance companies, creditors, the state motor vehicles department, friends, and relatives. The following services should be discontinued or transferred: telephone, electric power, water, gas, milkman, newspaper delivery, dry cleaning service, and diaper service.

The Day Before

The day before moving, make a list of all items that the mover will load on his truck. Beside each item, write down any appropriate information, including damage that might already exist on the goods. When the movers arrive, give them a copy of the list. When they eventually unload the truck, check off each item, one by one. Never sign a receipt until everything is accounted for and checked for damage as much as possible.

Packing

Although movers will pack all belongings, they will charge for the time it takes them to do so, and will also charge for the packing containers they provide. It is, therefore, preferable for the customer to do most or all of the packing himself. However, let them pack valuable china, crystal, ceramics, and other fragile items. Since some items won't be unpacked until after the movers have left, sign the receipt but add the phrase "subject to later inspection for concealed loss or damage."

Damage and Insurance

Even the most efficient movers sometimes break things (damage claims for $50 or more are filed on 16 percent of all interstate moves). When this happens, the mover is liable for only 60 cents per pound per article. Thus, the customer is only reimbursed $1.20 for a broken two-pound vase, or $12 for a severely damaged 20-pound electric typewriter. This is not nearly enough protection, particularly for valuable items, such as furniture and glassware. It is, therefore, wise to invest in insurance, available from the moving company. Note, too, that movers are not liable for cash, securities, coin collections, jewelry, and other such items—so move such items personally.

Exchange of Information

Movers should always be provided with an address and phone number where the customer can be reached while his possessions are in transit. In turn, the customer should obtain the name of the driver, the van number, the shipment number, and the planned route. This information will be necessary if there is a need to trace the shipment.

Payment

Be prepared to pay the moving bill when the belongings arrive at their destination. On local moves, a personal check is usually accepted. But on longer moves, a certified check, a cashier's check, a money order, or traveler's checks are necessary in the amount of the estimated cost of the move. Enough extra cash should be available to cover any extra charges. On interstate moves, if the actual cost exceeds the estimate by more than 10 percent, the balance may be paid within 15 business days.

Tipping

Movers need never be tipped. In fact, tipping is illegal in interstate moves, as well as in most states. If a mover ever applies pressure for a tip, contact the Interstate Commerce Commission, Washington, D.C. 20423.

Self-Moving

About 15 percent of all Americans who move transport all their possessions themselves, usually with the aid of a haul-it-yourself trailer or truck. By renting a trailer, the cost of a move is reduced by at least 50 to 60 percent.

Moving a House

The ultimate move is one that involves not only one's family and possessions, but one's very house. House haulers are listed in the Yellow Pages, frequently under "House Movers" (although they also move office buildings, bridges, towers, and sports stadiums). It is usually less expensive to move a house than to build a new one—unless the move is over a very long distance (most house moves are under 25 miles). A single-story frame house costs between $3,500 and $5,500 to move a few miles; a brick house of the same size costs as much as $9,000. Two-story houses are more expensive.

Preparing for a House Move

When having one's house moved from one location to another, most moving experts recommend that breakable items be removed from the house. Heavy furniture may be left inside the structure. Although the hauler carries his own insurance policies to protect the house itself, the possessions that remain inside are not covered. Homeowner's insurance policies offer some protection for moves of this kind, but if coverage is limited, request that a rider be added to the policy, increasing protection.

CHAPTER 5

Furnishings and Appliances

Although furniture prices continue to rise, furniture quality continues to drop—often to embarrassingly low levels. Even merchants sometimes complain to manufacturers about the poor quality of their products. Some merchants refuse to sell it; others are quite content to pass along shoddy merchandise to unwary customers, often at inflated prices.

How can one tell if a bargain is really a bargain? Consider the bed, which may be the most important piece of furniture a person ever purchases (we spend one-third of every day in it!). An item that is used so much has to be chosen carefully. But frequently those "drastic reduction" sales persuade consumers to buy beds that don't satisfy their sleeping needs.

Baby furniture, particularly cribs, are also very controversial items. Crib accidents result in 200 infant deaths and 50,000 injuries a year. Safety is an all-important consideration when purchasing cribs.

People are buying more carpeting and appliances now than ever before. Air conditioner sales leaped 20 percent in 1976, despite the energy crunch. Eight million new color television sets were sold the same year. But consumers don't often shop as carefully as they should. A 20 percent discount on a $400 refrigerator can cut its cost to $320. And since the average American family owns at least five major appliances, a discount on each one could add up to an impressive overall savings.

In a survey conducted by a national dealers' association, many retailers admitted that they engage in a practice called "selling up"—placing every low-priced carpeting line, freezer, or other major item next to a more expensive brand or model with more elaborate features, hoping to persuade consumers to buy the more costly one rather than the reasonably priced one. Shoppers always have to be wary of schemes like this.

While some new features and conveniences are nothing more than money-wasters, others are worth the extra investment. Keep track of innovations in carpeting and appliances by reading the newspapers and consumer magazines. The microwave oven, for instance, appears to be revolutionizing cooking. It emits electromagnetic waves, which set the food's own molecules in motion, creating heat and thus cooking the food in its own juices.

FURNITURE

Six Cardinal Rules of Furniture Buying

1. Before buying a piece of furniture, decide where it will be placed—and make certain it will fit. That sofa on sale isn't a bargain if it will block a doorway.

2. Buy furniture that will look good in more than one room. The greater the versatility of the furniture in a home, the more numerous the possibilities for changing atmosphere and environment.

3. Look for sales. Fine quality furniture is offered at reduced prices from time to time. Large items, particularly sofas and chairs, are frequently on sale in January-February and August-September.

4. Don't buy cheap furniture because it's cheap. Although tempting, it is often a bad investment. If the materials and the construction of furniture are inferior, its life expectancy will be brief. There are exceptions, such as unfinished furniture which is low-priced but is still of good quality. But as a rule you get what you pay for.

5. Don't be afraid to haggle. Even in the most exclusive furniture stores, it is often possible to bargain for a lower price. Furniture is marked up considerably, and in periods of sagging sales, stores may be willing to lower prices to make room for new items in their showrooms or warehouses.

6. Look for sales of floor samples, seconds, or slightly-damaged furniture. Savings on these pieces can be considerable, and the damage is frequently scarcely noticeable. An item is often automatically classified a second if it has a minor blemish, a flaw undetectable by the average customer.

Wood Furniture

Best Types

The best types of furniture wood are the hardwoods—walnut, mahogany, maple, oak, pecan. The soft woods—cedar, redwood, pine, cypress—are less expensive, but less durable.

Grain

Examine the grain of the wood on any piece of furniture before buying it. The grain should run parallel to the length of the wood, not across it. If certain parts of the furniture—particularly table legs and tops, or chair arms and legs—have anything other than this straight grain, they will be prone to splitting or warping.

Finish

The finish on wood furniture should be inspected closely. Ask the salesman if it will withstand water or food stains. If he claims that it will, ask for a written guarantee stipulating that the store will assume responsibliity if various stains damage the finish.

Defining Terms

Furniture cannot legally be labeled "wood" if it isn't. Beware of such terms as "walnut-style" or "walnut-finish" or "maple-like," that only describe the finish of an item, not the material of which it is made.

Unfinished Furniture

Good Buys

One can save between $5 and $25 on some furniture by buying it unfinished. Bookcases, chairs, and chests are all good choices for home finishing, and can be bought in furniture stores, department stores, and lumber yards, as well as stores specializing in unfinished items. Many merchants who sell such furniture will provide instructions on the best finishing techniques.

Upholstered Furniture

Fabric Grades

Fabrics are usually graded with either a letter or a number by the mills that manufacture them. The most common system uses letters, usually on a scale from A to Z, with A the lowest grade and Z the highest. The higher-graded fabrics are more durable, so it is advisable to buy the highest grade one can afford.

Color

When selecting colors for furniture, choose those that will harmonize with the furnishings already in the home. Keep in mind that dirt will be more obvious on light-colored fabrics, and dust and lint more visible on dark-colored ones. In addition, upholstered furniture that will be exposed to sunlight should be fade-resistant.

Cushions

Check to be sure that the cushions on sofas or chairs fit snugly. The best values in cushions are those made of foam, which are both durable and nonallergenic. Cushions that are down-filled are comfortable, but difficult to keep puffed up. A better selection is a combination of down and feathers. Also keep in mind the desirability of reversible cushions.

Reupholstering

The cost of reupholstering an old chair or sofa may be almost as much as buying a new one. Labor costs for reupholstering have become very high. The cost is particularly inflated for channel-back or tufted furniture.

Beds

Size

Twin beds range from 38" x 75" to 38" x 80"; double beds are 53" x 75"; queen-sized are 60" x 80"; and king-sized are from 76" x 80" to 76" x 84". A bed should be at least 10 inches longer than its tallest sleeper. Each occupant needs from 36 to 38 inches of width. The mattress should fit individual needs, but don't buy a bed that's larger than necessary; the larger the bed, the greater the outlay of money for linens and bedspreads.

Types

Two kinds of mattresses are available: innerspring and foam. Both cost approximately the same, and a foam mattress that is solid and at least five inches thick will be just as comfortable and durable as an innerspring mattress. Physicians often recommend foam mattresses for individuals who suffer from allergies.

Foam Mattress

A foam mattress is lighter than an innerspring, and is intended to give a floating sensation. A foam mattress requires a sturdy box spring beneath it, which will have to support much of the weight. The box spring to be used with a foam mattress should have between 70 and 80 coils.

Firmness

Even with a good box spring, choose as firm a foam mattress as is available. Look for one with a high density of rubber. A density rating of 30 to 37 is an indication that a mattress is very firm. A 25 to 29 rating indicates that the mattresss is less firm, but still quite good. A mattress with a density of 20 to 24 has a medium firmness, and less than 19 is probably unacceptable for most consumers.

Support

A good mattress will provide support for the entire body; it will not sink at the points where body weight is greatest. Its handles will be attached securely, and it will have ventilators on its sides to permit circulation. If the mattress is an innerspring model, the padding should be thick enough to protect a baby from the springs.

Testing

To test the quality of a mattress, sit on its edges. Does it sink down, or is it as firm along its borders as in its center? Edges that are vertically stitched will provide greater support. So will added fortification provided by a substance such as urethane.

Bottom Slat

A good box spring will have a horizonal wooden slat on its bottomside to support each row of its coils.

Best Buy

When *Consumer Reports* (January 1976) rated foam mattresses, it gave a rating of "A Best Buy" to Sears Siesta Sleep Set Serofoam Medium Firm ($58 for a double mattress, plus $58 for foundation). Other highly-rated mattresses were manufactured by Montgomery Ward, J.C. Penney, Englander, Serta, and Thera-pedic.

Used Mattresses

Never purchase a used mattress. Aside from risking the possibility that it may have lost some of its comfort, the danger exists that a used mattress may be disease-infested.

Waterbeds

Some people find waterbeds more comfortable than conventional mattresses. According to its advocates, a waterbed's pressure is equally distributed over the sleeper's entire body, and tossing and turning are lessened considerably.

Keep these factors in mind before investing in a waterbed: (1) it is not easy to fill and empty; (2) it requires its own heating system (unless you don't mind sleeping on a bed of cool water!); and (3) the water must be regularly treated with chemicals to prevent the formation of algae.

Baby Furniture

Cribs

The slats on the sides of a crib should be no more than 2⅜ inches apart to make it impossible for a baby to put his head between them. A rail height of 26 inches is also a necessity. The crib mattress should fit snugly, so that no part of the baby's body can slide between the frame and the mattress. If two fingers can be slipped between the crib and the mattress, a larger mattress is needed.

Although cribs with sides that slide up and down are convenient, be certain that the sides can be locked securely. Latches should be positioned at both the head and the foot of the crib in such a way that neither baby nor his older brothers and sisters can manipulate them. If the sides should accidentally collapse, the child could fall to the floor and injure himself. Although double drop-side cribs are available (at $20 over the price of single drop-side cribs), don't bother with them if one side of the crib will be placed against the wall.

Consumer Reports (June 1975) gave its top rating for a single drop-side model to the Hopkins 916 crib ($40-$50). Other top-rated cribs were manufactured by Montgomery Ward, Welsh, Nod-a-Way, and Simmons.

Strollers

A stroller should be weight-balanced so that a child seated inside is unable to tip it over. It should have no protruding or pointy parts, and should be equipped with a brake. The so-called "umbrella" or "folding" lightweight strollers can be equally as safe as the more conventional "pusher-type" models which are not nearly as compact when collapsed.

When shopping for a stroller, look for those with a backup safety catch to prevent the unit from folding if the main lock fails. (Check out the Silver Cross models—both conventional and umbrella—manufactured by Carriage Craft).

Car Seats

The label of a child's car seat should indicate that it was manufactured after April 1971, the month in which new Federal Trade Commission safety standards became law. A car seat should be sturdy and well-padded.

Two informative booklets can be obtained on buying car seats: "Stop Risking Your Child's Life" (25 cents plus a self-addressed stamped envelope) from Physicians for Automotive Safety, 50 Union Avenue, Irvington, New Jersey 07111; and "What to Buy in Child Restraint Systems" (20 cents) from the Superintendent of Documents, Washington, D.C. 20402.

CARPETING

Characteristics

Materials

Because of its high durability and resilience, its resistance to soiling, and its ease of cleaning, wool is by far the most expensive carpeting fiber. Synthetics are usually more moderately priced, including acrylic, nylon, polyester, and olefin. Nylon, for instance, has good resilience and durability, and it is your best carpeting buy. Acrilon is another good carpeting buy.

Flammability

Wool and nylon carpeting present little flammability hazard. Nylon simply won't burn; wool tends to smolder rather than burn. Other carpet fibers, particularly rayon, burn very quickly.

Durability

The type of carpeting purchased should depend in part on the amount of traffic the carpet will bear. When carpeting a family room, kitchen, or hallway—areas that get heavy traffic—choose a tough fiber, such as nylon, rather than a polyester or acrylic. Twists and shag carpets are good choices for heavily-traveled parts of the house (like vestibules and hallways). They are durable, disguise dirt rather well, and demand less care than other types of carpeting. When carpeting bedrooms or other light-traffic areas, the softer fibers are most often used.

Sales

Special sales are held on all kinds of carpeting periodically. But beware: if a price seems extremely low, be sure to examine the carpeting closely. As with most consumer products, the price of carpeting usually reflects its quality.

Woven vs. Tufted

Carpeting currently available is either woven or "tufted." "Tufted" carpeting is the cheaper to manufacture; its pile is sewed to the backing, and then is sealed with rubber latex. Carpeting woven on a loom is generally stronger than tufted, but good tufted carpeting is available. The better tufted carpets have a double backing rather than a single one. Single-backed carpeting tends to ripple, stretch, and even tear.

Broadloom

Some buyers believe that the designation "broadloom" automatically guarantees that the carpet is of superior quality. Such is not the case. The term indicates only that the carpet has been woven on a wide loom and is without seams.

Testing

When shopping for carpeting, dig your fingers into the various materials to evaluate depth and density. When you pull your fingers away, see if the indentations that have been made spring back to their original position. A good carpet will immediately do so.

Labels

Read carpet labels carefully. Be sure to take note of the date of manufacture; carpets made after April 16, 1971 must comply with the Federal Trade Commission's fire safety standards. The label will also note the name of the manufacturer, the country from which it came, and the fibers that the carpet contains—by name and percentage.

Carpet Texture and Color

Adding Feeling

Carpet texture gives a room a particular appearance and feeling. Rough textures project a casual appearance; smooth textures give a more formal feeling.

Choice of colors is also important. After all, except for the walls, carpets are the largest area of color in a room. Because soils show up readily on very light or very bright colors, the most practical selections are medium or deep shades of red, green, blue, violet, brown, beige, or grey. Carpets that are multicolored—tweeds or stripes—usually conceal dirt better than solids.

The so-called "warm" colors—reds, oranges, yellows—tend to make rooms appear smaller. By comparison, the "cool" colors—greens, blues, purples—make rooms seem larger.

Carpeting Costs

Determining the Cost

To determine the approximate cost of carpeting a room, measure the area to be covered, and multiply the length (in feet) by the width (in feet). Then divide by nine to obtain the number of square yards that will be needed. Finally, multiply again by the price per square yard.

Discontinued Lines and Remainders

Good carpet buys can frequently be found on discontinued carpet lines or on the remainder of a special order (a carpet store has custom-dyed an entire roll for a particular customer, but has not used all of it).

Imperfections

If a carpet has been placed on sale because it is "imperfect," find out what that imperfection is. Is it not uniformly dyed, is it improperly weaved, or is it missing some tufts? Identify the imperfection before purchase.

Examination Upon Delivery

When new carpeting is delivered, examine it carefully. Is it the same quality carpet that has been paid for? Check the labels carefully.

Installation Cost

Low-grade carpets are rarely worth having installed wall-to-wall. Installation would cost too much in relation to the price of the carpet itself, and the life of the carpet may be relatively short anyway. If the carpet lasts only five years, a new installation cost will have to be paid for the replacement.

Whether carpeting is expensive or cheap, the labor costs for installation should be the same. Don't let a merchant charge more for installing an expensive carpet; his own costs are identical.

Increasing Carpet Life Expectancy

Stairways

Carpeting for stairways should be a little longer than is actually needed. About every 1½ to 2 years, hire a carpet installer to shift the carpeting about three inches. Because carpeting on stairs wears out faster than carpeting in any other location, the repositioning of the carpeting can increase its life expectancy four or five times.

Cushion

A good-quality cushion, such as one made of hair and jute, placed underneath carpeting can extend the life of the carpet by as much as 135 percent. That, at least, is what tests conducted by the National Bureau of Standards have revealed. In addition to hair and jute, cushions made of foam rubber are available. Although the latter are more expensive, they help increase a rug's life expectancy even more—by 145 percent. Compromise between the two by buying a rubber-coated hair-and-jute cushion, which resists dirt better than a regular hair and jute cushion, and is also more durable.

Carpets or Rugs?

Advantages of Rugs

Most people prefer carpets over rugs. But rugs, unlike carpets, can be turned so that they wear evenly. If one part of a room has significantly more foot traffic than another, rotating the rug can solve the problem of uneven wear.

It is preferable to purchase a high-quality area rug instead of inexpensive wall-to-wall carpeting. Most of the buying tips applicable to carpets are also relevant for rugs.

APPLIANCES

Shopping Tips

Consider the Cost

Before purchasing an appliance, ask whether its use will justify its cost. Will the electric ice-cream maker be used more than once or twice a summer, or will it primarily be a shelf decoration? Will a juice extractor be merely a dust collector? Is it worth buying a rug shampooer, or would it be more economical to rent a rug shampooer when one is needed.

Extra Features

Do not spend money on extra appliance features that will not be used. Most automatic oven timers, for instance, are never used. And a washing machine industry study found that most women do not use all the settings and dials on their automatic washers, simply because they don't understand the purpose of each. In addition to increasing the sale price of appliances, these features are just something else that may someday be in need of repair.

Added Costs

The price tag hanging from a large appliance does not necessarily include all costs. Most discount houses and department stores add on delivery and installation fees.

"Year-Old" Models

Save money on appliances by purchasing "last year's" model when the new models are released. As with cars, many appliances carry a model year designation, and when the new models come out, the old ones are sold at considerable discounts.

Operation Costs

When shopping for appliances, keep in mind what they will cost through the years in terms of energy consumption. The more elaborate the appliances, the higher their electricity consumption.

Below are listed the average yearly operating costs for electrical appliances:

Appliance	Average Annual Kilowatt Hours Used	Average Annual Operating Costs at 4.2¢ per KWH
Water heater, quick recovery	4,811	$202.22
Water heater, standard	4,219	177.20
Refrigerator-freezer, 14 cu. ft. frostless	1,829	76.82
Room air conditioner, ¾ ton	1,389	58.34
Refrigerator, 12 cu. ft. frostless	1,217	51.11
Electric kitchen range	1,175	49.36
Clothes dryer	993	41.70
Color television (tube)	660	27.72
Color television (solid state)	440	18.48
Dishwasher	363	15.24
Black-and-white television tube	350	14.70
Microwave oven	190	7.98
Auxiliary room heater (radiant)	176	7.40
Electric blanket	147	6.18
Electric iron	144	6.04
Black-and-white television (solid state)	120	5.04
Automatic washing machine	103	4.32
Coffee maker	90	3.78
Radio	86	3.62
Sewing machine	75	3.15
Iron	60	2.52
Vacuum cleaner	46	1.93
Toaster	39	1.64
Floor polisher	15	.63
Carving knife	8	.34
Blender	.9	.04
Can opener	.3	.01

Gas vs. Electricity

Generally, gas is a cheaper energy source than electricity. A gas water heater, for example, may cost anywhere from 25 to 50 percent less to operate than an electric water heater. So if it costs $15 a month to operate an electric water heater, it might cost as little as $8 for its gas counterpart. However, if a home is already equipped with mostly electric appliances, don't run out to buy gas appliances to replace them. The savings in reduced energy bills probably won't offset the cost of the new purchases. As the old appliances break down through normal wear, however, replace them with new gas models.

Small Appliance Service

When shopping for a small appliance, ask the store clerk about the manufacturer's service facilities. Is there an authorized service center in town? Or will the product have to be mailed across the country if it needs repair?

Check to make sure that small electric appliances have their original serial number on them. If they don't, many manufacturers will not honor the guarantee.

UL and AGA Seals

Underwriters' Laboratories tests electrical products for their safety. It checks to make sure electrical items won't overheat, and that they are properly insulated. When basic standards are met, the manufacturer has the right to put the UL seal on its product. Never buy an electrical item that does not carry the UL seal. Gas appliances should be affixed with the AGA (American Gas Association) seal, indicating that safety standards have been met.

Refrigerators

Will It Fit?

Before shopping for a refrigerator, measure not only the kitchen space into which it must fit, but also the height and width of the doors through which it will have to be carried. A big refrigerator that meets the family's needs perfectly is not worth much if it will have to be kept on the front porch.

When to Buy

The best month of the year to buy a refrigerator is June, when discounts of 10 to 20 percent are common. At any other time of year, be sure to comparison shop. The "house brand" refrigerators sold by Sears or Montgomery Ward are generally less expensive than the nationally-advertised makes, except in June when the prices are about equal.

The Size

A family of two should purchase a refrigerator with a fresh food section eight cubic feet in size. For each additional family member, add at least one more cubic foot. Those who entertain frequently might want to add still another cubic foot or two. For the freezer section, figure on about two cubic feet per individual. Also consider future needs—perhaps eight cubic feet for fresh food is sufficient now, but what about in five years when there may be several children to feed?

Doors

Most refrigerator doors are hinged on the right side. Left-hinged doors are obtainable, but often at an extra cost. Ideally, a refrigerator door should open facing the work area in the kitchen.

Ice Makers

Although an automatic ice maker is a convenient feature, particularly for those who entertain frequently, it adds to the price of the refrigerator. Also, because additional plumbing is usually needed to transmit water into the unit to make ice, the installation costs are often higher than normal.

Condenser Coils

Inspect the condenser coils of a refrigerator before buying. If they are located *under* the refrigerator, the unit can be pushed almost flush against the wall. If the coils are in the *back* of the refrigerator, added space must be left between the appliance and the wall to allow for circulation.

Guarantees

Ask the refrigerator salesman what the guarantee actually covers. Guarantees differ. A "five-year guarantee" for a refrigerator often does not cover the entire appliance; it only covers the compressor. Other guarantees cover the complete refrigerator except for the motor, which is more likely to have problems than any other part of the unit.

Recommended Buys

When *Consumers's Research Magazine* (1976 annual) recommended refrigerators with top-mounted freezers, it gave its highest rating to Hotpoint CTF 18EP ($350), Kelvinator TCK180FN ($420), and Westinghouse RT174R ($360).

The Cost

How much will a refrigerator cost the consumer over its average 14-year life span? According to researchers at the Massachusetts Institute of Technology, a $400 refrigerator will cost its owner about $1,100 by the end of its life cycle. The purchase price figures out to be only 36 percent of the overall cost. Power will account for most of the ultimate expense, and service makes up the remainder.

Keep energy bills down by not buying a refrigerator containing freezer sections equipped with an automatic defrost feature. One industry analysis shows that the automatic defrost models consume two to four times as much energy as manual defrost models.

Freezers

A Good Investment?

A deep freezer, because of its high operating expenses, isn't nearly as good an investment as it used to be. Unless the contents of a 600-pound freezer will be "turned over" at least twice a year, little if any money will be saved at all. The biggest savings are on meats bought on sale and stored. Freezing less expensive, bulky foods saves little.

When considering the cost of owning and operating a freezer, the food stored in it costs about 10 to 25 cents a pound more than if bought and used immediately. Savings are accumulated on food that is bought at considerable discounts, and is then frozen.

Used Freezers

Used freezers can often be found at bargain prices. Check the classified section of the daily newspaper, and bulletin boards in supermarkets. People frequently sell freezers when they move, choosing to give them up rather than transport them across the city or country.

Ranges

Points to Consider

When shopping for a range, consider these points:

—Select only those features that will make cooking easier, not those that duplicate tasks that can be performed by small kitchen appliances one already has.

—If one has a particularly large family or entertains frequently, it may be practical to buy a two-oven range.

—Special dials should not be located so that it becomes necessary to reach over boiling or steaming pots to adjust them.

—A good oven or broiler should have shelf stops that prevent racks from being unintentionally pulled out.

—Consider the ease or difficulty with which a range can be cleaned. The door of the oven should be either removable or should open from the sides. All knobs should be removable as well, as should all components of the broiler and oven.

Self-Cleaning

A self-cleaning oven is a desirable feature, even though it may add from $50 to $100 to the sale price. Ovens equipped to clean themselves allow their temperature to be raised to as high as 1000 degrees F for a short period of time. This temperature activates chemical decomposition of the spills or splatterings in the oven, rendering them into an ash form that can quickly be wiped away with a damp cloth or sponge. This self-cleaning process uses very little energy, and will cost less per cleaning than a chemical cleaner that would otherwise have to be used.

Gas vs. Electric

Gas ranges cost less to operate in most communities than electric ones. The repair costs of gas ranges are also usually not as high, and they do not require special wiring.

Best Buys

The United States government's General Services Administration released recommendations in 1976 as to the ranges it felt were the best buys in terms of cheapest price and lifetime energy costs. Its recommendations, by model numbers:

Electric ranges—General Electric JASO 4; Sunray ASRE 22 AX 033, ASRC 24 CB 029, ASRC 26 GX OJK, ASRE 26 GX OJK.

Gas ranges—Crown 847-207 KGOWT; Roper 1234-W; Sunray SSP 22 BD, SSP 29 DA.

Microwave Ovens

Time-Savers

A microwave oven is a great convenience, particularly for families in which both husband and wife work, and time for cooking is limited. Microwave ovens reduce cooking time by as much as 75 percent: they can bake potatoes in four minutes, casseroles in 12 minutes, and hot dogs in under 30 seconds. What's more, microwaves use only 20 percent of the electricity used by conventional electric ovens.

Disadvantages

Before buying a microwave oven, be aware that it has some disadvantages: (1) it is expensive; (2) it is not suitable for all types of cooking (for example, baked bread will not rise, food cannot be browned or crisped, casseroles are cooked unevenly); and (3) there is some risk of radiation leaks.

Almost all microwave ovens are required to contain instructions on how to prevent exposure to dangerous microwaves. For instance, never clean the oven with scouring pads or steel wool that might damage seals, and never play with the safety interlocks. Have a repairman check for radiation leakage at least once a year. When using a model manufactured before 1972 (when strict safety guidelines were instituted), keep at least an arm's length away from it while it is on.

Best Buys

In its 1976 annual issue, *Consumers' Research Magazine* gave its highest recommendation to microwave ovens manufactured by Amana, Frigidaire, General Electric, Hotpoint, Litton, Sharp, and Montgomery Ward.

Costs can vary widely for microwave oven models of similar specifications—such as a $205 list price for a Montgomery Ward model in 1977, and $495 for a comparable Amana that same year.

Automatic Washers and Dryers

Washer Capacity

Automatic washers with large capacities allow for freer movement of clothes and, therefore, clean them more efficiently. Families that do much washing may find an 18-pound-capacity model worth the investment. Eighteen pounds is the largest capacity model generally sold for home use. Families using smaller size washers should be sure not to overload them; overloading sometimes results in a premature motor breakdown.

Water-Consumption Rate

Washing machines vary considerably in the amount of water needed per cycle. So before buying, ask the salesman about the water-consumption rate of the machine being considered; the less water needed, the better, particularly if the home water supply is limited.

Front vs. Top Loading

Most automatic washing machines currently on the market are top-loading models. Unlike the front-loading styles, some of which are still available, the top-loading washer can be stopped in mid-cycle. Front loaders use less water, however, and are convenient because their tops can be used as counters. Tests conducted by the U.S. Department of Agriculture have shown that neither type is better in terms of cleaning heavily-soiled clothes.

Permanent-Press Cycle

Because of the increased popularity of permanent-press clothes in recent years, it is useful to buy a washer equipped with a permanent-press cycle. During this cycle. both the agitator and spin speeds are reduced, and a cool-down phase is added. Clothes emerge with few or no wrinkles.

Lint Filters

Lint filters are features on all automatic washers, and they must be kept clean. Although for an additional expense, one can buy a washer with an automatic lint filter that cleans itself, don't waste the money on this extra component. Keeping the lint filter clean manually is hardly an arduous task.

Dryers

When shopping for an automatic dryer, look for one with an automatic moisture-sensing control. This feature, which cuts off the machine when the clothes are dry, not only saves on energy, but reduces wear on both the dryer and the clothes.

Washer-Dryer Combinations

Combination washer-dryers are great space savers: both washing and drying are done in one unit. The major drawback to these appliances is that only one load can be done at a time. As a result, laundry sessions will be longer.

Best Buys

In its October 1976 issue, *Consumer Reports* gave its highest quality rating for washing machines to Maytag A606 ($370). Close behind were Whirlpool LDA5800 ($284), Hamilton WA384 ($292), and Admiral LWA1835 ($274).

The magazine's ratings of clothes dryers (November 1975 issue) ranked models by Frigidaire, Westinghouse, J.C. Penney and General Electric at the top of its list.

Dishwashers

Types

Three types of dishwashers are available—built-in, convertible, and portable. The convertible models are most expensive and are essentially large portable models, which can be plumbed in permanently later as under-the-counter models. Don't buy a convertible machine unless absolutely certain that it will be installed someday.

Cycles

Dishwashers with a variety of cycles are usually worth the extra cost. Cycles can range from light to heavy for items ranging from fragile crystal to pots and pans. A good dishwasher also has several temperature settings.

Best Buys

According to its 1976 annual, *Consumers' Research Magazine* listed the Norge KDP-2450-A22 ($295) as the most highly recommended portable dishwasher. The most highly recommended built-in models were General Electric GSD281 ($200) and the Tappan 61-1131-11 ($230).

The same magazine's most highly rated dishwasher detergents were Acme Speedup for Automatic Dishwashers, Calgonite Spotless Automatic Dishwasher Detergent, Cascade Detergent, Dishwasher All, and Shop-Rite Dish Wash.

Televisions

Color vs. Black-and-White

Color televisions are much more enjoyable to watch than black-and-white ones, but they cost about three times as much for the identical screen size. Color televisions also usually require more frequent repair over the life of the set, and consume from three to four times as much electricity.

As color television sets become more expensive with each passing year, some consumers are turning to black-and-white models as second sets in the household. Black-and-white models offer the following advantages: they cost less; they are more compact and lighter in weight, making them easier to move from room to room; breakdowns occur less often because of simpler circuitry; and repairs, when needed, are usually less costly (for example a color picture tube costs three times as much as black-and-white).

"Instant-On" Capability

When shopping for a television set, avoid those with "instant-on" capability. They use electricity 24 hours a day—even when the television is not being watched. Those who already own one of these models can save electricity by keeping it unplugged when it isn't being used.

Tube vs. Solid State

Television sets are available in both solid state and vacuum tube models. Both can provide a good picture; the tube models usually need more repair work. However, the tube models are cheaper, and when the solid state models do need repairs, they are often more expensive. Weighing the pros and cons, choose the solid state.

Picture Quality

Compare the picture quality of various televisions when shopping for one. Don't allow the salesman to turn off one set while you're inspecting another. Look at them both, comparing brightness, contrast, focus, and distortion. A television with an image that is very bright when first turned on, and which maintains its focus at that brightness level, has a better chance for a long life than one that does not.

Portable or Console?

By buying a portable television instead of a console, the consumer can save as much as several hundred dollars. The console cabinet adds considerably to the cost of the unit, and lasts much longer than the television mechanism itself. A portable black-and-white set can be bought for $100-$145; a color console costs $375-$950.

Life Expectancy and Used Models

The life expectancy of the average television set is 10 to 12 years. So to save money when shopping for a good second set, consider buying a used model. Check the classified ads. A five- or six-year-old used model will probably provide several years of viewing.

Television Quality

In 1977, *Money* magazine had 60 viewers watch factory-inspected 19-inch color television sets provided by Zenith ($500 retail price), RCA ($500), Sony ($600), General Electric ($500), Sanyo ($400), Sharp ($440), and Toshiba ($460). These viewers showed a clear preference for the General Electric set, with Zenith close behind.

Trade-ins

Some television retail outlets will accept TV's as trade-ins, deducting as much as $100 off the price of a new set. These trade-ins are often resold by the dealers as used models, or are broken down and the parts kept for future use. Incidentally, some stores will accept not only an old television set as a trade-in for a new one, but also some small appliances—stereos, coffee makers, vacuum cleaners.

Stereos

Compact vs. Components

Except for those individuals very knowledgeable about sound systems, who also have a very sophisticated listening ear, a compact stereo system may be the best buy. A compact stereo system has the various individual components (turntable, tuner, amplifier, speakers) built into a single system. Most of these compact units range in price from $300 to $700, but some sell for as little as $200. By contrast, in component systems, each part must be bought separately and plugged into one another. The component setup offers more flexibility and versatility, but can cost more as well.

Selecting a System

In most cities, the stereo marketplace is extremely competitive, and discounts of up to 30 percent below list price are not rare. Before selecting a system, read the stereo ads in the daily newspapers for several weeks, shopping for the best deals. Name brands are important; buying the cheapest equipment may be a waste of money.

Speakers

The single most important component in a stereo system is the speakers. While amplifiers and tuners within any specific price range are usually of comparable quality, that is not necessarily the case with similarly-priced speakers. When buying components separately, don't scrimp on the speakers; they can enhance the performance of the rest of your system.

Weight is a good initial test of a speaker's quality. In general, the heavier the speaker, the better its quality. Also, never buy two or more speakers of differing makes or models; unless both speakers are identical, the stereo effect being sought will be jeopardized.

Amplifiers

As a general rule, the more powerful the amplifier, the freer it will be from distortion. However, "overbuying" power in an amplifier is very common; many people buy an amplifier potent enough to not only fill the room(s) of their own house with music, but also those of their neighbors! Almost all stereo retailers have charts to help you pick the amplifier power most appropriate for the dimensions of the room where it will be. Don't buy more power than is necessary.

Testing a System

Before buying a stereo system, listen to the sound it produces. Many stereo stores have specially-designed rooms for test listening. Bring one of your own records that you're familiar with for this test; the demo records the store will provide are often special ones that give excellent sound; they can make an average system sound superior. Also, ask for return privileges of the stereo system; if it doesn't sound as good at home as in the store, bring it back.

For Further Information

Before buying a stereo system, perusal of the stereo magazines will provide evaluations and recommendations of the newest units and components. The best of these periodicals are *High Fidelity* and *Stereo Review*, available on most newsstands and at many public libraries.

Air Conditioners

Measure the Room

Before purchasing an air conditioner, it is advisable to measure the room or area it will be expected to cool. Give this information to a dealer; he will estimate the size of the unit needed by consulting charts devised by appliance industry associations. It is important to select the appropriate unit: an air conditioner that is too small will never sufficiently cool the room or area; if it's to large, the room or area will be cold and damp.

BTU

The BTU (British Thermal Unit) rating of an air conditioner reflects the maximum load capacity of the appliance—how much heat it will remove from the atmosphere in one hour—and is the best indicator now available to determine the cooling ability of a unit. It is a much better yardstick than horsepower. Determining how many BTU's are needed to cool a room or a house is a relatively complicated process, but a worthwhile endeavor. As suggested above, a dealer can do it; or send for a "Cooling Load Estimate Form" from the Association of Home Appliance Manufacturers, 20 North Wacker Drive, Chicago, Illinois 60606.

Wattage

Inquire as to the amount of wattage that a particular air conditioner consumes. Determine the number of BTU's per watt by dividing the number of watts into the BTU capacity (a 1,000-watt model with an 8,000 BTU capacity provides eight BTU's per watt). An air conditioner with a higher BTU-per-watt rating will use less electricity.

Noise Level

The noise level at which an air conditioner normally operates is one of the factors to consider when shopping for a unit. Ask the salesman to turn on the unit and compare its noise level with the sound of other units. To be thorough, request that the salesman let you listen to the noise level of each unit when its front panel is both on and off. There will be a sizable difference in noise level in a unit with a well-constructed acoustical front.

Cost

Room air conditioners generally cost from $120 to $350 each. Central air conditioning to cool an entire house costs from $1,100 to $2,000.

Best Buys

In 1976 the General Services Administration of the federal government recommended the following air conditioners, based upon sale price and energy efficiency: Fedders (models ACL 16E 7H; ACL 18E 7H; ASL 19E 7H; ASD 24E 7H); and General Electric (models AG FE 90 9F; AGFS 81 3D).

Sewing Machines

Purpose

Before purchasing a sewing machine, consider how it will be used. If it will be used only occasionally (sewing a patch on a pair of jeans), a simple and inexpensive model will do. But to sew dresses, suits, and other more complicated items, a more elaborate machine would be appropriate.

Zigzag Machines

A zigzag sewing machine, which permits many stitching styles, is the most popular type of unit on the market. Most women, however, never use the elaborate features of a zigzag. There's no need for a zigzag for minor clothing repairs.

Portable or Cabinet Models?

A portable sewing machine usually is at least $50 cheaper than a cabinet model. Because of their cost, cabinet models are an extravagance these days.

Safety Features

Ask the salesman about the safety features of various machines. A very popular feature is a small light built into the unit; the machine automatically turns off when the light is switched off. A child crawling on the floor who depresses the foot control cannot start the machine as long as the light remains off.

Other Appliances

Vacuum Cleaners

Cylinder-type vacuum cleaners are circular units that lie flat on the floor. They are versatile, and their attachments are easy to use. Upright models are like carpet sweepers, in that the entire unit can be pushed by a handle that rises up to about waist level. They usually have greater suction, and are superior for cleaning carpets.

An acceptable compromise between these two systems is a third type—a high-powered cannister vacuum cleaner equipped with a revolving, motor-driven brush in its nozzle. The brush draws up dirt almost as effectively as an upright model.

Water Heaters

When gas and electricity were cheap, it was acceptable to buy a water heater big enough to fill a family's hot water needs during "peak periods." When a clothes washer, dishwasher, and shower were all running simultaneously, enough hot water was available for them all. Of course, the heater also kept its tankful hot during times when no hot water was being used. But with energy costs now so high, it is foolish to heat more water than is needed at one time. Instead, buy a heater that will fill the family's needs during "average" periods. Avoid washing clothes and dishes and using the bath or shower simultaneously. Remember that the water heater is the home's second largest user of energy (only the central heating system consumes more). So buy the smallest heater with which the family can reasonably manage. Also, keep in mind that electric models usually heat water more slowly than gas, so to get performance from an electric unit equal in performance to gas, a larger one will be needed.

Electric Skillets

When shopping for an electric skillet, check the wattage. As the wattage increases, cooking time decreases. A good skillet will have from 1,100 to 1,300 watts, and will be equipped with a plug that can be completely detached from the skillet so that the appliance can be immersed for cleaning.

CHAPTER 6

Household Economics

In the previous two chapters, we discussed buying a home, furnishing it, carpeting it, and purchasing appliances. Once this has been done, how should one keep the house running smoothly and economically?

Those who live in a house for any length of time will probably want to make some major improvements. Almost everyone wants to customize his home to some degree—by adding an extra bedroom, remodeling the kitchen, or installing a swimming pool. In fact, Americans spend $17 billion a year to renovate and remodel their homes.

Any kind of renovation or remodeling requires expertise. And hiring the proper workmen—which is the responsibility of the individual homeowner—requires equal expertise. It is a major achievement to deal effectively with a contractor. The homeowner must know precisely what improvements he wants made, and he must know how to ensure that they will be executed properly and at a fair price.

An ignorant homeowner will find himself easy prey for the many fraudulent home improvement contractors. About seven percent of all the money spent on home improvements is wasted on inferior craftsmanship and unfulfilled promises. The Better Business Bureau alone receives more than 300,000 complaints a year about negligent or dishonest home improvement contractors.

Building costs have increased about 10 percent per year in the 1970's. So an improvement that cost $150 in 1977 may cost $165 in 1978. In 1977, the addition of a bedroom cost about $30 a square foot; a new bathroom cost about the same, with an additional $300 per fixture (toilet, sink, bathtub). A fireplace in a one-story house carried a $1,350 pricetag, and enclosing a porch, about $14 per square foot.

One of the most common home improvements—the installation of a swimming pool—can cost from $3,500 to $10,000, depending on the amount of soil that must be excavated and the pool's size. With an investment that large, a pool installation must be approached cautiously and knowledgeably.

Of course, there's a lot that the homeowner can do on his own, without the help of a contractor. One out of every three American homeowners does his own house painting and wallpapering. Modern paints and paint accessories make it very simple for the novice to do a more than adequate job—at a much cheaper cost than hiring a professional painter.

The wise homeowner is also doing what he can to run his home more efficiently by cutting down energy bills. Unfortunately, the United States is using up fuel at a faster rate than it can be replaced. About 30 percent of all the energy this country consumes is wasted, and much of that occurs in homes in all parts of the country. Many families have as much as 35 to 50 household appliances, all of which guzzle energy. Every household can cut its utility bills—some by a little, most by a lot.

REMODELING AND RENOVATION
The Contractor

Finding a Contractor

Major home improvements—adding a room, putting in a patio, installing a sprinkler system—should be made with the assistance of a reputable contractor. Ask friends or the owner of the corner hardware store for recommendations. To check a contractor's reputation, ask him for the names of other customers who can vouch for his competence. Also request a written estimate for the improvements to be made; compare it with estimates obtained from at least two other contractors.

The Contract

Contractor-homeowner agreements should always be in writing. Read the contract carefully before signing, making certain it stipulates the precise improvements to be made, the materials and products to be used, and the total cost and method of payment. It should specify when the work will begin, and the approximate date of completion. Keep in mind that such contracts often include a deed of trust, which means using the property of the homeowner as collateral for the cost of the improvements.

Any reputable contractor will be willing to grant a one-year guarantee on his work. Insist upon such protection before signing any contract.

Under federal law, if home improvements are to be financed by a loan in which a house serves as collateral, the homeowner is granted a three-day "cooling off" period *after* signing the contract. During this time, he may change his mind and legally cancel the agreement. If for any reason the homeowner has second thoughts about proceeding with the work, he must notify the contractor before the three days have passed.

Paying the Contractor

Before paying the contractor, the homeowner should make certain that all companies that have supplied materials have signed a waiver of lien. If this is not done, and the contractor has not paid his suppliers, they can file a lien on the homeowner's property, requiring the homeowner to pay the bill, even if he has already paid the contractor for the supplies.

Recouping the Investment

Don't expect the full amount of money spent on home improvements to be returned when selling the house. As a rule, every dollar spent on an improvement will only add an average of 50 cents to the value of a house when it is sold. Some items, of course, add more than 50 cents per dollar—namely, a remodeled kitchen or a new bathroom, Others—a porch, patio, or swimming pool—will return less. (Indoor improvements usually add more to a house's value than outdoor improvements.) The money not recouped can be considered an investment in the pleasure that has been derived from having the improvements made.

Home Improvement Rackets

Door-to-Door Shysters

Some home improvement gypsters travel from door to door, claiming that they "just happened to be in the neighborhood," and offer to perform some job at a tremendous discount, using the materials "left over" from another job. Frequently, they offer to resurface a driveway for what may seem like a fair price. However, all they intend to do is spray the driveway with black oil. To avoid headaches, door-to-door home improvement salesmen should be shunned.

Promised Commissions

Contractors sometimes promise the homeowner commissions on work to be done by the contractor in the future. "All you must do," the homeowner is told, "is to hire me [the contractor] to do certain work on your house, and then allow this work to be shown to other people. They will be so impressed with the improvements, they'll decide to have the same work done on their own property. If enough people choose to have the improvements made, you will receive enough commissions to recoup all the money you have spent for the work on your own house." In reality, future rebates are never forthcoming, and, in addition, a higher price tag is usually put on the original work.

Completion Papers

Don't sign a completion paper until the entire home improvement job is finished. Some dishonest contractors place such documents in front of homeowners, requesting their signatures. Many homeowners simply sign the papers without hesitation; others at least read them through, after which the contractors usually explain that the documents must be signed in order for him to receive the final installment on a loan so he can finish the work on the house. As protection, *never* sign a completion document until *all* work is actually completed. There is no legal obligation to do so.

INSTALLING A SWIMMING POOL

The Cost

A swimming pool is a popular and enjoyable addition to a house. But remember that its costs continue long after the last construction payment has been made. In metropolitan areas, property taxes will increase by about $100 a year. Liability insurance will go up, too, as will fuel bills if the pool water is heated. And one can add to that the costs of normal maintenance, chemicals, and repairs, which run about $50 a month.

Zoning Regulations

Before contacting a pool builder, check carefully with local health and building code authorities about pool regulations. Make certain that local zoning laws permit pool construction. Inquire as to whether a pool must be a given distance from lot boundaries, and what kind of fence, if any, must be erected around the pool.

Pool Dimensions

When planning the dimensions of a pool, don't oversize it. Most people use only a small area for their normal swimming activities, but still insist on building large pools. The Swimming Pool Institute recommends that a pool provide 36 square feet of space for each user. Also, unless a diving board will be installed, little or no very deep area, which is expensive, is needed.

Location

Ideally, the pool should be located in an open area, in the sunlight, and away from overhanging trees. Not only will swimming be more enjoyable in the sun, but the problems of twigs and leaves falling into the pool will be avoided.

"Kid-Proofing" the Pool

Nearly half of all pool drownings occur in private home pools, and most victims are under four years of age. For this reason, every pool should be "kid-proofed." Fencing at least six feet high should surround the pool, and it should be very difficult to climb over. The gate opening into the pool area should be locked when an adult is not nearby.

Selecting a Contractor

There are dozens of swimming pool builders listed in the Yellow Pages of many cities. To select a good one, contact the local Better Business Bureau for a tally of complaints lodged against these contractors. Also contact previous customers of the builders. To ascertain their names, visit the city building department and inspect the swimming pool building permits for the past couple of years. The permits will list the names of the homeowners, and the pool builders who did the work. These past customers are an excellent source of information, and don't hesitate to call them.

Once the choices have been narrowed to three or four, ask each prospect to offer a bid on the construction. If the contractors appear to be about equal in expertise and dependability, cost will probably be the final determining factor.

The Construction Contract

Once a reputable pool contractor has been contacted and terms have been agreed upon, a construction contract will be drawn up. Read the document thoroughly before signing. It should stipulate the completion date, the detailed expenses for labor and materials, and the particular colors and styles to be used. Some contractors neglect to include the costs of retaining wall sand decks in the contract, and later charge an additional $1,000 or more for installation of these items.

Maintenance

When the pool has been completed and is in use, chlorine must be added regularly to destroy bacteria and algae, and to oxidize small earth particles. When using chlorine, follow the instructions on the container carefully . An overdose may make the water assume an unusual color, and cause a blue-green powder to settle on the pool bottom. Also, if too much acid accumulates in the water, the seals on the pool's filter may gradually erode.

It makes little difference what brand of chlorine is used, since all manufacturers produce pretty much the same quality chemical.

PAINTING AND WALLPAPERING

Do-It-Yourself Painting

What to Buy

Latex paint—also called vinyl or acrylic—is preferred by most people. It is easy to apply (brush marks are kept to a minimum), is fast-drying (usually within two hours), and produces little smell. In addition, brushes and clothes, as well as hands, can be cleaned with soap and water; paint thinner is not needed.

Oil base paints, or alkyds, are "dripless," and dry in a day or two. They are generally more difficult to apply than latex paints. They have a stronger odor than latex paints, and must be cleaned with mineral solvents instead of water.

Before buying a can of paint, read the label carefully. It will offer suggestions on the best way to apply the paint, and will provide information on whether the paint is appropriate for the surface to be painted.

Brushes and Rollers

When applying latex paints, it is best to use so-called calcimine brushes, which have long, stout bristles. For oil base paints, use flatter, chisel-shaped brushes. A total of two brushes—one for walls and one for trim—will handle most jobs.

Rollers with a ¼-inch nap are adequate for most household painting chores if one prefers a roller over a brush (Personal preference is the main determining factor here). For stucco surfaces, use a ⅜- or ¾-inch nap. Although V-shaped rollers are on the market, most amateur painters will have trouble handling them; so use a brush for corners.

Preparing the Surface

In order for paint to adhere properly to most surfaces (like wood that has been previously painted), use some sandpaper lightly on it prior to taking the brush in hand. If walls have a film of dirt or grease on them, scrub them with a household cleanser, rinse, and wipe dry.

How Much Paint?

Most house paints cover 450 to 500 square feet per gallon for smooth surfaces. About 20 percent more paint is needed for porous or rough surfaces. Use these guidelines after calculating the number of square feet to be painted.

Applying the Paint

Don't skimp on paint. Fill the brush with paint and spread it evenly. When heavy pressure needs to be applied to the brush, dip the brush again. If paint, particularly exterior paint, is stretched too thin, it may chalk excessively.

On very cold days, postpone any planned outdoor painting. For paint to set properly, air temperature should not be less than 50 degrees F. Also do not paint a surface when it is directly exposed to the sun's rays and is extremely hot. Wait until the surface is shaded, and has had time to cool down somewhat.

Hiring a Painter

Selection

A hired painter should preferably be recommended. Ask friends or the local paint dealer for recommendations, contact three of them, and ask for estimates. Tell them specifically what is to be painted and the type of paint to be used. Based on these estimates, select the painter and set up a convenient time to have the painting done.

Written Contract

The arrangements made with the painter should be put in writing—including his fee, how it will be paid, when the work will be done, and whether the work is guaranteed. Check to make sure that the painter carries his own liability insurance.

Wallpapering

Measuring the Room

Perk up the appearance of a room by covering its walls with an attractive wallpaper. But before heading down to the local department store or paint shop to select a design of wallpaper, measure the room to see how much will be needed. First measure the perimeter of the room in feet, and multiply that figure by the height from floor to ceiling. Next, divide the result by 30 (the approximate number of square feet per roll of wallpaper). This figure is the number of wallpaper rolls that will be needed to cover the area. But since there are doors and windows that won't have to be papered, this amount can be reduced some. So for every *two* average-sized openings (doors, windows, wall heaters, fireplaces), deduct one roll.

Let's take an example. Assume the room to be wallpapered is 13 feet by 16 feet, with an 8-foot ceiling. It has three windows and one door. First, the perimeter of the room is 58 feet (13+16+13+16). Multiplying by 8 (the ceiling height) gives a total of 464 square feet. Dividing this figure by 30 equals 15.47 rolls—or 16 rolls, when rounded off to the nearest full roll. Now subtract a total of two rolls for the four openings (16-2=14). Thus, 14 single rolls (or seven double rolls) will be necessary to wallpaper the room.

Prices

Wallpaper prices vary considerably, so shop carefully. Single rolls may be as inexpensive as $3 or $4, but most will be priced in the $7 to $20 range, with some selling for as much as $45.

Selecting a Design

When browsing through the sample books at the wallpaper dealer, keep in mind the furnishings of the room to be papered. What color are the drapes, the carpets, the furniture? Will the wallpaper blend with them? Some dealers might allow a small sample to be taken home to make a final decision.

More Information

A worthwhile guide to wallpapering is available free from dealers. Titled *How to Hang Wallcoverings*, it is distributed by dealers who belong to the National Decorating Product Association.

BURGLAR-PROOFING THE HOUSE

Security Alarms

An alarm system can cost from $100 to several thousand dollars, depending on the type and the size of the house. The most expensive systems are connected by special wiring directly to the police station. Cheaper units just set off a loud ringing that is designed to scare away the intruder.

Of all home security systems, alarm units are the least expensive, less than electrical systems (even though alarm batteries have to be replaced periodically). After the alarm system has been installed, put stickers in the windows, warning potential intruders that the house is protected.

Best Alarm Systems

In its 1976 annual, *Consumers' Research Magazine* gave its highest recommendation to three alarm units:

—Heathkit Home Protection Receiver (model GD-77), $50, and Heathkit Utility Transmitter (model GD-97), $36.

—Northern Intruder Alarm (model 1703), $225.

—3M Intruder Alarm (model 451), $99.50.

Locks

It's foolish to spend money on mediocre locks, which can be picked by even a novice burglar. To be safe, every exterior door should have a deadbolt lock, with the bolt extending at least ¾" when in the locked position. These locks can be purchased and installed for about $25.

"Double-Cylinder" Deadbolts

On doors that contain glass, install deadbolt locks which require a key to be used on the inside of the door as well as the outside. These "double-cylinder" deadbolts prevent burglars from breaking the glass and opening the door by reaching through and turning the inside knob. (Be sure that the key is nearby when anyone is not at home, so the door can be opened quickly in case of fire.)

Apartment Locks

In some cities, codes require the landlord to install pickproof locks, chain guards, and one-way viewers on doors. If you are living in an apartment without these, call the local building department. It can tell you if your landlord is responsible for paying the cost of putting in these security devices.

Windows

Prevent double-hung windows from being opened by burglars, by using just two sturdy nails. First, holes should be drilled at a slight downward angle through the upper rail of the bottom sash into the lower rail of the upper sash. The nails should then be slid into the holes, which will make the windows impossible for a potential intruder to open. When you want to open them, simply remove the nails.

Electric Timers

To give a house an occupied appearance when no one is there, buy some inexpensive electric timers to turn the indoor and outdoor lights on and off during the day and night. These same timers can be used to turn a radio on and off.

Garage Doors

An electronic garage door opener is a convenient device, but not necessarily an adequate means of protection. When a particular beam of light makes contact with the electronic mechanism, the door opens. But if *you* can open it that way, a sophisticated burglar may also be able to. A safer garage door opener is one in which a key must be inserted into a box and turned.

REPAIRING APPLIANCES

Owner's Manuals

The frequency at which appliances need repairing can be

reduced by following the advice furnished in owner's manuals. If a manual recommends that a machine be cleaned regularly, or that lint be removed from a filter after each use, or whatever, then do it.

Do-It-Yourself Repairing

There are books for sale that guide an individual through the do-it-yourself repair process. A book may cost $5 to $10, but it may save many times more than that in repair bills.

Check the Obvious

When an appliance has broken down, and fixing it yourself seems too complex, check a few obvious things before calling a repairman. Are all the dials and controls set properly for operation? Is the plug inserted snugly into the socket? Is the outlet supplying power to *other* appliances, and if not, is the plug, not the appliance, flawed? Has a fuse blown at the electric board, or has the circuit breaker been tripped? After determining that the problem lies in the appliance itself, whenever possible take it to the repair shop and avoid paying for an expensive house call.

The Cost of Repair

When leaving an appliance at a repair shop, ask for an estimate for the repair cost before giving the go-ahead. Repairs on small appliances (toasters, irons, vacuum cleaners) sometimes almost equal the cost of buying a new one. If that's the case, it's not worth investing in repairs.

Life Expectancy

Consider the average life expectancy of an appliance as a factor in determining whether it's worth spending money to repair the unit. How much more use will be gotten out of it after it is repaired?

Below are the number of years of service that can be expected from common appliances:

Sewing machine	24 years
Vacuum cleaner, upright	18
Range, electric or gas	16
Refrigerator-freezer	16
Freezer	15
Toaster	15
Vacuum cleaner, tank	15
Clothes dryer	14

Clothes washer 11
Television set............................ 11
Hot-water heater........................ 10

Effective Complaining

If a manufacturer refuses to honor an appliance guarantee for a seemingly unjust reason, contact the state consumer affairs office, the state attorney general, or the Federal Trade Commission. In addition, write to the Major Appliance Consumer Action Panel (20 North Wacker Drive, Chicago, Illinois 60606), which has been established by appliance manufacturers themselves to settle such disputes.

Television Repairs

Tubes

Before calling a television repairman, first test the tubes by gently removing them and checking them on a tester at an electronics parts store or a supermarket. If one or more tubes are burned out, buy replacements and reinsert them. Faulty tubes are the cause of 90 percent of the problems that occur in television circuits.

Antenna

If reception has become very bad almost overnight, perhaps the antenna has blown down or been disassembled by heavy winds. Check the condition of the antenna before calling a repairman.

Do-It-Yourself

There are several books on the market for individuals who want to tackle their own television repairs. One of the best is *Make Your Own TV Repairs* by Art Margolis (Arco Publishing).

Repairmen

Ask friends for recommendations of honest and competent television repairmen. If no suggestions are forthcoming, call various repairmen listed in the Yellow Pages, and ask if they are Certified Electronic Technicians. This certification, issued by the National Electronics Service Dealers Association, is not simple to obtain, requiring several years of training and at least a 75 percent score on a very difficult examination.

Air Conditioner Repairs

Filters

Reduce air conditioner repair bills by replacing air filters whenever they become worn. Also, clean the filter regularly. If the filter is dirty and hinders the free flow of air, the unit will not cool as efficiently; more serious repair problems may develop as debris builds up in the machine.

Checking Malfunction

When an air conditioner begins to malfunction, first clean the filter. Then see if a fuse needs replacing. If neither solves the problem, turn off the entire air conditioning system for two to three hours. If the filter had been totally clogged, the evaporator coil may have iced up. Frequently, not using the air conditioner for just a few hours will allow the coil to defrost.

Dripping

If water is dripping from an air conditioner into a room, call a serviceman. The unit may have been mounted improperly, or its drain may be obstructed.

SAVING ENERGY

Cutting Heating Expenses

"Insignificant" Savings

Reducing heating (as well as cooling) bills involves taking advantage of small savings each day, which add up over a period of weeks and months. Don't pass up the chance to cut a few cents off the monthly bill because the savings seem insignificant. Those pennies add up over a year's time.

Lower Thermostat

Keep the house temperature as low as the family can comfortably tolerate. They may find that 68° F is as pleasant as 72° F. By lowering the thermostat just four degrees, 12 percent less fuel will be consumed. To help acclimate the body to lower temperatures, lower the thermostat gradually—one degree at a time. After a few days of becoming accustomed to 71° instead of 72°, drop down to 70°, and so forth.

Insulation Savings

Warming a house in the winter consumes nearly 60 percent of all the energy used in that home. Although turning the thermostat down a few degrees can help, probably the best way to save is to properly insulate the home. Doubling the thickness of insulation already on the floor of a poorly-insulated attic will reduce by half the loss of heat from the rooms below.

Is Insulation Needed?

How does one determine if a house needs added insulation? During cold weather, try placing the palm of your hand firmly against the inside surfaces of the exterior walls of the house. If these walls feel cold, they are losing too much heat. Compare these walls to interior wall partitions. If the interior partitions are significantly warmer than exterior walls, insulation is needed on the exterior walls. Use the same palm test on the ceiling.

Buying Insulation

When purchasing insulating material, examine its R, or resistance, factor. This rating is an appraisal of the insulation's aptitude for impeding the flow of heat (rather than transmitting it). The same insulating material may have several R factors, depending on the manner of installation and the direction from which the heat flows. Particular R factors are recommended for certain parts of the house. For instance, walls should be insulated with an R factor of at least 11 to achieve the greatest savings. Insulation on the attic floor should have a higher R factor—at least 19—because of heat's natural tendency to rise from the rooms below.

Installation

An amateur can install insulation in a house in a single day—probably for less than $200. If a professional is hired, the cost would be about 50 percent higher. In either case, the insulation will more than pay for itself in reduced energy bills.

Storm Windows

Wall and ceiling insulation is only the first step in keeping the home warm and reducing heating bills. When the outside and inside temperatures differ by 50° or more (for example 70° F indoors and 20° F outdoors), install storm windows to minimize heat loss and provide protection from wind. Storm windows will cut energy bills by about 15 percent. Cracks around the doors and windows should be sealed with caulking or weatherstripping.

Unoccupied Rooms

Fuel costs can be further reduced by closing off unoccupied rooms, and turning off the heat in those rooms. Actual savings will vary, depending on where the rooms are located and how successfully they can be isolated. In these unused rooms, weatherstrip around the doors to prevent cold air from escaping into other parts of the house.

Firewood

By selecting the right type of firewood at an inexpensive price, burning wood in a fireplace will also help reduce energy bills. The best slow-burning, heat-producing woods are oak, beech, birch, hickory, locust, maple, and pecan. Wood prices vary from one part of the country to another, but during the summer wood can be obtained at National Forest lands, either for free or a very small charge. Permits issued by the United States Forest Service allow individuals to take their pick of "downed" trees or stumps.

Cutting Cooling Costs

Thermostat Setting

Air-conditioner thermostats should be set no lower than 78°F. At this temperature, the air conditioner will reasonably cool the room, and still be somewhat energy-efficient. By setting the thermostat at 78° rather than 72°, home cooling costs will be reduced by about 46 percent.

Fan Speed

An air conditioner is most efficiently run by setting the fan speed at "high" on hot days. On humid days, however, place the fan speed at "low," which will produce less cooling, but will remove more moisture.

Range Exhaust

When cooking while an air conditioner is in use, turn on the range exhaust fan so that the waste heat from the stove will not be added to the air conditioner's load. A fan requires much less energy to rid the house of excess heat than does an air conditioner.

Scheduling Household Chores

A house will be kept cooler by scheduling for early morning all cleaning tasks that discharge considerable moisture into the air. Washing windows or mopping floors makes for mugginess, so either postpone these chores until a cooler day or do them during the coolest part of the day. Ironing clothes also releases large amounts of moisture into the air, so choose the coolest time of day for this as well.

Sunlight

During the hot summer months, keep cool without adding to air conditioning bills by preventing the sun's direct light from entering the house. Shade trees can do the job, but if there are none, use awnings on the *outside* of the windows. Roll shades are much more effective in keeping the sun out than drapes or curtains inside the house.

Savings in the Kitchen

Boiling

Fierce boiling cooks no faster than a gentle, rolling boil, but it consumes much more fuel. So turn the heat down to a level that prevents furious boiling. Also use lids on pots and pans to prevent steam from escaping.

Defrosting

Although defrosting the refrigerator's freezer compartment is not the most pleasant of chores, do it when needed. If an excess amount of frost builds up in the refrigerator, it acts as an insulator, and prohibits the appliance from operating at peak efficiency. The refrigerator's motor must run longer, and in the process, more electricity is consumed. Even a quarter inch layer of frost in a freezer compartment will force the unit to use 20 to 25 percent more electricity.

Position of Refrigerator

A refrigerator should not be positioned next to a range or other appliances that generate a lot of heat. When they are placed side by side, the refrigerator uses more electricity than normal to keep itself cold.

Reducing Lighting Bills

Wattage

To reduce energy bills, use bright lights only in those areas where necessary—such as where reading is done. In some rooms, like the kitchen and the bathroom, install fluorescent lights in place of incandescent bulbs. Fluorescents generate more light per watt than incandescents, and are therefore a cheaper way to illuminate rooms which need light for long periods of time. One 40-watt fluorescent light will provide more illumination more cheaply than three 60-watt incandescent bulbs. If a porch light is customarily left on throughtout the night, fluorescents are the most economical choice.

Extended-Life Bulbs

When shopping for incandescent light bulbs, buy extended-life bulbs for places that are difficult to reach (for example, a high ceiling that can only be approached with a ladder). These bulbs are intended to last up to five years. Buy in large quantities when they are on sale at drug or hardware stores.

Dimmers

Dimmer controls that lower the illumination of light bulbs are effective for special occasions (a romantic dinner) or for night lights. But they are not necessarily good for the bulbs themselves, which do not operate as efficiently at dimmed settings. For example, when a 150-watt bulb is dimmed to give the light of a 90-watt bulb, it is actually using the energy of a 115-watt bulb. So if saving energy is of primary importance, it would be more desirable to replace that 150-watt bulb with a 90-watt bulb, and abandon the option of using the 150-watt brightness.

Hot Water Costs

Water Heater

The water-heater thermostat should be set at the lowest temperature at which hot water is required—usually equal to the hottest faucet water that a human hand can bear, or about 140°F. Depending on the specifications of a clothes washer or dishwasher, however, it may be necessary to raise the temperature somewhat higher—to 160°-180°F. An even higher setting will only waste fuel.

Once a month, drain about a gallon of water from the bottom of the hot water heater. This process will dispose of accumulated sediment, which thwarts heat from moving from the heating surface to the water in the tank.

Dishwasher and Clothes Washer

If a dishwasher and clothes washer are the only appliances in a house that need extremely hot water, have a plumber install a dual-supply valve on the water heater. This valve divides the water supply into two circuits—extra-hot (160°-180°F) for those appliances that require it, and a more normal hot level (140°F) for all other uses.

When a washing machine is run without a full load, both hot water and energy are being wasted. A typical wash cycle requires 32 gallons of water. Washing one small load everyday, as opposed to a single full load every second day, wastes 5,840 gallons of water a year.

Faucet Washers

Further save on hot water by maintaining faucet washers in good condition. Washers deteriorate more rapidly at high temperatures; hot water faucets, therefore, tend to drip more often than cold. And a dripping faucet may waste an incredible 200 to 300 gallons of water a month.

Showers or Baths?

Cut hot water bills still further by taking showers instead of baths. The average bath uses 36 gallons of water; the average shower, 25 gallons.

Watering the Lawn

Periodic Soaking

Curtail the total amount of water used in the household by soaking the lawn thoroughly once every seven to ten days, rather than watering it lightly every two or three days. When the lawn is heavily watered, the water is absorbed deep into the soil, and keeps the grass moist for many days. When the watering is shallow, most of the liquid remains on the surface and evaporates. In the long run, less water will be used by heavily soaking the lawn.

CUTTING PHONE BILLS

"Unlimited" or "Measured" Service

In most cities, a variety of telephone services are available. By choosing the one that's most suited to family needs, money can be saved. For most people, "unlimited service" is the best and cheapest. A flat rate is paid each month, and an unlimited number of local calls, and at any length, can be made. At the front of the telephone book is a list of the various prefixes that can be called without extra charge under this plan. Under the "measured service" plan, 30, 60, or 80 local calls are allowed for a cheaper monthly rate. For every call made over the allotted number, an extra charge is added.

"Call-Pak"

If many phone calls are made to a given area outside of the local calling zone, it may be wise to spend a few extra dollars a month to expand the area considered "local." This service, called Optional Residence Telephone Service, or Call-Pak, allows for toll-free calls within the expanded area. The choice of either having an unlimited number of calls to that area, or an hour's worth of calls per month for a set fee, is usually available.

Mistakes on Bills

Because mistakes are sometimes made on telephone bills, check the statement carefully each month to ensure its accuracy. If calls that have not been made are listed on the bill, contact the phone company and ask that these calls be deleted from the record. If the company refuses to give credit, don't pay for the calls anyway. Be sure to write to the telephone company and the utility commission that regulates the company, and explain why the bill is not being paid in full.

Wrong Numbers

There is no need to pay for any wrong numbers you may have dialed. Simply call the operator, and request that credit be issued for the calls. Misdialing occurs in about 10 percent of all calls, so the phone company is accustomed to receiving and processing requests for credit.

Credit Cards

Those who frequently make calls while away from home may be wise to obtain a credit card from the telephone company. All credit card holders need do is give the operator the credit card number when placing a call: that call will be billed to the credit card account. This eliminates the hassle of searching for the right number of coins when calling from a pay phone. Apply for a credit card from the business office of the telephone company.

Out of Order

When a phone is out of order, notify the phone company immediately. The regular service charge need not be paid for the period of time that the phone is unusable.

Vacationing

Check with the phone system about its policy regarding customer vacations. Most companies will agree to disconnect a telephone if the phone will be unused for more than a month, eliminating any charges at all during that time. An advantage of disconnecting the phone is safety: potential burglars won't be able to determine whether you're home or not. But before agreeing to the vacation disconnection, make sure that the telephone company will not charge a reconnection fee; if it does, the fee may more than offset any savings.

CHAPTER 7

Automobiles

An estimated 80 percent of all American families own at least one car. Next to their home, it is usually their most expensive possession. One out of every four retail dollars is directed toward an auto-related product or service.

An automobile is costly around the clock. Even when sitting in a garage, it is depreciating in value by the minute. Insurance payments and auto loan payments continue whether a car is idle or not. And when in use, a car costs the average American nearly five cents a mile (for gas and oil).

The world of the automobile is a complex maze. To buy a new car today means to choose from among 350 American-made and 250 foreign-made models, each offering its own array of optional accessories. The thought of shopping for an automobile and having to confront fast-talking, high-pressure salesmen is enough to make most people recoil. For that reason, the consumer must know how to choose a car, and where to buy it at the cheapest price.

Financing an automobile is also sometimes difficult. Four out of five car buyers take out installment loans to pay for their vehicles, making monthly payments over a 24-to-48-month period. When negotiating a loan, it is best to know precisely how the transaction works—and how to protect one's own interests. Although many people end up with loan payments they are able to meet, in the long run these arrangements cost them several hundred dollars more than they should have paid.

The used car market is, in its own way, as much of a jungle as the new car industry—and perhaps more so. Finding a reliable used car sometimes seems to be an impossible task. The consumer must know what to look for when shopping for an older car, or he may end up cursing the "lemon" all the way to the repair shop.

These repair shops pose problems of their own. Americans spend $30 billion annually on auto repairs, not feeling quite capable themselves of tackling a piece of machinery with 1,300 moving parts. But all too often, they fall victim to rip-off artists. A car may need only a small part—such as a spark plug—but an unscrupulous mechanic may convince the owner that the engine needs a complete overhaul. The United States Senate Judiciary Subcommittee concluded in a 1973 report that one-third of all auto repairs are "either unnecessary or not done properly."

Not long ago, the Automobile Club of Missouri conducted a study that diagnosed the problems of 4,000 cars. The owners of these cars were instructed as to what repairs were needed, and were asked to choose a mechanic and have the repairs made. When the club rechecked 2,000 of the cars, more than one-third of the work ordered and paid for by the owners had not been done.

Consumer dissatisfaction with car repairs is second only to mail-order fraud in volume of complaints. Small wonder, then, that the consumer must be careful when choosing among the nation's 400,000 car service outlets.

The times are changing very rapidly in the car industry. Gone are the days of the huge gas-guzzlers. In fact, all 1978 passenger cars average no less than 18 miles per gallon. Also, the days when gasoline cost 30 cents (or 40 or even 50 cents) a gallon have disappeared forever, too. The energy crisis has changed what we drive and how we drive. More than any other time in history, the automobile owner and driver must be informed and aware in this fast-changing marketplace.

BUYING A NEW CAR

Should You Buy a New Car?

The Present Car's Condition

Is now the time to buy a new car? The typical motorist, who drives about 12,000 miles a year, usually considers trading his car in for a new one every three to five years. When trying to decide whether to buy now, the consumer must consider the condition of his present car. If it is in relatively good running condition, but needs only some minor improvements (new tires, for example), it's advisable to have those improvements made and postpone the much larger investment of buying a new car. The extra year or so that the present car can be used will allow extra time needed to save money toward the new one. However, if the current auto has major problems—the body is corroding, it needs a new front end, etc.—then a new car may be worth the cost.

A Second Car

Families that can live without a second car should by all means do so. Two cars will almost double the family's total automobile expenses. Maintenance and insurance costs will go up; two sets of registrations will need to be purchased each year.

Those that must own two cars should make one of them a small, economy car. Use the small car for running neighborhood errands; use the bigger, roomier car for vacations and for times when more space is required.

What Kind of Car

Standard vs. Compact

According to the Department of Transportation, it costs 43 percent more to buy and run a standard-size car than a subcompact. So shop for the smallest car that meets your needs. Gasoline alone is very expensive. The Federal Energy Administration reports that a 2,500-pound car needs only half as much fuel to be driven around the city as a 5,000-pound car. A four-cylinder Chevette with an 85-cubic-inch engine, for instance, achieves double the gasoline mileage of an eight-cylinder Chevrolet station wagon with a 454-cubic-inch engine.

Engine Size

There's no need to buy a car with a powerful engine, on the assumption that it will provide an extra margin of safety in an emergency. In reality, the opposite is true: a very powerful car sometimes tends to be unstable. Ralph Nader's Center for Auto Safety suggests that a car should have 70 horsepower for each 1,000 pounds of body weight.

Selecting the Color

Light-colored cars are generally safer than dark-colored ones. Cars painted white, cream, and yellow are simply easier to see than red or black models.

Buying a Diesel

Those who do a lot of driving, and who plan to keep the same car for several years, might consider purchasing a diesel-powered automobile. Over the years, it is much less expensive than operating a gasoline-powered car. In recent years, diesel fuel has cost an average of seven cents less per gallon than gasoline. And cars powered by diesel fuel get much better mileage. Experts say that if one drives about 20,000 miles a year and holds onto the same diesel car for five years, he can accrue about $1,000 in savings on fuel costs.

Who Sells Diesels

Although American automakers have been slow in turning to the diesel engine, General Motors began offering a diesel in its 1978 Oldsmobiles—the first American model to use the engine. At least three foreign manufacturers are also selling diesel cars in the United States—Peugeot, Mercedes-Benz, and Volkswagen.

Finding Diesel Fuel

Buying fuel for a diesel-powered automobile may be a

problem. There were only 8500 diesel stations in the United States in 1977, and most of them were in major cities or along interstate highways. However, diesel-powered cars do not need to have their tanks filled as often as gasoline-powered models. The diesel cars currently on the market have large fuel tanks, which when coupled with their relatively high miles-per-gallon figure, make trips to the service station necessary less frequently. At 30 mpg, a tankful of diesel fuel in a Mercedes or Peugeot will last for over 500 miles of driving. For a directory of diesel stations in the country, send $6 to Diesel Fuel Services Incorporated, P.O. Box 256, South Salem, N.Y. 10590.

Options

The dealer makes his biggest profits by selling luxury options, such as power steering, power brakes, automatic transmission, a V-8 engine, air conditioning, and an AM/FM radio. These extra features not only add considerably to the purchase price of a car, but most raise operating costs as well. The initial added cost of buying a car equipped with automatic transmission ranges from $190 to $275; power steering on a new car adds from $120 to $300 onto the price; air conditioning costs from $420 to $850.

Auxiliary Gas Tanks

For those who drive during hours or in areas where open gas stations are many miles apart, an option worth investing in is an auxiliary fuel tank. These tanks usually have an 8-to-10 gallon capacity. When the main tank is empty, the driver can change to the auxiliary tank by flipping a switch on the dashboard. The cost of these tanks averages between $30 and $40.

Buying to Save Fuel

Fuel-Saving Accessories

Aside from the initial cost of various car options, weigh how much they will cost in gasoline consumption. For instance, an automatic transmission in a car reduces its miles-per-gallon total by two-to-five miles per gallon. Air conditioning accounts for a fuel penalty of four miles per gallon. Power steering and power brakes, on the other hand, have no effect on gas mileage.

EPA Mileage Figures

Generalizations about car gas mileage are difficult to make. An auto loaded with accessories gets far fewer miles-per-gallon than one with a minimum of them. However, the Environmental Protection Agency's statistics on *average* gas mileage are still a good guideline. In 1977, the cars with the best gas mileage were the Honda Civic CVCC and the diesel-engined Volkswagen Rabbit, both of which got 44 mpg in combined city and highway driving. The Chevette (36 mpg) was the top-ranking American car. At the bottom of the gas-mileage ratings were the Plymouth Fury and the Dodge Monaco, at 11 mpg.

How Much Savings?

How much money can be saved by buying a car with better gas mileage? Well, if a car is to be driven 10,000 miles a year, and gas costs 70 cents a gallon, here's how much gas will cost in cars with various mileage figures:

Gas mileage	Annual gas cost
10 mpg	$700
20 mpg	350
30 mpg	233
40 mpg	175

You may decide that the $175-a-year added expense between the 20-mpg car and the 40-mpg is worth the cost, in return for the increased size and comfort of the larger 20-mpg car. But be aware of how much greater other operating expenses will be for the bigger car.

Negotiating the Deal

Prepare to Bargain

Once the decision has been made as to what kind of car is preferred, how much can be spent, and what options are desired, then shop at various dealerships. Be ready to negotiate the price of a new car. The manufacturer's suggested list price posted on the car is only a starting point for bargaining. Less than 20 percent of all new car buyers end up paying an amount even close to the list price.

Trade-In Strategy

Those who have a car they would like to trade in would be wise not to mention that fact to the salesman until a price for the new car has been agreed upon. If the salesman is told about the used car in advance, he may quote a high figure for the trade-in, but make up for it by boosting the price of the new car.

The Dealer's Costs

It is possible to determine what a car dealer actually paid the manufacturer for a new American car, which should help in bargaining for a good price. First, take the total price on the official sticker and subtract the transportation charge listed on the sticker. Multiply the resulting figure by 0.85 for a compact or subcompact car, 0.815 for an intermediate model, and 0.77 for a full-sized car. Finally, add back the transportation charge: the resulting figure will be very close to what the manufacturer charged the dealer. In some large cities where competition among car dealers is intense, it is possible to buy a new car for less than 10 percent over the manufacturer's price. But the normal acceptable markup is a full 10 percent, which is considered a fair price for everyone involved.

Cost Printouts

Those who prefer not to do the above price computing can buy a computer printout indicating what the dealer paid for the car. This is available, at a cost of $10, from Car/Puter International Corporation, 1603 Bushwick Avenue, Brooklyn, N.Y. 11207. Car/Puter will send a form on which one writes the car he is interested in—plus up to 30 options for it—and, by return mail, he receives both the wholesale and the retail price of the car and each option.

On-the-Lot Savings

It is usually easier to negotiate a good price on a new car already on the dealer's lot rather than on one he has to order. Everyday the dealer is accumulating insurance and finance charges for each car on his premises, and he is eager to sell them to reduce his expenses.

When to Buy

The Best Time

The best time of the year to buy a new car is just before the following year's models are released. Thus, late summer and early fall are the times to get the best deal. Dealers are eager to move these cars off their lots to make room for new models, and low prices are easier to obtain, at savings of from 5 to 35 percent more than at other times of the year. However, there may no longer be a wide selection of colors and options. Keep in mind that these seasonal savings will only pay off if the car is kept for a minimum of three or four years. This is true because once the new models are released, the "new" car just purchased will already be one year old (in terms of the model year), and will immediately decline in value. Depreciation on a car is greatest during the first two years.

Month-End Savings

No matter what the time of the year, a better deal is usually obtained at the end of the month than at the beginning. Near month's end, the dealer is often trying to fill his sales quota to earn a bonus from the manufacturer.

The Best Deal

Broker Buying

Probably the least expensive way to purchase a new car (anytime of the year) is through United Auto Brokers, 1603 Bushwick Avenue, Brooklyn, N.Y. 11207, a subsidiary of Car/Puter International Corporation. UAB will provide a car, along with all the options desired, for only $125 above dealer's cost. The firm orders the car through a local dealer in the customer's neighborhood, and he picks it up at the local showroom. It will carry the same manufacturer's warranty as if bought the normal way.

Deceitful Practices

Trade-In Price Ploys

Beware of the many disreputable tactics employed by some new car dealers in negotiating their transactions. One common ploy is used when the car the customer buys will not be delivered for several weeks. When the customer finally comes to pick up his new car, the dealer informs him that his trade-in allowance has been decreased because "used cars just aren't selling well now." Too often, with his heart set on the new car, the customer agrees to the new financial arrangement.

Used-Car Price Changes

A similar trick used by dealers is to tell a customer that he believes he can sell his old car for him within a short period of time at a given price. The new car deal is written up with this in mind. When the customer returns to pick up his new car, however, the dealer informs him that the old car has been sold, but at a much lower price than had originally been anticipated. The customer then is asked to make up the difference himself.

Fine-Print Changes

Another common unethical practice of new car dealers is to make a verbal deal, but then have it appear quite differently in the sales contract. Therefore, ask the salesman to put *everything* into writing before finalizing the deal. Also be aware that at many dealerships, a salesman's signature is not binding; the contract must be signed by the owner of the franchise.

Financing the Car

Paying Cash

If at all possible, pay cash when buying a car. True, in some instances, particularly when the seller is the creditor, there might be some benefit to financing the purchase. In such instances, the consumer might have greater leverage if large and unexpected repairs are needed before the loan is paid off. But usually, the car dealer is only the middleman in the consumer's financing, and the dealer is paid in full by the creditor who carries the consumer's loan. So if at all possible, the consumer is advised to pay cash and avoid interest charges.

Informing the Dealer

Never tell the car dealer how the car will be paid for until a written commitment stating the price of the vehicle has been prepared. The dealer may offer a lower price if he thinks he'll have the opportunity to arrange the financing, for which he'll get a commission.

The Best Financing

When an automobile purchase must be financed, remember that commercial banks and credit unions usually offer the best terms (including an interest rate almost two percent lower than dealer-financed loans). Banks and credit unions usually require a down payment of at least 25 percent of the car's sale price; the balance is then financed at a 10 to 13½ percent interest rate. The trade-in value of an old car is normally applied as part of the down payment. Make as large a down payment as possible—at least one-third of the purchase price—and pay off the loan as rapidly as possible.

No-Down-Payment Loans

With new car prices increasing so rapidly, a few banks are adapting to the situation by being more flexible when making auto loans. If the consumer's credit rating is good, he may find a bank willing to make the car loan for no money down, and with payments extended over a 48-month period.

Extended-Term Loans

Although nothing-down loans are still rather rare, extended financing to minimize monthly payments is becoming commonplace. About 20 percent of all auto loans are currently financed for longer than 36 months, which was a rarity as recently as 1974. When negotiating a loan, however, try to keep the payment schedule as short as possible to reduce the overall cost of the car. Let's say one assumes a loan of $4,000 at an annual interest rate of 13 percent. A 36-month loan, for which one would pay $135 a month, will cost a total of $4,852. If the loan is extended over 48 months, one would pay $107 a month—a total of $5,151. The shorter-term loan would save $299.

Cost of an Auto Loan

The chart below shows what auto loans of various rates and durations would cost in terms of total interest and monthly payments. Dollar figures are rounded to the nearest single dollar.

Annual Interest Rate	Amount of Loan	2 Year Loan Monthly Payment	2 Year Loan Total Interest	3 Year Loan Monthly Payment	3 Year Loan Total Interest	4 Year Loan Monthly Payment	4 Year Loan Total Interest
10%	$3,000	138	323	97	485	76	652
	4,000	185	430	129	647	101	870
	5,000	231	538	161	808	127	1,087
	6,000	277	645	194	970	152	1,305
11%	3,000	140	356	98	536	78	722
	4,000	186	475	131	715	103	963
	5,000	233	593	164	893	129	1,203
	6,000	280	712	196	1,072	155	1,444
12%	3,000	141	390	100	587	79	792
	4,000	188	519	133	783	105	1,056
	5,000	235	649	166	979	132	1,320
	6,000	282	779	199	1,174	158	1,584
13%	3,000	143	423	101	639	80	864
	4,000	190	564	135	852	107	1,151
	5,000	238	705	168	1,065	134	1,439
	6,000	285	846	202	1,278	161	1,727
14%	3,000	144	457	103	691	82	935
	4,000	192	609	137	922	109	1,247
	5,000	240	762	171	1,152	137	1,559
	6,000	288	914	205	1,383	164	1,870

Collision Insurance

Lenders usually require that collision insurance be maintained for the duration of the loan. They may also insist that the borrower have life and disability insurance in the amount of the loan.

Repossessing the Car

Almost always, the collateral for an automobile loan is the car itself. So keep in mind that if one defaults on payments, his car can be repossessed and sold to someone else. If this resale price does not equal the balance of the note (and it usually doesn't), the borrower might be sued for the difference, plus the court costs, the lawyer's costs, and the repossession fees.

USED CARS

Buying a Used Car

Where to Buy

Buying a used car can be treacherous. Unless the buyer is a mechanic—or has a close friend who is—it's often impossible to know exactly what he's buying. Finding a reliable used car dealer is almost as difficult as finding a reliable used car. So ask friends and associates about their experiences with various local dealers. The best bet is probably to deal with the used car department of a reputable new car dealership.

When to Buy

The best time to purchase a used car is in the fall, when many used cars are being traded in for new model-year cars.

Checking with Previous Owner

Before buying a used car from a dealer, ask him for the name and phone number of the previous owner. A reputable dealer will gladly oblige. Ask the former owner about any serious mechanical problems of which he was aware. Then make certain that these problems have been repaired by the dealer. Incidentally, if the dealer says he doesn't have the name of the previous owner, he's probably lying. Federal law requires that he keep it on file.

Used-Car Warranties

Used car warranties are not nearly as impressive as their new car counterparts. Most, although not all, used car warranties are for 30 days or 2,000 miles. Almost all stipulate that during the warranty period, the dealer and the new owner split all repair costs 50-50. But these repairs are usually done in the dealer's own garage, and the bills are often so inflated that the consumer's 50 percent nearly equals the total amount it would have cost him to repair the car elsewhere. Also, warranties often only cover the drive train (engine, transmission, differential, and related parts).

Private-Party Purchases

Buying an automobile from a private party frequently brings the consumer a better car and a better deal. Rarely have odometers been tampered with or car defects been concealed—or at least not as cleverly.

Avoiding Stolen Cars

Good used cars are often advertised in the classified sections of local newspapers. But be sure to do some checking on the private party selling the car to guard against buying a stolen car. Almost one million cars are stolen each year, and many are sold to unwary buyers. Inquire at the state motor vehicles department as to the car's owner—never buy a car from someone other than the owner. Look for signs that a car may have been stolen. (Are the door lock cylinders loose or off-center?) Also check the VIN plate, displayed above the instrument panel on the driver's side in most cars built since 1969. It lists basic information about the car (make, body style, year, etc.). If it is not firmly attached, or does not match the interior color scheme, it may have been transferred from a wrecked automobile.

The Price

When buying a car from a private party, try to avoid paying more than $100 over the wholesale price. Your bank's loan officer will be able to let you look at his up-to-date used-car price book, which will list both the wholesale (or "trade-in") and retail prices of every car.

Car-Defects History

Check to see if the make and model of the used car in question has ever been recalled because of a safety defect. This information can be obtained in writing from the National Highway Traffic Safety Administration, c/o Department of Transportation, 400 Seventh Street, N. W., Washington, D.C. 20590. Or the data is available by calling a toll-free number, 800-424-9393. If the car has been on a recall list, have it checked by a mechanic to see whether the defect has been corrected.

Inspecting the Used Car

Because paint is often applied to conceal a problem-ridden past, avoid buying cars that have been repainted. Look under the hood or in the trunk; and if the body paint doesn't match the exterior color, you can be assured that a new coat of paint has been applied. Also examine the car's sides, hood and trunk for ripples. These are signs that the vehicle has been in an accident and has had poor body work. Continue the inspection by standing back about 30 feet to see if the car sits level; if not, it may be an indication of faulty suspension or a bent frame.

Check for rust spots around the body edges and behind the bumpers. Using a finger, probe the area to determine if the rust is only on the surface or if it has worked its way through from beneath.

Take the car on a road test of at least 30 minutes duration. A short ride around the block is not sufficient. Take the car up and down hills, over bumpy roads, and on high-speed freeways. Operate the car in all gears, and watch for any sticking or jerking. Pay close attention to the brakes; if they feel spongy, if they grind or squeal, or if they cause the car to swerve, they will need some work.

At some point during the test drive, stop the car and hose down the tires. Then drive the car in a straight line for approximately 50 feet. Look closely at the tire tracks. If four tread marks are visible instead of two, the frame of the car is bent, and it has probably been in a serious accident. Place a penny into each tire tread; if the top of Lincoln's head doesn't disappear into any part of the tread, the tire will have to be replaced. If tires are worn unevenly, the car is probably in need of a front-end alignment.

After the test drive, leave the car idling on its own. Five minutes later, move the car and check for leaks—a black substance on the ground means an oil leak; a brown residue is gasoline; a red substance indicates transmission problems.

A Mechanic's Opinion

Spend the $15 to $20 it may cost to have a mechanic inspect the used car being considered. He can offer advice as to what problems are likely to be encountered, and can estimate repair costs. Not only can his advice help to avoid purchasing a "lemon," but the information he provides can be used as a bargaining tool.

Ask the mechanic to estimate the worth of the used car. Compare that with the seller's asking price, and try to bargain down to the mechanic's estimate. As a rule, offer the seller from $100 to $150 under his asking price, and do not depart far from that figure.

LEASING A NEW CAR

Does it Pay?

Comparing the Cost

For most individuals, leasing a car does not make sense economically. For a $4,000 car, leasing payments would come to approximately $10 a month less than if the car were bought with an average down payment and the balance were financed. So over two years, buying would cost only $240 more than leasing, and the value of the car (that would then be the property of the individual) would more than make up this difference.

Tax Advantages

Most individual car leasees are well-to-do doctors, lawyers, and businessmen. They use their leased cars almost exclusively for business, and deduct all automobile-related expenses from their taxes. Keep in mind, however, that car owners may deduct those same business expenses. It is true that with a lease, everything is a bit easier to calculate. But from a business point of view, leasing offers no more tax advantages than buying.

The Convenience of Leasing

Car leasees sometimes lease for convenience: everything from license plates to taxes to insurance is taken care of at once. So are maintenance contracts, which cover repairs from oil changes to complete overhauls, but which add $25 to $45 to monthly leasing payments. And there's no worry about bargaining over the value of a used car when it's time to trade in the vehicle.

Investing the Down Payment

Those who are masters at making high-return investments—say, 14 percent or higher—might be wise to lease rather than buy a car. For one who can take the capital that would otherwise be used as a down payment on a car and invest it at a 14 percent return, leasing is sensible. However, if one plans to place the down payment in a savings account or buy United States savings bonds, leasing is foolish.

Selecting a Leased Car

Choosing Between Plans

Car leasees are asked to choose between two plans. One is the *closed-end lease,* which is essentially an agreement to rent the car for a designated period—often 24 months—after which the leasee will return it to the agency. The other option is the *open-end lease,* which works the same way as the closed-end arrangement, but which specifies no date at which the car must be returned. When the car is brought back, the leasor will try to sell it on the wholesale market; if he gets less than he originally estimated, the leasee is responsible for paying the difference. If he gets more, however, the customer will receive a refund. (The leasor, by the way, always has the option of buying the leased car at or near the wholesale price.) Open-end leasing, which costs about $10 to $15 a month less than closed-end leasing, is usually the preferred method.

Shopping for Terms

Before leasing a car, shop around for the best terms. A large leasing company is recommended because of the discounts they are able to offer since they buy cars in such large volume. Large companies also have more influence with auto manufacturers and can better promise that warranties will be honored.

The Small Details

Read carefully the fine print of any leasing contract. Some stipulate that the leasee will pay for all body repairs—from major dents to minor scratches. Others hold the customer responsible for replacing tires if the treads have been worn down more than one-eighth of an inch. Remember that most of these clauses are negotiable, so be prepared to bargain. The mileage limitation clause is particularly flexible. It stipulates that if the given mileage limit is exceeded the leasee will pay between three and five cents for each extra mile. Always request a higher mileage limitation than the one initially offered.

RENTING A CAR

Looking for Bargains

When on vacation or in temporary need of a second or third family car, more and more people are now renting. Keep in mind that automobile renting is expensive, and its rate schedule is very complicated. However, there are ways to save money, particularly by renting smaller cars from smaller auto rental companies. Also, ask about special holiday and weekend rates, usually available in large cities. With these discounts, the rented car must usually be returned to the city in which it was rented.

Unlimited Mileage

Vacationers who are doing long-distance driving can almost always save money by asking for a special unlimited mileage rate. Under this system, the renter pays a flat fee, and is responsible for paying for gas as well. Although Hertz, Avis, and National rental companies require that the car be rented for at least three days under this plan, smaller firms usually allow rentals for shorter durations.

Contingencies

Make certain that every rental contingency is well-explained, or the bill may turn out higher than originally expected. Typical of the contingencies is the requirement that a car be returned to a specific location; if returned elsewhere, a higher rate will be charged. Also understand fully whether you will be responsible for putting gas in the car, and how the company defines a "day" in its contract—that is, is a day 24 hours long, or only eight hours?

Discounts

Always request discounts, even when you don't think you qualify. Some car rental companies routinely offer discounts to policemen, businessmen, writers, and anyone else they may particularly like.

SELLING A CAR

Trading-In or Selling?

When buying a new car, most people trade in their old model to the dealer from whom the new car is being purchased. Others sell old models privately. If a car isn't worth much, it's probably foolish to try to sell it on your own. But if it is worth at least several hundred dollars, a better price can be obtained by selling it privately than by trading it in. Check a used car price book (a bank should have one) to find out the value of a car for a given make, model, and year. Add or subtract from that price, depending on the condition of the car and its accessories.

Remember that a car's greatest depreciation occurs in the first two years. After that, its decline in value is slower. The first year's depreciation is about 25 to 30 percent of the original price. Second year depreciation is 15 to 20 percent of the original price; third year, 12 to 15 percent; fourth year, 10 to 12 percent; fifth year, 8 to 10 percent. Thus, a new car purchased for $4,000 will be worth $2,800-$3,000 by the end of the first year, $2,000-$2,400 after two years, and so forth.

Preparing the Car for Sale

Be sure that a car is clean when it is put up for sale. Wash and wax it, clean the trunk and under the hood, and vacuum the interior. Replace burned-out light bulbs. (Don't spend money on major repairs; the investment will never be recovered.) Then place a classified ad in the local newspaper—preferably in the Sunday edition, which has a larger circulation than the daily editions. Also place a sign on the car itself, and place notices on school and supermarket bulletin boards.

CAR MAINTENANCE

What You Can Do

The Owner's Manual

It is wise to carefully read the owner's manual that comes with a new car. Read it when the car is first bought, and then weeks later when you are more familiar with it. Pay particular attention to its suggested maintenance schedule. If an oil change is recommended every 4,000 miles, do not neglect to do so. Dirty oil can severely damage engine parts, and cause friction that will decrease gas mileage. In the long run, regular maintenance will help avoid the major repairs caused by neglect. With proper care, the typical American-made automobile can run up mileage from 60,000 to 100,000 before costly repairs are needed.

Good Driving Techniques

Reduce repair bills by developing good driving habits. These habits should include the avoidance of unnecessary "riding" of the clutch (for stick-shift cars), fast starts, and racing the engine. Good driving habits will make major car repairs unnecessary for several thousand miles.

Home Maintenance

Many minor repairs and maintenance procedures can be performed by the car owner at considerable savings. The car's owner's manual can be an important guide. It will show, for example, where the fuse box is, and burned-out fuses can be changed very easily. Air filter replacements can be bought for only $2 to $4. Burned-out tail and headlights can be replaced at a cost of $1 or less per bulb. Radiator hoses, which average $2 to $3, can easily be installed. A new fan belt sells for about $2 to $3. Oil filters cost about $2, and oil itself can be bought at discount stores at nominal prices.

Using the Proper Oil

Oil is the lifeblood of an automobile engine, and top-quality oil is essential for good performance and maximum engine life. Don't use a cheap oil. Instead, buy a high-grade product, but buy it in bulk from an auto supply store to save up to 40 percent on the cost. Don't mix different brands of oil, which may cause a harmful chemical reaction in the engine.

Auto-Repair Books

For instructions on doing your own auto repairs, visit the public library and look for a recent volume on the subject. Two of the best of these books are *Auto Repairs You Can Make*, by Paul Weissler (Arco), and *How to Service and Repair Your Own Car*, by Richard Day (Popular Science Publishing).

Dealing with Diagnostic Centers

One of the real problems in the car repair industry is that the same garage usually performs both the diagnosis and the repairs. An alternative to this system is to have a car analyzed at a diagnostic center and the actual repairs done elsewhere. A diagnostic center has nothing to gain by recommending un-needed work. These centers are listed in the Yellow Pages, usually under "Automotive Diagnostic Service."

Choosing an Auto Mechanic

When searching for an auto mechanic to repair a car, ask for certification documents from the National Institute for Automotive Service Excellence. Such certification attests that the mechanic is qualified to work on car transmissions and brakes, to tune up engines, and so forth. The NIASE program requires that its certified mechanics have at least two years' experience in their specialized fields. About 100,000 auto repairmen in the United States have been certified by the institute, and they work in car dealerships, gas stations, and independent garages.

First-Hand Test Drive

Try to find a repair shop where the mechanic is willing to test drive the car, diagnose its problem, and determine what repairs are needed. In too many shops, the individual who writes up the repair order is a salesman, not a mechanic. All the mechanic relies on is the repair order prepared by a nonexpert, who may recommend repairs that are unnecessary or ill-advised.

Getting a Written Estimate

Ask for written price estimates on all repair work. Make it very clear that if the mechanic finds other problems that need to be repaired, you want to be contacted before that work is begun.

Defining the Guarantee

Request that the mechanic make a full disclosure of the terms of any guarantee. What's the length of the guarantee? Does it cover only parts, or both parts and labor?

A Long-Distance Breakdown

When one's automobile breaks down far away from home, it's impractical to have it towed to one's own mechanic. Should the situation arise, try to find a reliable repairman in the area in which the car is stranded. Members of automobile clubs ought to call the nearest club office, and ask for a recommendation of a mechanic. No matter who finally works on your car, keep your cool, and don't automatically agree to whatever repairs are suggested.

Retrieving Old Parts

When new parts are installed in a car, insist that the old ones be returned. This will at least ensure that the parts have been replaced. If possible, stay with the car while the repairs are being made. It's not as likely that a mechanic will do a shoddy job if the owner observes him at work and seems to understand what work is being done.

Common Deceptive Ploys

Beware of the following common ploys of fraudulent auto mechanics:

—A car that's smoking badly or leaking transmission fluid doesn't necessarily need a new transmission, as some mechanics will insist. It may only need new seals, or something even less costly, such as replacement of the modulator valve.

—If one is told that his car's ball joints need replacing because the wheels wobble when the car is on a hoist, keep in mind that all wheels wobble when off the ground. The play in a new ball joint will be anywhere from one-eighth to one-fourth of an inch. Ball joints often don't need to be replaced until the car has been driven 100,000 miles.

—Some play is also common in the car's idler arms, which help the wheels move when the steering wheel is turned. If a mechanic points out the movement in the idler arm, and recommends that it be replaced, have the car checked elsewhere. Idler arms last a long time.

—Unscrupulous repairmen sometimes squirt oil on shock absorbers and then claim new ones are needed. To determine the truth of the claim, push down hard once or twice on a fender or bumper until the car begins rocking. If the bouncing continues after you have let go, the shocks need to be replaced.

Making Complaints

When a consumer thinks he has been cheated by a service station, write to the president of the oil company. Complaints about the service departments of car dealerships should be directed to the general manager of the firm, and a copy of the letter sent to the regional or zone office of the car manufacturer (General Motors, Ford, American Motors). Some states now have automobile consumer offices that investigate complaints, and have the power to take legal action against any individual or garage suspected of fraud.

Saving on Gasoline Costs

Testing Various Grades

To determine the best and most economical type of gasoline for a car, experiment with several grades. Recent government studies indicate that the lowest grades of gasoline are adequate for all but a few high-powered automobiles. If an engine begins to knock, however, a higher grade of gas is recommended.

Brand Similarities

All brands of gasoline are essentially the same. The nonadvertised brands sold at independent stations are cheaper, and they are often bought directly from the major oil companies.

Limiting the Speed

Driving within the national 55-mile-per-hour speed limit, even on the open highway, makes real sense from a fuel economy standpoint. As a car's speed increases, so does the wind resistance, which substantially affects gasoline mileage. The typical automobile gets about 21 percent more miles per gallon at 55 miles per hour than at 70.

Gentle Acceleration

Gradual rather than sudden acceleration can reduce fuel consumption by two miles per gallon in city traffic. The only time to accelerate fast is when passing another car or when entering high-speed traffic lanes.

Maintaining Steady Speeds

Driving at steady speeds for as long as traffic will allow also reduces gasoline consumption. Varying the speed by as little as five miles per hour can cut gas mileage by 1.3 miles per gallon. Excessive idling is another gas guzzler. A typical car uses a cup of gasoline every six minutes when idling. Never idle the engine for more than a minute; less gas is consumed by turning the engine off and restarting it.

Early-Morning Starts

It's uneconomical to sit in a driveway gunning a cold engine in the morning. All that is being accomplished is the burning of gasoline at zero miles per gallon. Instead, drive off immediately, maintaining moderate speeds until the engine is warm.

Proper Hill Driving

Better gas mileage will be achieved by anticipating hills. When approaching a hill, gradually accelerate up to the maximum speed that road conditions and the speed limit will permit. Speed costs less on level ground than on a hill, so the added velocity gained on a flat road will allow the hill to be climbed more economically. If you find that you have to depress the gas peddle to the floor on hills, it is probably better to reduce your speed in the interest of fuel economy.

TIRES

Deciding When to Buy

When to Replace Tires

Don't wait for a car's tires to become completely bald before replacing them. Ninety percent of all tire troubles occur during the last 10 percent of tire life. Not only are flats and blowouts more likely on worn tires, but there is also the increased risk of hydroplaning on wet pavement—that is, having the tires ride on top of the water without touching the pavement, making skidding more likely.

What Kind of Tires to Buy

Radial Tires

Those who do much high-speed, long-distance driving should buy radial tires. Although the initial outlay of money for radials is greater than for regular tires, they will last longer. When calculated on a cost-per-mile basis, radials will prove cheaper: a car will get from 5 to 10 percent more miles per gallon with radials. In addition, the more flexible sidewalls of radials allow treads to make better contact with the road, thus permitting better handling and braking.

Foldaway Tires

If trunk space is very limited, consider buying one of the new foldaway tires as a spare. These totally collapsible tires can be inflated with an aerosol can. A safety valve in the tire prevents overinflation. Save even more trunk space by doing without a spare completely. Some new tires, such as Uniroyal's Air Guard, can be driven on at low speeds even when they contain holes as large as one quarter inch.

The Economy of Defective Tires

Save money on tires by purchasing those that are cosmetically defective. Whitewall tires with some black showing through its sides, or tires with cosmetically imperfect tread patterns, are often sold at 20 to 25 percent discounts.

Purchasing Tires

Where to Buy

Tires sold by a department store (Montgomery Ward, J. C. Penney's, Sears), which carry the store's own label, are frequently good buys. These tires are often manufactured by the major rubber companies.

Tire Sales

Tire sales are usually held in January, May, July, and September. The identical tire can be bought for at least $5 less during a sale period.

Balancing Tires

It's wise to have all new tires balanced when purchased. Although manufactured under strict uniformity standards, it's impossible for tires to be perfectly round and balanced for all wheels. A car will ride considerably smoother with balanced tires.

Caring for Tires

Break-in Periods

Like a new car, new tires need break-in periods. As a general guideline, drive at under 50 miles per hour for the first 500 miles.

Maintaining Proper Inflation

A government study has shown that underinflated tires rank only behind brake failure as the leading mechanical cause of auto accidents. Yet more than 25 percent of all cars on the road have at least one tire underinflated by four pounds or more. Buy a pocket pressure gauge (which will cost anywhere from $1 to $5), and check tire pressure at least once a month. Pressure should be checked when tires are cool.

Long-Distance Driving

When planning to drive on a highway for long stretches, increase tire pressure by three to four pounds. Do not, however, exceed the maximum pressure printed on the tire.

Rotating Tires

The Rubber Manufacturers Association recommends that car tires be rotated every 6,000 miles. Note however, that tires are being rotated differently now than in the past. The old technique of cross-switching the rear tires to the front and moving the front tires straight back is considered outdated. Advances in tire design and construction have made a new rotation system necessary: if a car has bias or belted-bias ply tires, move the right front tire to the left rear; then move the left rear tire to the left front. The left front takes the place of the spare, which is placed in the right rear position. Finally, the right rear is moved to the right front. (If the spare is not being used in the rotation, simply bring the rear tires straight ahead to the front, and cross-switch the front tires when they are moved to the rear.)

Special Radial Rotation

Radial tires follow a different rotation system: The right front tire should become the spare, which is moved to the right rear. The right rear replaces the right front, and the two tires on the left side simply change positions. (If the spare is not being used in the rotation, simply move the rear tires directly forward, leaving them on the same side of the car. Likewise, the front tires should be moved directly back.)

BATTERIES

Purchasing Batteries

Maintenance-Free Batteries

"Maintenance-free" car batteries have emerged on the market in recent years. These batteries never need to have water added (a different chemical makeup—calcium instead of antimony— halts the loss of water). They are $20 to $25 costlier than the normal battery, but they'll obviate concern that the battery water level is too high or too low.

Warranties

The longer the warranty, the higher the price of the battery. A so-called "lifetime" battery is only worth the investment if the car is expected to be kept for longer than five years. Other warranties are available for 24, 36, 42, and 48 months.

Caring for Batteries

Checking the Battery Charge

The life of a car battery will be lengthened by having the charging system of the car checked periodically. The primary cause of battery failure is an excessively high or low charging rate. Ask a mechanic to test the car's alternator and voltage regulator every time the car is tuned.

Using a Hydrometer

A battery hydrometer allows for close monitoring of the electrical charge of the car battery. These devices cost from $1 to $5, depending on the sophistication of the particular instrument. If the hydrometer reads 1.260 or higher, a battery cell is fully charged. A reading of 1.230 to 1.250 indicates that the battery needs charging.

Inspecting the Terminals

With the electrical cables connected to the battery, regularly inspect the terminals. They should be affixed securely, and free of corrosion. The top of the battery should be cleaned every six months. Battery terminals can be cleaned with a file, sandpaper, or steel wool. An inexpensive terminal cleaner is also available.

The Water Level

The water level of a battery should be checked at least every 2,000 miles. When water needs to be added, use only distilled water; tap water is filled with many damaging minerals. A battery constantly in need of water may be overcharged, due to an improper setting of the voltage regulator.

Battery Rejuvenators

Avoid using any of the so-called battery "life extenders" or "rejuvenators" now on the market. Many of these additives are harmful to battery cells. Their use will also probably void any existing battery warranty.

Bolt the Battery

A battery that has not been securely bolted down can create problems. Vibrations can cause the chemically-active material on the battery plates to shake loose. As this material accumulates at the bottom of the battery case, it may touch the plates and result in a short circuit, causing the battery to go dead. In older cars, battery retainers sometimes corrode through, leaving the battery free to dislodge in the event of a full stop.

CHAPTER 8

Banking and Investing

Everyone saves or invests—or at least wishes he did. With the cost of living in a seemingly endless upward spiral, saving and investing is becoming increasingly difficult. But millions of people are somehow managing to do it—and each for his own good reasons.

Some individuals save and/or invest as a means of accumulating capital to buy a home, an automobile, or a houseful of furniture. Others are looking ahead to the college education of their children. Still others are planning for retirement, or are saving for an emergency.

Most Americans save their money in savings accounts at banks and savings and loan associations. The rate of return at such institutions is reasonable, particularly since money deposited there is essentially a risk-free investment, with funds being insured up to specified limits.

Investing in the stock market is more complex. When an individual buys stock in a company, he is in essence becoming a part owner of that firm. In return for his investment, he hopes to receive dividends from the company's earnings, and to watch the value of the stock climb.

Most of the 25 million Americans who now own one of the nation's 4,000 stocks do so because their investments have a higher profit potential than is available at any bank or savings and loan association. The possibility for making sizable profits certainly exists, but the risks are high. Yes, maybe you'll find another stock like International Business Machines, which literally made millionaires out of some of its early investors. But the possibility of disaster is just as likely—recall the former high-priced stock, the Penn Central Railroad, whose shares dropped in value from $80 to less than $5 in just a few years, causing the company to eventually declare bankruptcy.

Very simply stated, making money in the stock market is not easy. There are no foolproof systems or magic formulas that guarantee success on Wall Street. In fact, no one wins all the time in the market, so don't expect to. A realistic goal should be to win most of the time and for the gains to outweigh the losses. Risks can be limited by continual monitoring of one's investments. Few stocks are so safe that they can be bought and then forgotten about for an extended period of time.

When an individual buys the *common stock* of a company, he in effect becomes part owner of that firm. Common stock is considered riskier than *preferred stock,* but it does provide a greater opportunity for growth: the common stockholder shares in both the profits and losses of the firm. Preferred stock is a class of stock with a claim on the company's earnings before payment may be made on common stock. It is not as susceptible to dramatic increases in value, but it is also not as vulnerable to sharp decreases. In fact, preferred stock dividends are often set at a fixed amount. Thus, preferred stock offers more security than common stock.

The role of the stockbroker is important to the investment-minded consumer. A good stockbroker not only buys and sells stock; he also works out investment programs for the nonexpert, suggesting the particular stocks which offer the best opportunity for either short-term or long-range growth, depending on preference. If the stockbroker is truly knowledgeable, his advice is invaluable.

Unfortunately, expert investment advice is not readily available—particularly to the small investor. That is why mutual funds have become such a popular investment in recent years; their popularity is based on the assumption that the average individual is relatively ignorant about investments and lacks the time, temperament, and resources to acquire such information. The fund hires its own professional investment managers, who are able to offer the small investor a diversified and well-planned array of stocks, bonds, and other assets.

There are many kinds of bonds in which one can invest— from United States savings bonds to municipal bonds. Essentially, when an individual purchases a bond, he lends money to the company or governmental body that issued it. The bond itself is an acknowledgment that a loan was made, that it will be repaid in a designated period of time, and that a particular amount of interest will be paid on the loan.

Municipal bonds exist in two forms: (1) *general obligation bonds,* which are backed by the issuing government (states, counties, cities); and (2) *revenue bonds,* which are backed by the tolls on the facility (bridge, turnpike) being financed by the bonds. General obligation bonds are considered the safer of these two investments.

Another popular form of investing is purchasing real estate. According to the National Association of Realtors, one out of every five families owns real estate other than its own home. But buying something like a small apartment building, for instance, is a complex process, and operating it at a profit is demanding.

Other forms of investment—from buying gold to gems to stamps—also have advantages and disadvantages. Gold has traditionally been a prized commodity throughout the world. Many people have turned to it over the years in times of uncertainty, viewing it as the ultimate protection. Since 1975 Americans have legally been able to own gold bullion.

Wise investments are worth whatever efforts it takes to make them. Investing shrewdly now can ease many financial concerns later in life.

SAVINGS

Savings Institutions

Commercial Banks

There are three major types of savings institutions in which one can place one's money. *Commercial banks* are the largest holders of savings in the United States. Although the interest they pay on savings accounts is often less than the rate paid by other types of savings institutions, they usually provide services not always available elsewhere, such as checking accounts, trust services, and credit cards. It is permissible to have a checking account at a commercial bank without also having a savings account at the same bank. Because interest rates are higher at mutual savings banks and savings and loan associations, it is advantageous to the consumer to keep his savings accounts at these kinds of institutions.

Mutual Savings Banks

Mutual savings banks operate in only 18 states. Besides making loans (primarily for home mortgages and home improvements), they offer a wide selection of savings accounts— from *regular* accounts (paying interest from day-of-deposit to day-of-withdrawal) to *term* accounts (paying higher interest rates on money left in accounts for a specified time period).

Savings and Loan Associations

Savings and loan associations (also called *savings associations* or *building and loan associations*) are, in effect, cooperative efforts in which all depositors are shareholders in the institutions. The deposited funds are used to make loans to other individuals. Savings account interest rates are higher than those of commercial banks. Although savings and loan associations do not usually offer the wide range of services offered elsewhere (including checking accounts and business loans), they are the wisest places to keep savings.

Safety—a Consideration

When deciding on the type of institution in which to place savings, make safety one of the primary considerations. A mutual savings bank should be a member of the Federal Deposit Insurance Corporation (FDIC); a savings and loan association should belong to the Federal Savings and Loan Insurance Corporation (FSLIC). Both insure the money in every account in a single bank up to $40,000. If an individual's savings exceed this insured limit, he would be wise to withdraw the excess and open an account in another savings institution, or set up another account in the same institution in the name of his spouse or children. Incidentally, there is no cost to the saver for this insurance protection; each savings institution pays the insurance premium.

Credit Unions

Some people choose to place their savings in *credit unions*, which are "cooperative" organizations owned and operated by a particular group of people (teachers, labor union employees, church members, social lodge members). There are 23,000 credit unions in the United States. Since 1971, federally-chartered credit unions (about half of all credit unions) have come under a federal share insurance plan (the National Credit Union Administration) which protects members' savings up to $40,000 per account. State-chartered credit unions are usually insured, too, but the protection varies from state to state. This insurance, or something comparable to it, is vital. In past years, some credit unions have collapsed during periods of economic depression. (Technically, deposits in credit union accounts are not savings. The depositor is said to be investing in the credit union, and receiving, not interest, but dividends on his investment.)

Credit Union Interest Rates

The interest rate offered on savings by credit unions differs from one organization to the next. It varies from four percent to seven percent, usually depending on how well the credit union is run. A skillfully operated credit union will not only offer good interest rates for savings, but will provide loans more readily than other sources.

Credit Union Insurance

Credit unions usually give their members free life insurance coverage equal to or double the amount an individual is investing or saving, usually up to a limit of $1,000 or $2,000.

Thus, besides paying dividends on investments, credit unions offer the bonus of life insurance protection.

Computing Interest

Smallest Monthly Balance

Because savings institutions compute their interest in different ways, it is important to study a given bank's policy before depositing one's money there. Some institutions, for example, pay interest on only the smallest balance in an account during an interest period. So let's say, for example, that interest is compounded quarterly (compounding interest means that interest is paid on interest as well as on the deposit itself), and you have $2,000 in an account at the start of the quarter. Then, a month later, you deposit another $2,000, but withdraw it before the quarter ends. In this case, interest will only be paid on the first $2,000. From the depositor's viewpoint, this is a dismal approach to computing interest. Avoid it whenever possible.

Day-in to Day-out

The method of computing interest that is most advantageous from the depositor's point of view is day-of-deposit to day-of-withdrawal, in which he is paid interest on every cent of his savings for every day it is deposited. This approach is particularly beneficial for those with active accounts—that is, those who frequently make deposits and withdrawals. When interest is compounded daily, a 5 percent interest rate actually yields 5.12 percent annually. By comparison, a bank with an interest rate of 5 percent that compounds and pays interest only four times a year really yields only 5.09 percent interest.

The rate of interest is a more important factor to consider than the frequency of compounding. For instance, 5.5 percent compounded annually is preferable to 5 percent compounded daily.

The chart below indicates how much an individual would have to deposit monthly in an account paying 5.5 percent interest compounded daily, in order for a particular amount of money to be accumulated.

To save this amount	Make this deposit monthly for			
	5 yrs.	10 yrs.	15 yrs.	20 yrs.
$ 5,000	$ 72.57	$ 31.33	$ 17.92	$ 11.46
10,000	145.13	62.65	35.84	22.92
15,000	217.70	93.98	53.76	34.38
20,000	290.27	125.30	71.68	45.85

25,000	362.83	156.63	89.60	57.31
30,000	435.40	187.96	107.51	68.77
35,000	507.97	219.28	125.43	80.23
40,000	580.53	250.61	143.35	91.69
45,000	653.10	281.93	161.27	103.15
50,000	725.66	313.26	179.14	114.61

Grace Days

Some savings institutions offer "grace days" on accounts; that is, they pay interest on money which was deposited after the beginning of a period. For instance, in some banks, money deposited by the tenth day of each quarter earns full interest as if it had been deposited on the first day. Likewise, the final three days of each quarter might be designated as "grace days"—meaning money withdrawn on, say, December 29 will receive interest as if it had remained in the account through December 31.

Bank-by-Mail

Banks in rural areas may not offer interest rates as attractive as those in urban areas. In such cases, it might be wise to bank by mail with an out-of-town institution.

Certificates of Deposit

The Worth of CD's

Term savings accounts, or certificates of deposit (CD's), allow deposits of a specified amount of money (usually a minimum of $500) for an agreed-upon time at a higher interest rate. If that money is withdrawn before its date of maturity, a penalty is issued, usually equal to three months' interest. Thus, only that portion of one's savings that will not be needed during the duration of the term should be put into certificates.

Time Periods

Certificates of deposit can usually be established for any time period—not necessarily only those offered in advertisements by the savings institution. If, for instance, an individual knows that he will need cash in two years and two months, he can establish a time deposit for that precise period of time. Banks or savings and loans can make the arrangements.

The table below shows how additional interest can be earned by putting some of one's savings into a six percent certificate, rather than a five percent regular account:

Interest rate	Original deposit	One year later	Two Years	Three Years	Four Years	Five Years
5% interest	$1,000	$1,050	$1,103	$1,158	$1,216	$1,276
6% interest	1,000	1,060	1,123	1,191	1,262	1,338

Remember: it is advantageous to find a certificate account which computes interest on deposits daily rather than quarterly. Also, if the bank offers the choice of leaving the interest in the term account, or transferring it to a regular savings account, choose the former, since the interest will then compound at the higher rate.

Taxes on Interest

Income tax must be paid annually on all interest earned in term accounts, even if the depositor will not have access to that money until the date of maturity several years hence. At the beginning of each year, the bank mails each depositor a computation of the amount of interest his account has earned in the previous year. This figure must be stated as income on the 1040 tax form.

Maturity Dates

Carefully watch the maturity dates on all certificates of deposit at both banks and savings and loan associations. There are two types of CD's—*fixed-maturity certificates* and *multiple-maturity certificates*—and each has its own regulations as to what occurs when a certificate becomes due. When a fixed-maturity certificate matures, it either stops earning interest completely (usually at commercial banks) or its interest rate drops to the current passbook rate (usually at savings banks and savings and loans). On the other hand, a multiple-maturity certificate is usually automatically renewed for another term if the depositor does not make other arrangements within a specified period of time past the original maturity date—often 10 days. Depositors should therefore read the fine print of all CD's carefully, and keep track of the due dates.

INVESTMENT CLUBS

Forming Clubs

Government regulations limit the amount of interest that can be paid on all savings accounts with balances under $100,000. But for accounts over $100,000, banks are free to offer any interest rate they desire (as much as 11 percent in recent years for $100,000 certificates of deposit). Most of us obviously, don't have $100,000 in cash to place in a savings account. But the average person can still take advantage of these investment possibilities by pooling his resources with friends and neighbors, and forming a club to raise the $100,000 to buy a high-interest certificate of deposit. The government limits the number of people who can join together to form a club—35 in most states (except Wisconsin and Illinois, where the limit is 15). No public advertising is allowed, and no management fee can be paid to a member.

Choosing a Bank

Select a bank carefully when deciding where to buy the investment club's $100,000 certificate of deposit. Shop around for the best interest rates. Certificates that mature in only 90 to 120 days have earned the highest interest recently. A banker can offer guidance on setting up the investment club.

Ways to Save

Forced Savings

Find ways to force savings. If, for instance, an individual receives a pay raise, he might place half of the raise into a savings account each week, and add the other half to his spending money. Or he may request that his employer mail the entire paycheck directly to his bank. It is possible to arrange with the bank to divide this money up and deposit specified amounts in checking and savings accounts.

Christmas Clubs

Avoid Christmas Club plans at commercial banks: they require a deposit of a certain amount of money each week for 50 weeks, presumably to save money for December holiday shopping. These clubs are actually a form of forced savings, and have little else to offer. Some clubs don't pay any interest at all; other pay less than a regular account. If money is withdrawn from a Christmas Club account before the full 50-week period of payments, some banks charge a penalty.

Bank Gimmicks

Banks are continuously offering services intended to attract more customers—from free checking accounts and free safe-deposit boxes to free traveler's checks and free photocopying service. These services, if used frequently, can add up to considerable savings for the consumer.

Mexican Banks

Those who live near the Mexican border can take advantage of the high savings interest rate offered by Mexican banks in cities like Tijuana and Mexicali. Although regular passbook accounts at Mexico's banks pay interest rates comparable to those at United States banks, certificates of deposit of at least 90 days can earn 10 to 14 percent. The Mexican government, however, levies a minimum 15 percent tax on bank interest as it accrues. The interest is also fully taxable on the depositor's United States income taxes. Nevertheless, the depositor still comes out ahead with his CD's in Mexican banks, assuming his United States tax bracket is not exceptionally high.

CHECKING

The Convenience of Checking

Every adult, particularly those who run households and pay bills regularly, should consider opening his or her own checking account. Checks are probably the safest and most convenient way to pay bills. And at the same time, a checking account provides an orderly record of spending, which will help when preparing a budget and completing income tax forms. A canceled check is legal proof that a particular bill was paid.

Two Basic Types

There are two basic kinds of personal checking accounts: A *special checking account* requires no minimum balance, but the depositor must pay a fee (usually 15 cents) for every check he writes, and sometimes an additional service charge of fifty cents to $2 a month. A *regular checking account* requires that a minimum balance ($100 or more) be kept in the account. Check writing is cost-free as long as this balance is maintained or exceeded. If the required balance is not maintained, a fee (usually $2 to $3 a month) is charged. Those who can afford to maintain the minimum balance should consider the regular checking plan. As a general rule, those who write more than 10 checks a month will find the regular checking account is the most economical.

Free Accounts

Be alert for the few banks that offer free checking accounts to customers, with no minimum balance required. The customer is not billed for a maintenance charge nor a per check charge for as long as he maintains the account. These accounts are sometimes offered to charter customers when a new bank opens.

Update Balances

Checkbook balances should always be kept updated. As each check is written, calculate the new balance. Compare these calculations with the bank's monthly statement when it arrives. If there is a discrepancy, determine the source of the error.

Overdraft Protection

Probably the most controversial of the many services now

offered by banks is "overdraft protection," which provides that a check can be written—up to $1,000 or more—even when there is no money in the checking account. When an individual writes a check for more than he has in his account, the bank in effect loans him the money to cover the check—at an interest rate of either 12 percent or 18 percent, depending on the state. This service, useful in emergencies, should not be used unwisely. Keep in mind that many banks will loan money only in multiples of $100. Thus, even if a loan of only $10 is needed to cover a check, the bank will automatically transfer $100 to the account—and charge interest on the full amount.

Late Deposits

If an account does not have "overdraft protection," a check exceeding the balance in the account should not be written on the assumption that there will be time to make a deposit before the check is processed. With the modern electronic processing systems used by almost all banks, checks clear very rapidly— sometimes the same day. By the time a deposit is made, it might be too late.

Stopping Payment

After sending out a check, it is possible to decide against making payment by telephoning the bank and requesting that a "stop payment" order be put on the check. (Confirm this request in writing.) Once a stop payment order has been issued, the bank will not honor the check. There is a charge of $1 to $4 for this service.

Check-Cashing Cards

Some banks provide check-cashing cards to their customers. These cards, granted free of charge, make it easier for the holders to use checks when buying merchandise at stores, or when cashing checks at banks. By issuing the card, the bank guarantees payment of the holder's checks up to a specified limit, usually $50 or $100.

Limiting Deposits

Don't keep more money in a checking account than is necessary. This same money could be earning interest if it were deposited in a savings account. Also, should a checkbook be lost, an experienced con artist could easily use the checks and drain the account. But if the account contains little money, the checks will not clear, and the loss to the checking account holder will be minimal.

Interest-Paying Accounts

Some mutual savings banks, mostly in the New England area, offer checking accounts that pay interest—usually 5.25 percent. These so-called NOW accounts (Negotiable Order of Withdrawal) are technically savings accounts against which checks can be written—but they are, in effect, checking accounts that pay interest. The draft received through these accounts looks like a check, and can be used as one. If these accounts are available at banks near you, definitely take advantage of them. Some of these banks accept accounts from out-of-state residents, but not all. (Banks have been barred from offering interest on checking accounts since 1933, in hopes that this would end the rivalry among banks that eventually led to unwise investments; however, the NOW accounts have legally sidestepped this law since, technically, they are not checking accounts.)

STOCKS

Should You Invest?

For years, stocks have been considered intriguing and glamorous investments. But before buying stocks, the investor should have a cash reserve set aside to meet present obligations and to handle any emergencies that might arise. This reserve should be kept in a savings account or in an easily-converted investment, such as government bonds. A general guideline is: an individual's cash reserve should equal his total living cost for six months plus an extra 10 percent—*less* insurance benefits and any supplemental income.

Brokers and Brokerage Houses

Choosing a Broker

The first step for the novice stock investor is to choose a capable stockbroker. Expert investment information is essential, and unless the investor has the time and the background to ferret out the facts himself, he will need to turn to someone to provide that data. Although a skilled broker may not be easy for the small investor to find, it is possible to locate one. Most large brokerage houses (such as Merrill Lynch Pierce Fenner & Smith, E. F. Hutton & Co., Dean Witter & Co.) will accept new clients regardless of the size of his or her investment program.

Analyzing a Firm

Before deciding to let a particular brokerage house handle your investment business, try to ascertain how good the firm's past recommendations have been. Ask to see the house's research reports dating back a year or two, and study the recommendations that were made. Did the firm make wise investment suggestions? Or did it make as many poor recommendations as good ones?

Membership Status

Never do business with a brokerage house that is not a member of the Securities Investor Protection Corporation. An individual who deals with a firm that belongs to this government-sponsored corporation will be insured for a maximum of $50,000 (including up to a $20,000 cash balance). This protection, incidentally, does not insure against losses in the market itself, but against the brokerage house's inability to return the cash and securities belonging to its customers should it go out of business.

Top Brokerage Houses

In 1976, when *Financial World* magazine surveyed institutional investors as to their choices for top brokers (based on research, execution of orders, and overall services), several firms that orient themselves to individual investors ended up near the top of the list. They included: Merrill Lynch; Smith Barney, Harris Upham; E. F. Hutton; Loeb, Rhoades; and L. F. Rothschild.

Discount Houses

Some brokerage houses make no stock recommendations, and thus have no research department or immense sales staffs. They are therefore able to offer their purchase and sales services at a lower fee than the better-known brokers. Money can be saved by dealing through them if an individual knows exactly what he'd like to do, and is not in need of counsel and advice.

The following discount brokers are all members of the National Association of Securities Dealers and the Securities Investor Protection Corporation. Most accept collect calls from within their own state, or have an "800" toll-free area code.

Baker & Company, Incorporated, Cleveland, Ohio.

Blinder & Company, Boston, Massachusetts.

Burke, Christensen & Lewis Securities, Chicago, Illinois.

W.T. Cabe & Company, Incorporated, New York, N.Y.

C.W. Clayton & Company, Boston, Massachusetts.

Columbine Securities, Incorporated, Denver, Colorado.

Daley, Coolridge & Company, Cleveland, Ohio.

John Finn & Company, Incorporated, Cincinnati, Ohio.

Kahn & Company, Incorporated, Memphis, Tennessee.

Kulak, Voss & Company, Incorporated, Springfield, Virginia.

Letterman Transaction Services, Incorporated, Newport Beach, California and Houston, Texas.

Marquette de Bary Company, Incorporated, New York, N.Y.

Odd Lots Securities, New York, N.Y.

Quick & Reilly, Incorporated, New York, N.Y.

Rose & Company, Incorporated, Chicago, Illinois.

Charles Schwab & Company, Incorporated, San Francisco, California.

Source Securities Corporation, New York, N.Y.

Springer Investment & Securities Company, Incorporated, Indianapolis, Indiana.

Stock Cross, Boston, Massachusetts.

Thrift Trading, Incorporated, Minneapolis, Minnesota.

Complaints

If you believe that your broker has made an egregious error—for example, has bought stocks other than those requested, or more shares than were ordered—first complain to the broker himself. If you're unable to resolve the problem with him, contact the branch manager of the brokerage house. If you are still unsuccessful, write directly to the Securities & Exchange Commission, 500 North Capitol Street, Washington, D.C. 20549. The SEC will order an investigation of a complaint if it feels one is warranted. Also send a carbon copy of the letter of complaint to the New York Stock Exchange (11 Wall Street, New York, N.Y. 10005), which will exert pressure on the individual broker to settle the matter.

Selecting a Stock

The Exchanges

For safety, invest in companies listed on one of the major securities exchanges, such as the New York Stock Exchange, the American Stock Exchange (New York City), the National Stock Exchange (New York City), the Boston Stock Stock Exchange, the PBW (Philadelphia-Baltimore-Washington) Stock Exchange, the Midwest Stock Exchange (Chicago), and the Pacific Exchange (Los Angeles-San Francisco). Before a company may list its stock on a major exchange, it must meet specific standards. Its transactions are all carefully checked by the exchange and the federal government, which certify that these companies are meeting basic criteria of openness and honesty.

Investigating the Company

Prior to investing in a particular stock, find out as much as possible about the company. Write to the firm itself and request an annual report and prospectus. Check various business periodicals in the library (including *The Wall Street Journal, Fortune, Barron's,* and *Forbes)* for information about the company. If you have a broker whose judgment you trust, ask his opinions of the firm. Most brokerage houses have their own research departments, which can be useful sources of information.

Ratings

Standard & Poor's *Stock Guide* rates thousands of common stocks, basing its recommendations on earnings and dividends. The ratings are A+ (highest), A (high), A- (above average), B+ (average), etc. As a general rule, don't invest in a company rated below B+.

P/E Ratio

Among the other yardsticks that can be used to measure a stock's attractiveness is its P/E ratio, or price/earnings ratio. This is the ratio of the stock's current price to its earnings over the most recent 12-month period. Thus, a stock now selling for $35, and which earned $7 a share in the past year, has a P/E ratio of 5. Some experts say that the safest investment is in a stock with a low P/E ratio, which appears headed for a growth period. In such instances, the investor's risks are small, and his chances for profit are good.

A Stock Market Investment Plan

"Blue Chips"

A new investor in the stock market should start with some good common stocks, including "blue chips" (stock issued by a company long known for its ability to make money and pay dividends). From this solid base, he will be able to further diversify as he becomes more familiar with the workings of Wall Street. The blue chips include General Motors, AT&T, IBM, Standard Oil, and some of the major utilities and railroads.

Record of Earnings

A company that has had a record of continuous earnings or dividends over the past decade is quite likely a healthy and stable firm, and a good one in which to invest.

Don't Limit Investments

No matter how limited or large the investment, don't put all you money in a single stock, particularly if you're seeking a long-term return. Invest in several companies in several industries. If one or two companies do poorly, the other four or five may offset those losses.

Vital Industries

When choosing stocks for long-term investment, select some from vital industries, such as energy, transportation, and food. Even in times of economic recession, essential industries usually maintain stability.

Patience for Profits

A common mistake made by inexperienced stock market investors is expecting immediate profits and acting too hastily when the profits don't materialize. Some new investors simply don't give a stock time to perform as anticipated. If the stock goes down slightly, they may sell in a panic and take a short-term loss. In many cases, if they had waited and given the stock the chance to work, they would have realized a profit.

Sell Weaker Stocks

Regular investors in stocks should sell their weakest stock every year or two, without regard to its original cost. Invest that money in another stock which gives indications that it will be more profitable.

Government Regulations

Don't invest in a company subject to government regulation. Restraints placed upon a company by regulatory agencies can substantially limit its profits. Also avoid companies that are burdened with long-term debts: this is a clear indication of a firm's poor management.

Monthly Investment Plan

A simple way to invest in the stock market, particularly for the small investor, is through a Monthly Investment Plan (MIP) account. These accounts can be opened at any brokerage house that is a member of the New York Stock Exchange. MIP's allow individuals to invest anywhere from $40 to $999.99 either monthly or quarterly—in any stock on the NYSE. Either whole or fractional shares of stock can be purchased—for example, $40 will buy 6.67 shares of a stock selling for $6. Dividends can be reinvested, or they can be taken in cash. Although commission fees are higher for MIP funds, they are a convenient way of regularly investing.

Buying on Margin

Never buy stocks on margin unless you are willing to assume

great risks in hopes of obtaining short-term profits. In effect, buying on margin is buying with borrowed money. Under such a system, if you put up, say, 65 percent of the stock's total price, the remaining 35 percent is loaned to you by your broker or by a bank. However, when an investment is financed by margin loans (at an interest rate from 7 to 13 percent), all will be lost if the stocks substantially drop in value.

Stock Certificates

Keep all stock certificates in a safe place; they are proof of ownership. Store the certificates in a safe deposit box, and for easy reference, keep a list of the stocks at home, including the name of the corporation, the number of shares, the identification number, and the price paid for them.

NYSE Courses

One of the best ways to learn more about stocks and the stock market is to enroll in one or more of the courses offered by the member firms of the New York Stock Exchange. Contact the brokerage houses in your city for more information on the classes offered. NYSE also publishes several informative pamphlets, including *The Language of Investing* and *Understanding Financial Statements*, available from the NYSE, 11 Wall Street, New York, N.Y. 10005.

MUTUAL FUNDS

Advantages

For those with limited investment funds, a mutual fund is particularly advantageous. An individual investing on his own might find himself making uneconomical, small stock purchases, and paying proportionately high commissions. Invest instead in a mutual fund. Guided by an investment counselor whom the average investor could never afford, a mutual fund may invest in 100 different stocks and bonds.

Past Performance

A clear benefit of investing in mutual funds is the ease with which their past-performance records can be acquired and examined. It's a matter of public record. By comparison, to ascertain the performance of stockbrokers or other money managers is usually difficult: to ask them directly is not necessarily to get a full or honest reply.

Types of Funds

There are various types of mutual funds from which to

select: (1) *Maximum capital gain funds* seek the largest profits possible and usually invest in developing companies and industries. Investments in such funds should only be made when high risks are willing to be assumed. (2) *Growth funds* are less speculative in nature, and seek long-range rather than immediate positive performance. (3) The most conservative type of funds are *growth-and-income funds,* which put their greatest emphasis on protecting capital investments while still trying to produce attractive dividend income.

Limited Investment

No matter how small his investment budget, most mutual funds will not exclude a potential investor. Many, in fact, will let an individual launch an investment program with only $25 or $50. Others have no minimums at all.

No-Load Funds

By seeking out mutual funds privately, and buying them without the aid of a salesman, sales charges can be avoided. So-called *no-load funds* are sold without salesmen and without commission fees, in direct contrast to *load funds,* which are bought through salesmen who charge a fee of about 8.5 to 9 percent. Over the years, no-load funds have performed as well as the load variety, and they are available in just as broad a selection. Explore both loads and no-loads, but remember that no-loads allow one to avoid sales charges. For specific information about various funds, consult *Investment Companies,* a fact-filled reference source available at the public library or at brokerage firms.

"Muni" Mutual Funds

A new and appealing type of mutual fund invests only in municipal bonds. Available since October 1976, these "muni" mutual funds require an initial investment of at least $100. Their major advantage is that the dividends are exempt from federal income taxes. The higher an investor's tax bracket, the better these funds appear. For instance, if an individual has a taxable income of $15,000, and his tax-free funds can earn a six percent return, that is equivalent to an 8.7 percent taxable return from, for example, a savings certificate or a corporate bond.

Mismanagement

In recent years, some mutual funds have been terribly mismanaged, and the money of many small investors has been pitifully squandered. So before turning your funds over to a mutual fund, investigate it. Talk to stockbrokers, attorneys, accountants, and friends. Only when you are assured of the competency of the fund's administrators should you make an investment. Remember that while a fund releases the investor from the responsibility of selecting individual stocks, it does not relieve him of the risks that accompany any form of investing.

BONDS

United States Savings Bonds

Security

United States savings bonds are attractive to those individuals looking for a secure investment. Savings bonds are backed by the United States government, and are not subject to fluctuations in the economy. They can quickly be transformed into dollars and cents, and they can never be redeemed for less than the total amound invested.

Interest

Savings bonds are a particularly desirable investment because the interest earned is not subject to state or local income taxes. Also, although federal taxes on the Series E interest may be paid each year as it accrues, these tax payments may also be deferred until the bonds are cashed in. Also remember that if savings bonds are lost or stolen, they can be replaced at no cost. (For replacement information, write the Bureau of the Public Debt, P.O. Box 509, Parkersburg, West Virginia 26101.)

Disadvantages

Before buying United States savings bonds, also be aware of their disadvantages: (1) Interest rates on savings bonds have consistently fallen short of rates offered by banks and savings and loans. (2) Savings bonds cannot be used as collateral for loans. (3) When compared to such investments as real estate or securities, savings bonds offer neither growth potential nor the opportunity for capital gain. (4) If savings bonds are redeemed less than six months after their purchase date, they will earn no interest at all.

Purchasing

Although savings bonds can be conveniently purchased at banks, an even easier way to buy them is through a payroll savings plan. Under such programs, an individual authorizes his employer to deduct the proper amounts of money from his pay checks and, with that money, buy bonds. The individual can authorize that as little as $1.25 a week be set aside for the purchase of bonds.

Series E and H

The United States Treasury is currently selling two types of United States savings bonds—Series E and Series H—both of which carry interest rates of six percent when held to maturity. The *Series E bond* is the most popular, and is sold in denominations of $25, $50, $75, $100, $200, $500, $1,000, and $10,000. All Series E bonds mature five years from the date of issue, and are sold for 75 percent of their face value. Thus, a $25 savings bond will cost $18.75; a $100 bond will cost $75; a $500 bond, $375. If savings bonds are redeemed prior to their maturity date, they will yield less than their face value. If they are held past the date of maturity, they continue to earn interest.

Series H bonds are current income bonds. They are sold in four denominations ($500, $1,000, $5,000, $10,000), and mature 10 years from the date of issue. A Series H bond sells for its face value (that is, a $500 bond costs $500), and the interest earned is paid semiannually by check. It earns 6 percent interest when held over the entire 10-year period. A Series H bond can be cashed in for its face value on one month's notice after it has been held for a minimum of six months. If held beyond its maturity date, it will continue to pay interest.

Treasury Bonds

The United States government offers several other types of investment possibilities. *United States Treasury bills* are sold at less than face value, and mature in 3, 6, 9, or 12 months. They can be bought from a broker or a commercial bank. *United States Treasury bonds* mature in more than seven years, and their interest rates have ranged in recent years from 3½ percent to 8½ percent. They can be purchased at the same outlets as Treasury bills.

Corporate Bonds

Becoming a Creditor

Unlike an investor in stocks, an investor in corporate bonds does not become an owner of a corporation. Instead, he becomes a creditor: he is loaning money to the issuer of the bonds, who promises to pay him a specific amount of interest, usually twice a year. The owner may retain the bond until its maturity date, or may sell it on the open market at the price then being quoted.

Ratings

Most corporate (as well as municipal) bonds are rated by prominent financial services, such as Moody's Investors Service or Standard & Poor's. Moody's gives the best bonds (those of the least speculative nature) a rating of Aaa; and the ratings progressively move down the scale to Aa, A, Baa, Ba, B, and so forth. Standard & Poor's ratings begin with a top of AAA, and they continue with AA, A, BBB, BB, and so on. Most libraries and banks keep these ratings on file. Examine them before making an investment, and as a general rule, never buy a stock rated below A by either service.

The rating symbols and basic explanations of Moody's and Standard & Poor's are listed below:

Moody's		S & P's
Aaa	highest grade	AAA
Aa	high grade	AA
A	upper medium grade	A
Baa	medium grade	BBB
Ba	lower medium grade	BB
B	speculative	B
C	very speculative	CCC

Purchasing

The best place to buy corporate (as well as municipal) bonds is from an investment firm (listed in the Yellow Pages under "Investments"). These firms offer assistance in selecting the right issue, yield, and maturity for one's needs. Commissions usually average under one percent of the principal amount, but are sometimes slightly higher.

Short-Term vs. Long-Term

Some bonds, called *short-term issues,* mature in only a few months or years. Others, called *long-term issues,* mature after many years. If one wants the option of transferring his bonds to cash at short notice, one ought to buy short-term, top-grade bonds. However, if one desires a consistent income with a relative price stability, one ought to invest in long-term, high-grade or medium-grade bonds.

Interest Rates

Generally, the longer the term of a corporate bond, the higher its interest rate. In the mid-1970s, for example, long-term bonds (20 years or more) were available that provided returns of 9 to 11 percent.

Risks

Bonds that offer high yields are not necessarily the safest investments. In fact, a higher yield usually means a higher risk.

United States savings bonds, for instance, have relatively low interest rates, but are a very secure investment. However, new and unstable corporations, in order to attract investors, must offer high interest rates.

Municipal Bonds

Denominations

Municipal bonds are generally available in either $1,000 or $5,000 denominations. Smaller investments can be made, however, by purchasing shares in tax-exempt bond funds, rather than buying the bonds themselves.

Tax Exemptions

Although interest earned on corporate bonds is taxable, income from municipal bonds is tax-exempt on the federal level, and also on the state level in the state where they are issued. Thus, for people in high tax brackets, municipal bonds are very attractive.

The table below indicates the approximate yields which taxable investments must earn in various income brackets to produce, after taxes, a yield equal to that of tax-free municipal bonds earning five percent. For instance, an investor earning $22,000 would have to earn 7.35 percent on a taxable investment to equal the after-taxes return on a five percent bond:

An Investor's Net Joint Tax Income:	The Federal Tax Bracket:	The Return on a Tax-Free 5% Bond:	To Keep 5% from a Taxable Investment, It Would Have to Pay:
$16-20,000	28%	5%	6.94%
$20-24,000	32%	5%	7.35%
$24-28,000	36%	5%	7.81%
$28-32,000	39%	5%	8.21%
$32-36,000	42%	5%	8.62%
$36-40,000	45%	5%	9.09%
$40-44,000	48%	5%	9.62%
$44-52,000	50%	5%	10.00%

REAL ESTATE

Rental Property

Advantages

There are at least three major reasons why investors buy rental property: for (1) rental income, (2) tax shelter benefits, and (3) long-term gains as the property value increases. Experts claim that if a landlord's total monthly rental income at least equals his expenses, he'll likely do well by holding onto the property for a few years and then selling it for a profit at its inflated value.

Tax Savings

Tax savings on rental property are often substantial. Even when the owner of a multifamily building has made a profit on his rental income, he can often show an overall loss on his income tax forms once depreciation is taken into consideration. Under "straight line" depreciation, an apartment building that costs $120,000 (excluding land) can qualify for a $3,000-a-year depreciation for each of its 40 years of expected life, meaning a $3,000 tax deduction each year. Under "accelerated" depreciation, an even larger depreciation can be claimed in the initial years, at the expense of smaller deductions later on.

The Responsibilities

Investing in rental property is usually a greater responsibility than most people realize. Many cities have a surplus of rentable units, so finding tenants isn't always easy—even when rents are kept at competitive levels. Add to that rising taxes and increasing fuel and maintenance fees, and the problems of being a landlord are sometimes greater than its benefits.

Start Small

Most experts recommend that a novice landlord start by buying a single-family home or a duplex, rather than an apartment building. If the experience is a positive one, the landlord may consider purchasing a larger complex. Should he decide that a landlord's way of life isn't for him, he can more easily sell a house or duplex than an apartment building.

Shopping Guidelines

When shopping for rental property, keep the following factors in mind:

—Select property in a community where values are climbing.

—Ideally, choose property close enough to your own residence so you can manage it yourself. Property management firms usually keep 6 to 10 percent of the landlord's rental income as their fee for obtaining tenants and collecting rents.

—Avoid communities that currently have rent controls or seem likely to establish them in the near future.

—Choose property in close proximity to mass transit systems. Such property often attracts tenants more easily.

Tenants

Choose tenants cautiously. Check their credit ratings, and ask for a list of personal references. Avoid future problems by taking the time to screen out irresponsible people before they become tenants.

Leases

Each tenant should sign a lease. Be sure the lease clearly defines the terms of the agreement, including the amount of the rent and security deposit, and the conditions under which the security deposit will be returned (the security deposit is usually equal to one month's rent). If tenants are permitted to have pets, ask for a larger security deposit. The lease should also require that tenants obtain permission before hanging wallpaper or doing any other extraordinary decorating.

Repairs

Ask tenants to report all needed repairs immediately, and have them done as soon thereafter as possible. Tenants will take better care of the house or apartment if the landlord demonstrates his interest in providing them with a well-kept place to live.

Buying Raw Land

The Dangers

Some real estate investments become nothing more than nightmares. For instance, raw land sold as part of a future development produces no revenue at all, but is nevertheless costly (taxes must be paid). In recent years, high-pressure salesmen have sold unwary investors "lakeside" property that purportedly would increase in value as the community developed into a prosperous recreational area. Too often, these lots are bought sight unseen, and the land turns out to be all but worthless. So approach raw land transactions cautiously.

On-Site Examination

Never buy investment property without first seeing it. Too often the property does not match the photographs on the sales brochures. To find out what a subdivision is really like, examine it in person.

Property Report

Before buying property, ask the real estate developer for a property report, which by federal law he must provide. Read the report carefully. All information pertinent to the purchase of the land—both positive and negative—must be included. It will state such important facts as who is responsible for paying for installations of water and utility facilities, and it will note the nearest schools and hospitals. Show it to a lawyer before deciding whether to purchase the land.

Contracts

Every promise that's made to you as a potential investor should be part of a contract. All oral agreements should eventually be put in writing. Then allow yourself several days for reflection before signing the contract.

Complaints

Complaints about real estate developers and developments should be directed to the Office of Interstate Land Sales Registration, United States Department of Housing and Urban Development, Washington, D.C. 20410.

INVESTING IN GOLD

Where to Buy

Gold should be purchased only from well-established, reputable dealers. Only through them can the buyer be certain that he isn't buying counterfeit or adulterated coins, or gold bars of inferior quality. Before investing large amounts of money in gold coins, it would be worthwile to have them authenticated for a fee of about three percent of the cost of the coins. (Experts estimate that as many as 30 percent of all the gold coins on the market are counterfeit.)

Purchase Price

When gold is purchased, the buyer must pay a premium of 2 to 20 percent over its market value, plus any applicable sales taxes. This premium represents the coin's numismatic value—based on its condition, scarcity, and collector interest. There will probably also be charges for assaying (evaluation by an expert), insurance, delivery, and storage. Because the market value of gold fluctuates, be willing to adjust insurance coverage frequently.

Low-Premium Coins

When purchasing gold coins, buy only low-premium coins, which are those that cost only a small amount more than the worth of their metal content. In recent years, such coins as the Mexican 50-peso gold coin and the Austrian 100-corona coin have sold for only about 8 to 15 percent more than the value of the gold content. For this reason, these coins have been considered among the best buys in the gold coin market.

Probably the most popular and most publicized of these coins has been South Africa's gold coin, the Krugerrand. Its premium is just five to eight percent, depending on the quantity purchased. The Krugerrand is a convenient coin to purchase because it weighs exactly one troy ounce, which is the unit of measure for gold on the international marketplace. Thus, its value can be checked instantly each day simply by reading the general price quotations in the newspaper.

INVESTING IN GEMS

Expertise Necessary

Inexperienced individuals should avoid investing in precious gems unless they do so with professional guidance. The field is complex, and precious stones—diamonds, rubies, emeralds, sapphires, and the like—are usually bought and sold successfully only by those who are knowledgeable in the field.

Diamonds

Diamonds are the most expensive stones, and when buying them, dealers recommend that four factors be considered: color, cut, clarity, and carat weight. According to the experts, the most precious diamonds have an absence of color. If a diamond is cut either too deep or too shallow, its light reflection may be impaired.

Clarity of Diamonds

The clarity of a diamond is reflected in its overall worth. Essentially, a diamond is said to possess clarity when it has no visible internal or external marks when viewed under a 10-power jeweler's magnifying glass. Incidentally, although carat weight is significant, it is not an infallible indicator, since a heavy but blemished stone may be worth less than a lighter but flawless one.

Weight of Diamonds

Experts recommend that diamond investments be limited to those weighing four carats and up, and with price tags of at least $5,000. All but these highest-priced diamonds are considered unwise investments.

Gem Analysis

For a fee of $15, the Gemological Institute of America will analyze any gem and provide a report that describes the stone's weight, measurement, and color. Such reports are useful when the gem is bought and sold, as well as when application for insurance coverage is made. (The Gemological Institute has offices in several cities, with its national headquarters located at 11940 San Vicente Blvd., Los Angeles, California 90025.)

POSTAGE STAMPS

Wise Investing

Investing in postage stamps—if the particular stamps are rare, in good condition, and in demand—can be profitable. The value of rare stamps has always stayed high, even in times of economic recession. Rare stamps have increased in value by about 20 percent annually in recent years. Some individual stamps have done even better. The $1 Omaha Centennial stamp, printed in 1898, sold for $270 in 1971, and $650 in 1976.

Specialization

When investing in stamps, specialize in a particular type— that is, stamps from a specific country, from a particular era, or of a particular type (air mail stamps). Older stamps are by far the best investment; post-World War II stamps have done poorly, barely maintaining their face value.

Advice

Knowledgeable stamp dealers are available to assist those planning investment programs. They normally charge fees of from 5 to 10 percent of the cost of the stamps bought. For the inexperienced investor, the expert's advice is invaluable.

CHAPTER 9

Credit and Loans

Will Rogers once proposed that the quickest way to ease traffic congestion would be to remove from the road all those cars that hadn't yet been fully paid for. If his suggestion were followed today, the streets would undoubtedly be nearly deserted.

Most Americans buy their cars—and a good many other things—on credit. Whereas, prior to World War II, the use of credit by the average person was minimal, it is now accepted as part of the American way of life. By the end of 1975, more than $190 billion worth of consumer credit was outstanding in the United States. One study says that two-thirds of all American families use credit to meet their everyday expenses—clothing, drugs, gasoline, household items, and even food.

The individual who buys on credit is, in effect, using someone else's money to make a purchase; for that privilege, the individual pays a fee—usually interest. The credit itself can be granted in the form of a loan, a charge account, or a mortgage.

The attractiveness of credit is obvious: It enables one to enjoy the things one needs or wants while earning the money to pay for them. Unfortunately, though, too many people abuse the credit privilege by buying merchandise that they would not have purchased if credit wasn't available. Studies indicate that credit buyers purchase up to one-third more goods and services than those who pay cash.

Just 30 years ago, buying on credit was considered a very poor method of consuming. Indebtedness was socially unacceptable, and lending agencies did little advertising to try to change the negative connotations of borrowing. Saving up one's money to make a purchase was considered most desirable.

But attitudes about credit have changed dramatically in recent years. What is largely responsible for this change is a 2-by-3½-inch piece of plastic called a credit card, of which there are many kinds. In addition to the all-purpose bank credit cards (Visa, Master Charge), millions of other cards are issued by oil companies, airlines, department stores, and even telephone companies. Visa (formerly BankAmericard) and Master Charge have grown so quickly that, in 1977, each of them had nearly two million outlets worldwide.

Credit cards not sensibly used can lead to trouble. Easy credit has put literally millions of Americans in financial straits from which it will take them years to extricate themselves.

Installment loans—high-interest transactions in which the money is repaid in monthly installments—rank close behind the credit card as a popular means of obtaining credit. At any one time, about 50 percent of all American families owe money on an installment loan. Unfortunately, the interest rate charged on some of these loans is outrageous—usually ranging toward 18 percent, and sometimes higher. The Senate Banking Committee recently found a New Jersey man who bought a $124 television set, and paid for it with 24 monthly payments of $17.50, or a total of $420. That works out to an annual interest rate of 229 percent!

Credit will probably continue to be an important part of the American way of life for many years. Even individuals uncertain about the worthiness of credit can't help being influenced by the social climate of acceptance of credit. To keep up (or down) with the Joneses, everybody seems to rely on credit at one time or another.

CASH OR CREDIT?

When to Pay Cash

Advantages

The least expensive way to buy anything is to pay cash. Credit purchasing involves the addition of finance charges to the purchase price. For this reason, it is preferable to get into the habit of paying cash for what you buy whenever possible.

Discounts

Money can be saved on some purchases by paying with cash instead of with credit. The Fair Credit Billing Act of 1975 allows merchants to grant discounts of up to five percent to cash-paying customers. Some hotels and motels, clothing and furniture stores, and even a few restaurants now offer such discounts, so ask before making a purchase or renting a room. The discount may be the incentive people need to refrain from overusing credit.

When to Use Credit

Advantages and Disadvantages

Credit cards have obvious advantages: They are convenient, they remove the necessity of carrying large amounts of cash, and payment is postponed until after receipt of the bill. Even for those who don't plan to use them regularly, credit cards are security in times of emergency (for example, your car breaks down 200 miles from home, and you have little or no cash on hand to pay for repairs). However, credit cards are disadvantageous in that they encourage the purchase of merchandise which the holder does not need or cannot afford, and finance charges tend to accumulate faster than the holder realizes.

Convenience

It's reasonable to use credit to buy goods and services when the convenience of credit is worth much more than its cost. This would hold true for a traveling businessman, whose credit cards allow him the luxury of carrying very little cash on his trips. The mother of two small children is quite justified in buying an automatic washing machine on credit, if the appliance makes her life considerably easier.

Essential Products

The use of credit also makes sense for the purchase of essential items. An automobile, for instance, can be considered a necessity in cities that lack a competent public transportation system. A new hot water heater is a necessity, too, when the old one has deteriorated. If the cash to buy these products is unavailable, then the use of credit is justifiable.

Sales

Credit cards can be used to advantage when stores are holding sales, and personal spending reserves are low. Use a credit card to make the purchase if you anticipate being able to pay the credit card bill before finance charges accumulate.

A Means of "Saving"

Making use of credit might also be warranted as a last-resort method of saving. If you're so undisciplined that you're never able to save for things you want to buy, then availing yourself of credit is one way of forcing you to set aside money for the goods and services you want or need, in the form of the payments you'll *have* to make. The payments are something you'll have to meet; regularly putting money into a savings account takes added self-discipline.

One Approach to Credit

In general, an article can justifiably be bought on credit if the time needed to pay off the loan will not exceed the lifetime of the item itself. Thus, while durable goods such as automobiles, appliances, and furniture may be bought on credit, nondurable items, such as clothing and linens, should not. (Take a vacation on credit if the money to pay it off will be available before the next vacation comes around.)

ARE YOU CREDITWORTHY?

Pertinent Considerations

Many factors are considered when a bank, small loan company, or other lending institution decides whether to grant a loan or credit. If you can answer "yes" to most or all of the following questions, your chances of obtaining a loan are quite good.

—Does your employment history indicate that you can keep a job and earn enough money to pay off your debts?

—In the past, have you promptly paid off your credit-card accounts, charge accounts, and other loans?

—Does your list of present creditors show that you have not borrowed beyond your ability to repay?

—Do your assets—home, savings, stock, life insurance, etc.—exceed your liabilities?

—Do you own your own home, or have you lived in the same rented apartment for an extended period of time?

Frequency of Moving

Lenders often do not consider a person who moves frequently to be a good risk. They want to loan money to stable people, not transients who may disappear before their loans have been repaid. Lenders also hesitate to loan money to individuals who have been involved in frequent lawsuits, even if the verdicts have been consistently in their favor. The consensus is that such people are troublemakers; and troublemakers are not good risks.

Occupations and Sexism

There are many other reasons why an individual may be refused credit. In the minds of some lenders, beauticians, bartenders, foreign diplomats, freelance writers, artists, and longshoremen are credit risks. Women have also often been refused credit over the years on the assumption that their income is less dependable than that of men. Recent federal and state laws, however, now make it illegal for a lender to apply separate standards for men and women. Stores can no longer refuse to open separate accounts for husband and wife if both are creditworthy. A wife can also choose to use her maiden name.

If an individual believes that she has been denied credit because of sex, she should write a letter of complaint to the institution that rejected her and send a copy to the Office of Saver and Consumer Affairs of the Federal Reserve System, Washington, D.C. 20551. If her rights have been violated, she can sue for any losses that result and for punitive damages up to $10,000.

HOW MUCH CREDIT-BUYING?

A Debt Ceiling

How much debt is too much? Some banks recommend that a family's monthly credit repayment obligations never exceed 20 percent of its income after taxes (not including a mortgage). Other banks suggest a figure of 10 to 15 percent, which is probably more realistic for most families. Thus, if one's take-home pay is $1,000 a month, his debt limit should be $100 to $150 (10 to 15 percent).

Consult with your spouse before purchasing major items on credit. Since both partners will share the financial burden of these purchases, both should agree on what is to be bought. If one partner is not enthusiastic, the purchases may lead to future conflicts.

SHOPPING FOR CREDIT

Where

Credit can be obtained from a variety of sources, including banks, savings and loan associations, department and retail stores, automobile dealers, credit unions, and finance companies. Because credit costs vary tremendously from one source to another, do some comparison shopping. The best way to compare the cost of credit is to ask each lender for the true Annual Percentage Rate of Interest (APR); the lender must provide this information before the contract is signed. The APR not only includes the finance charge, but also any maintenance fees.

A second way of comparing costs is to calculate the total amount of all payments to be made over the term of the contract, including the down payment. From this total, subtract the price of the product purchased; the remaining figure is the cost of the credit.

Savings on Various Rates

Shopping for the best interest rate can save you more money than you might initially realize. For example, let's say you borrow $1,000 at 9.25 percent interest, and repay it over a 36-month period. The total amount you'll pay back, including finance charges, will be $1,149.12. However, for the same $1,000 loan at 18 percent, you'll pay back $1,301.40—a difference of $152.28.

Monthly vs. Annual Rate

When loan interest charges are presented as a monthly rate, they can be very deceiving. For example, a loan at 1.5 percent per month is really 12 times that figure for the entire year, or 18 percent. A loan of three percent has a true annual rate of 36 percent.

Tax Deductions

Keep in mind that interest charges for credit are tax deductible. However, charges that are described as "service fees" or "maintenance costs" are not deductible.

Life Insurance

With some types of loans, the lender requires that the borrower purchase a life insurance policy in the amount of money being borrowed. The lender, as the beneficiary on the policy, is thereby protected in case of the borrower's death. The cost of this insurance is often built right into the interest rate paid by the borrower, and is included in the APR.

CREDIT CARDS

Two Types

There are basically two types of credit cards. The most common type is made up primarily of *bank cards* (Visa and Master Charge), *department store cards,* and *oil company cards.* They cost nothing to obtain, and if bills for purchases are paid within 25 days of the billing date, no interest is charged. (Most Minnesota banks have begun to levy an annual service fee of up to $15 for bank cards; a few other banks, like New York's Citibank, are now charging a 50-cent-a-month service fee if the entire balance is paid off and no interest charges have been incurred.)

The other type of credit card is the *T&E card* (Travel & Entertainment), which is offered by American Express, Carte Blanche and Diner's Club. T&E cards require an annual membership fee of $20. Holders of these cards are expected to pay their bills in full shortly after receiving them, and no finance charge is levied if they are paid within 60 days. After the 60-day period, a charge of 2.5 percent a month on the amount due is added. When interest is levied on bank card purchases, the rate is either 1 or 1.5 percent a month (12 or 18 percent annually), depending on the state.

Limiting Credit Cards

Don't become overdependent on credit cards. One or two general credit cards (bank or T&E), plus an oil company card and a couple department store cards are sufficient. Additional credit cards might only tempt overuse or abuse of credit.

Applying for Bank Cards

To obtain a bank credit card, all that is generally needed is an income of at least $7,000 a year and a decent credit rating. It's best to apply at a bank other than the one where you have a savings or checking account. The reason is simple: if you fail to pay your credit card bill, a bank in which you have an account could legally take the amount that is due from your savings or checking account. So, for instance, if you are incorrectly billed for a purchase that you didn't make, and you refuse to pay it, the bank could still withdraw money from your other accounts.

Interest Rates

Credit card interest charges vary, depending on how they are computed. The system most advantageous to the consumer, and the one you should try to obtain, is the *adjusted balance method*, in which the finance charge is calculated on the unpaid balance of the previous month, *after* payments made in the current month have been deducted. The *average daily balance method*, used by most banks offering credit cards, will cost about 16 percent more than the adjusted balance method. Under this system, the finance charge is computed by adding up all the balances outstanding for each day of the billing period, and dividing this sum by the number of days in the period. This figure is then multiplied by the daily interest rate. So if the consumer makes his payment late in the month, both his average daily balance and his finance charge will be higher.

Cash Advance

Bank credit cards allow the holder to obtain a loan known as a "cash advance" up to the credit limit on his card. Thus, if you need $500 cash for an emergency (or for any other reason), the bank will grant the loan providing that this transaction does not exceed your assigned credit limit. Although a cash advance is simple to obtain, the finance charges that accompany it are high. In California, for example, the credit card holder is immediately charged a service fee of two percent of the cash amount ($10 on a $500 advance); a monthly interest rate of 1.5 percent (18 percent a year) will then be levied on the running balance until the loan is paid back.

Special Services

Holders of American Express cards can have a check for up to $500 cashed in any of American Express' 600 offices. Actually, cash is not handed over to the card holder; American Express traveler's checks are, for a fee of one percent of their face value.

At some hotels in the United States and abroad, checks can be cashed upon presentation of a T & E credit card. For this hotel check cashing, American Express will guarantee a check up to $50; Diners Club and Carte Blanche guarantee up to $250.

Credit Card Fraud

Before signing a credit card charge slip, check to be sure that the amount indicated is correct. Also, when charging merchandise in stores, keep an eye on the clerks as they handle your credit cards. Dishonest clerks have been known to use charge plates on several blank sales slips. After the customer leaves the store, they fill in the slips and forge the card holder's signature, charging him for merchandise that he never received. If the customer doesn't check his monthly statements closely (which too many people don't), he may never catch these acts of fraud, and may innocently pay the bill.

Disputes

Receipts from all credit card transactions should be saved. When a monthly statement arrives in the mail, check it for accuracy against the receipts. Errors are not uncommon, particularly as the credit card billing procedures become more computerized. If you notice a mistake, call the company's customer service division, and follow up with a letter. By law, you must receive a response from the company within 30 days, and a final settlement within 90 days; if no response is received, you're entitled to keep the first $50 of the amount in dispute, and you can sue for another $100, plus lawyer's fees. Incidentally, until the matter is finally settled, you don't have to pay for the item being disputed.

Receipt of Bill

In past years, credit card holders have sometimes received monthly statements *after* the due date of their next payment. For instance, they receive a bill on December 1 telling them that the amount due must be paid by November 30. Obviously, under such circumstances it would be impossible to make payment on time, and a finance charge would be levied. Since late in 1975, though, the Fair Credit Billing Act has required that creditors mail their statements no less than two weeks before the due date.

If you are still receiving your bills late, write to the Office of Saver and Consumer Affairs of the Federal Reserve System, Washington, D.C. 20551.

Loaning the Card

Unless you're willing to assume full responsibility, never lend your credit card to anyone.

Lost Card Liability

If your credit card is lost or stolen and it is used by someone else, you are not liable for any amount over $50. By notifying the credit card company before it is illegally used, you won't even be liable for the $50. Keep a list of all your credit cards and account numbers; if one is lost or stolen, contact each company immediately by phone or wire, and follow up with a letter.

LOANS

Loans on Insurance Policies

Cash Value Borrowing

Probably the lowest loan interest rate available nowadays is on a loan taken against a whole life insurance policy (a policy which is guaranteed to have a certain cash value at designated intervals of time). An individual who carries whole life insurance can borrow on its cash value at an interest rate of from four to six percent, depending on how the policy reads. He can obtain up to 95 percent of the money in the cash-value portion of his insurance, and can repay it as quickly or as slowly as he chooses.

Drawback

There is, however, a serious drawback to borrowing from one's own life insurance policy. Should one die before having repaid the loan, one's beneficiaries will not receive the full face value of the policy; instead they will receive the face value minus the amount of the unpaid loan and interest.

Credit Unions

Reasonable Rates

Next to insurance policies, credit unions are one of the better sources of loans, usually providing funds at a reasonable annual interest rate of 9 to 12 percent. (*Credit unions* are voluntary associations of individuals with a common interest—for example, they all may be teachers or all may belong to the same lodge.) These loans are usually provided for a specific reason, such as to finance a new car, and are repaid in monthly installments. The loan payments are sometimes automatically deducted from the borrower's paycheck. Many credit unions will not make unsecured personal loans (those with no collateral) for over $2,500, or secured loans for over $10,000.

Passbook Loans

Borrowing from Yourself

Passbook loans, another relativey inexpensive kind of loan, can be obtained from banks and some savings and loans. They essentially involve borrowing against one's own assets—that is, using a savings account as collateral, which is held by the bank until the loan is repaid. An individual can borrow an amount equal to 90 or 95 percent of the balance in his account. The interest on these loans is one or two percent above the interest rate that the bank pays on regular passbook savings accounts. The money held as collateral continues to earn savings interest during the loan period, so the ultimate loan interest rate is actually just one or two percent.

Is It Sensible?

At first glance, it might seem better to withdraw money from a savings account rather than to obtain a passbook loan. But many people feel more comfortable leaving their savings intact in the bank, believing that they are more likely to pay back a loan than restore their savings to its previous level. It is also true that unless an account pays interest from day-of-deposit to day-of withdrawal, a great deal of interest can be lost by withdrawing funds shortly before the end of an interest period.

Establishing Creditworthiness

A passbook loan is an excellent way of establishing credit if an individual has never before proved his creditworthiness. So with $500 deposited in a savings and loan, he can borrow $450, using his account as collateral. Pay off the loan as soon as possible, and he will have established a good credit rating.

Banks and Savings Institutions

Largest Loan Source

Commercial banks and savings and loan associations make more loans than any other source, although their rates are not always the lowest. True, the cost (an annual interest rate of from 10 to 13 percent) will be less than from some sources, but borrowing on a life insurance policy, from a credit union, or against one's own savings is cheaper still. A bank will usually offer its most favorable terms to those able to present some substantial collateral—a savings account passbook, stocks, bonds, insurance policies. It is also advantageous to be a customer of that bank.

Strict Loan Criteria

Bank loans are probably the most difficult kinds of loans to obtain. Banks closely examine credit records before agreeing to loan money. The loan requests of those with flaws in their past credit dealings may be rejected outright.

Negotiating

When shopping for a loan, try to negotiate a lower interest rate than the bank has initially offered. Although loan officers try to give the impression that their rates are firm, they often have a range of acceptable rates which they can make available.

"Money Sales"

Be alert for the "money sales" that some banks occasionally advertise. These "sales" are usually held to attract new customers. During these periods, banks offer credit at one percent less than the normal interest rates. So whenever possible, wait to take out loans when these "sales" are held.

Use

How one plans to use the money one hopes to borrow is a factor in determining where to seek a loan. A savings and loan institution, for instance, usually offers better rates than banks on home improvement loans, including the financing of that swimming pool or the new roof you want. A bank should be thought of first when money is needed to pay for a trip or medical bills.

Small Loan Companies

High Rates

Although loans are easier to obtain from small loan companies than from banks, they are also more expensive. These firms (also called personal finance companies or consumer finance companies) lend amounts ranging from $25 to $1,500, and are notorious for their very high finance charges. Some impose interest rates as high as 30 to 45 percent a year. Others may only demand 19 or 20 percent per annum, but even this is excessive when compared to the interest charges of banks. Small loan companies justify their high rates with the explanation that most of their loans are to high-risk borrowers who default more frequently than borrowers from banks.

Investigate the Lender

Before borrowing from a small loan company, make certain that it is licensed by the state. Also check with the local Better Business Bureau to see if any complaints against the firm are on file. Over the years, several small loan companies have been shown to be unscrupulous, so investigate the one you plan to deal with before signing your name to a contract.

Should You Borrow?

Note: If you are unable to obtain a loan from any source other than a small loan company, perhaps you shouldn't be borrowing at all.

Mortgage Loans

Last Resort Loans

Last-resort loans can be obtained from "second mortgage companies." These firms, in return for the money they loan, receive a "second lien" against the borrower's house. This means that if he can't repay, they stand second in line behind the holder of the first mortgage to collect their money upon mandatory sale of the borrower's house. Interest rates on these loans are exorbitant.

Installment Loans

Monthly-Payment Loans

A common form of credit is the *installment loan,* usually limited to purchases of large items—cars, furniture, or appliances. Under this so-called "closed-end credit," the customer usually signs a contract, makes a down payment, and agrees to pay the remaining balance in monthly installments. The payments are sometimes made directly to the store from which the merchandise was bought; at other times, payments are made to finance company to whom the store sold the sales contract. The customer almost always receives a book of coupons, and he returns one coupon with each of his monthly payments.

High Interest Rates

Installment loans can carry high finance charges—from 9.25 to 18 percent, but sometimes as high as 36 percent a year. Loans of 15 and 18 percent are becoming much more common than loans at the lower rates. If you're making a major purchase that will take many months to pay off, it would be wise to try to arrange financing from one of the cheaper sources discussed above.

Here is what a $1,000 installment loan will cost when repaid at various interest rates over various periods of time:

annual percentage rate	length of loan (in months)	monthly payments	finance charge	total cost
9.25%	6	$171.19	$ 27.14	$1,027.14
	12	87.57	50.84	1,050.84
	24	45.80	99.20	1,099.20
	36	31.92	149.12	1,149.12
12%	6	172.55	35.30	1,035.30
	12	88.85	66.20	1,066.20
	24	47.07	129.68	1,129.68
	36	33.21	195.56	1,195.56
15%	6	174.03	44.18	1,044.18
	12	90.26	83.12	1,083.12
	24	48.49	163.76	1,163.76
	36	34.67	248.12	1,248.12
18%	6	175.53	53.18	1,053.18
	12	91.68	100.16	1,100.16
	24	49.92	198.08	1,198.08
	36	36.15	301.40	1,301.40

Holder in Due Course

When an installment contract is sold by the retailer to a bank or a loan company, the latter becomes the "holder in due course" of the payment agreement. Until recently, if the merchandise purchased turned out to be shoddy, the consumer was nevertheless required to continue making payments to the loan company, no matter how justified the complaint against the retailer. But in 1976, the Federal Trade Commission enacted a rule stipulating that the consumer has the same rights against the "holder in due course" as he does against the retailer. So if the item bought is of inferior quality and the retailer refuses to remedy the situation, the consumer may legally withhold payment until the matter is resolved. This ruling, however, is not applicable if the purchase price of the item is under $50 or if the purchase was made in a state other than the one in which the consumer lives, or one more than 100 miles from his home.

Installment Contracts

Before signing an installment contract, carefully read all fine print for undesirable provisions:

(1) Some contracts stipulate that should the consumer fall behind on payments, the creditor can demand that the remaining

balance be paid in its entirety immediately. Others stipulate that until the final payment is made, the merchandise cannot be moved from the buyer's address without the consent of the creditor. Still others provide that if payments are missed and the creditor takes the debtor to court, the debtor is responsible for paying the creditor's court costs and lawyer's fees—plus an additional 15 percent of the amount owed.

(2) Avoid the inclusion of so-called "add-on" clauses in installment contracts. These clauses provide that other purchases made by the debtor will serve as collateral for the new ones. Thus, if the debtor does not make the payments as stipulated in the contract, goods for which substantial payment has already been made can be repossessed, along with the new merchandise. "Add-ons" are most commonly found in loan contracts offered by furniture stores.

(3) Avoid so-called "balloon payments" in loan contracts. A balloon payment is a large sum of money to be paid *in toto* at the end of the loan term. It is much larger than the monthly payments that have preceded it. If the debtor is unable to pay the balloon payment when it comes due, he may lose the item he's been paying off for many months. Or at best, the debtor will be given the option of refinancing the balloon payment, meaning he will have a new series of smaller payments at an even higher interest rate.

(4) About 75 percent of all states permit installment sales contracts to include a clause allowing wage assignment. This clause permits the creditor to approach the debtor's employer to collect on debts directly from the debtor's salary. No court judgment is needed for such action to occur. However, federal law prohibits creditors from taking more than 25 percent of the debtor's after-taxes earnings. Creditors also cannot leave the debtor with a weekly salary that is less than 30 times the federal minimum hourly wage. Whenever possible, avoid loan contracts containing this stipulation. If this clause already exists in one of your contracts, and your wages have been assigned, make certain that the creditor is not taking more than he is legally entitled to.

Education Loans

Wise Investment

Borrowing money to finance a college education is one of the wisest and, in the long run, most productive loans one can assume. Interest rates are relatively low, and the return—a college degree and greater opportunities for employment—is enormous. Many government and private agencies make student loans available.

NDSL Loans

Education loans are available from commercial lenders at a variety of rates. But probably the most widely used are low-cost government-sponsored loans administered by the colleges themselves. The National Direct Student Loan (NDSL) is available at an annual interest rate of only three percent, and the loans may amount to between $2,500 and $5,000. Neither principal nor interest payments begin until after graduation, and the student has up to 10 years to repay the loan. If the student becomes a teacher of the handicapped or of the poor, the loan may be canceled. The funds for these loans are limited, and are usually awarded on the basis of need.

Guaranteed Loan Program

The federal government also sponsors an education loan program administered through banks, savings and loan associations, and credit unions. Called the Guaranteed Loan Program, the plan charges an interest rate of seven percent on loans up to $2,500 a year. But the government usually pays the interest charges for the first 9 to 12 months after graduation, at which time repayment begins. Applications for these loans are available at local lending institutions.

Loan Recipients

Although many government-sponsored education loans are given to students from low-income families, individuals in higher income brackets are also eligible. The American Council on Education, in a 1973 study, found that 37 percent of the recipients of the National Direct Student Loans come from families with gross incomes in the $12,000 to $20,000 range. The same study indicated that 49 percent of the students receiving Guaranteed Student Loans were from families of that same income group.

Emergency Loans

Many colleges offer short-term emergency loans of their own, ranging anywhere from a few dollars to several thousand dollars. Rates are usually very reasonable, and repayment can be deferred until after graduation. The financial aid officer can tell you whether such loans are available at your college

Private Lenders

The nonprofit United Student Aid Fund, 845 Third Avenue, New York, N.Y. 10022, is the largest private lender of money to students. Its programs change from year to year, so contact it directly for information about the student loans currently available.

Information Sources

In addition to loans, parent and child should begin investigating college scholarships when the student is a junior in high school. The best sources of such information are the high school guidance counselor and the financial aid personnel at the colleges being considered.

What Will College Cost?

With the inflation rate so unpredictable, it's impossible to anticipate the cost of a college education. In the 1977-78 school year, tuition and fees at four-year private colleges was $2,476 for nine months of schooling. Once books, supplies, room, board, transportation and personal expenses were added, that total rose to $4,905. At public colleges, tuition and fees averaged $621 in 1977-78, but when the other expenses were added, the total bill came to $3,005.

But what about the cost of a future college education? If we assume that the inflation rate will level off at six percent, a child who is now five years old and who will begin attending a state university at age 18 will need $37,530 to pay for four years of education. If he attends a private college, his education will cost $65,680. If a child is now 10 years old, his college education can be expected to cost $27,270 for four years at a state university and $47,720 at a private college. These figures include room, board, tuition fees, and miscellaneous expenses.

Using these figures as a guide, to save up the needed funds for the five-year-old's future education, his parents would have to save $1,780 a year (at a five percent after-tax return) for the state university education, and $3,120 a year for the private college. The 10-year-old's parents would need to save $2,300 and $4,030 annually (at a five percent after-tax return) for the state and private college, respectively.

Loan Sharks

Guarding Against Dishonesty

Despite attempts by government agencies to drive them out of business, dishonest "loan sharks" still exist today. The consumer's best protection against them is to be cautious when arranging for a loan. Remember the following:

(1) If the lender does not prominently display his state license, be suspicious.

(2) Beware of anyone who offers a loan with "no questions asked" and at a very high rate of interest.

(3) Never sign a document containing blank spaces.

(4) Demand copies of all papers for your own files.

(5) Make certain that the amount of the loan, the date of the loan, and the repayment terms are clearly stated on the contract.

CREDIT RATINGS

Bill-Paying History

A "credit rating" is essentially a record of how an individual has paid his bills in the past. It includes information about loans, credit cards, charge accounts, tax liens, court judgments, and bankruptcies. These records are compiled by so-called "credit bureaus" or "credit reporting agencies," which obtain much of their information from credit grantors themselves.

Applicant Rights

Whenever an individual applies for credit and is denied it, the creditor is required by law to give the applicant the name and address of any credit bureaus that influenced the decision to deny credit. The individual also has the right to obtain from the bureau a free report on the "nature and substance" of the material in his file, including who supplied the damaging information that has been collected.

The Credit Bureau

Whether or not an individual has been granted credit, he is entitled to know what information is included in his credit file. He should look in the Yellow Pages under "Credit Reporting Agencies" and "Credit Bureaus," and call the nearest bureau, asking for its procedure on allowing a person to examine his own file. Most will charge a fee of approximately $5, and will send out a computer print-out of the information. Under the Fair Credit Reporting Act, an individual also has the right to know who has received a copy of the file for credit purposes in the last six months, and for employment purposes in the last two years.

Inaccurate Information

If an individual can prove that certain information in his credit file is inaccurate, the erroneous information must be removed. If a difference of opinion exists about any information, he is entitled to submit a 100-word rebuttal that will become part of his file.

Discarding Information

Federal law requires that adverse information collected by

credit rating bureaus must be discarded after seven years (except for information concerning bankruptcy, which can be kept for an additional seven). Be aware, however, that there are loopholes in this law. For instance, if an individual applies for more than $50,000 in life insurance, information about him dating back more than seven years can be gathered. The same is true if an individual applies for a job that pays over $20,000.

WHEN DEBTS ARE OVERBURDENING

Adjusting Repayment Schedules

If you've borrowed to the point where you find it impossible to repay loans on schedule, discuss the situation with your creditors. Creditors are often understanding; if they see that your intentions are honorable, they may be willing to bend a little to help you through the financial crisis. Because most creditors are as eager to stay out of court as you are, a new repayment schedule—one with which you can cope—may be recommended. Or it may be suggested that you give each creditor a portion of the amount owed until you are able to resume making the full payments. Or you may be asked to pay only the interest on the loans each month until you can resume paying off the principal as well.

Collection Agency Abuse

If a collection agency representative becomes abusive—uses foul language or calls you in the middle of the night—report it to the telephone company. If you do not receive satisfactory help from the telephone company, complain to both the Federal Trade Commission and your local district attorney.

Debtor Responsibility

When merchandise is repossessed, it is taken back and resold by a creditor, and that money is applied to the account of the debtor. But in most states, if the sale does not pay off the debt in full, the debtor remains responsible for the balance. If, for example, you owe $350 on a color television, and it is sold for $200 by your creditor, you are liable for $150. (If the sale of the merchandise brings in more money than is owed, the creditor must pay the excess to the debtor.)

Debt Consolidation Loans

So-called "debt consolidation loans," which are intended to give the debtor money to pay existing debts, should be avoided. By taking out a loan of this kind, the debtor will be assuming another loan, which ends up costing more than the original debts in the long-run. The interest rate on a debt consolidation loan ranges from 18 to 38 percent. From the lender's point of view, it is a magnificent loan; from the debtor's, it is highly undesirable.

Financial Counseling

Those who are consistently in debt are prime candidates for financial counseling. Most cities have nonprofit credit counseling agencies that offer guidance on how to get out and stay out of debt. A counselor will study a family's lifestyle, determine how much of its income is needed for day-to-day living, and show how the remainder can be used to pay outstanding bills. This service is free in most states, but a $15-per-month fee is levied in others. To locate the credit counseling agency nearest you, write to the National Foundation for Consumer Credit, Incorporated, 1819 H Street, N.W., Washington, D.C. 20006.

CHAPTER 10
Insurance

Insurance is big business in the United States. Everyone, it seems, has some coverage, and most of us are heavily insured. The desire to protect ourselves against financial reverses caused by unexpected events has turned the insurance industry into a trillion dollar enterprise.

Life insurance alone is carried by 140 million Americans. Even more people—205 million—are protected by some form of health insurance. Other types of common coverage, including automobile and homeowners insurance, are purchased by a majority of families in the United States.

Despite the high reliance that Americans place on insurance, it remains poorly understood by consumers. Many people do not clearly comprehend the extent of the coverage they're buying, and only come to understand it—often the hard way—when they file a claim.

One of the real problems is that insurance policies are simply unreadable by the average consumer. Policies have been analyzed using the readability standards established by Rudolf Flesch, author of *The Art of Readable Writing*. Flesch's system is based upon sentence length and number of syllables per word. Using his method of analysis, some insurance policies actually prove to be less readable than Einstein's theory of relativity.

Insurance companies argue, of course, that a policy is a legal contract, and technical phrasing is therefore essential. Ralph Nader, however, has challenged this, along with other insurance company pronouncements, declaring that the insurance industry is "a smug sacred cow feeding the public a steady line of sacred bull."

Most consumers not only do not fully understand the types of insurance available, but also the extent of coverage they need. This is reflected in a recent study by the University of Minnesota, which indicates that 45 percent of all American families have inadequate life insurance protection.

Health insurance often presents less of a dilemma to the consumer than life insurance. Some people never have to shop for their own health protection, since it is commonly provided as a fringe benefit by employers. But many group health policies do not cover hospital bills in full; others do not cover care in the doctor's office. So even though millions of Americans have some health insurance provided by their employers, many feel the need for more protection.

The health insurance industry has been complicated in recent years by the enormous growth of mail-order health coverage. Mail-order protection is the fastest-growing aspect of the insurance industry, but it has been tainted by deceptive advertising.

Another kind of insurance important to most Americans is disability insurance. Over 8,000 workers become disabled every day in the United States, and for many of these people and their families, disability insurance is a real blessing. This protection pays a specified amount of money per month when injury or illness keeps the policy holder off the job.

Automobile insurance is very expensive. Americans spend $19 billion a year for car insurance, and they complain about it more than they do about any other aspect of their insurance program. People are generally unhappy about the skyrocketing insurance rates, the nonpayment of seemingly legitimate claims, and the long delays in the settlement of claims.

Homeowners insurance is a part of the typical family's entire insurance coverage. In the United States, a home burglary occurs every 22 seconds, and a home fire every 46 seconds. A solid homeowners policy is the only source of protection for the victims of these unforseeable events.

A competent insurance agent or broker should be able to solve many of your insurance problems. An insurance *agent* is employed by and works exclusively for a single insurance company. In effect, he is working for the insurer, not for you. By contrast, an insurance *broker* sells insurance for many companies, acting as middleman between these firms and his customers. A good, honest broker will gladly discuss with you the policies of many companies, thus enabling you to compare the prices and features of each.

To find a good insurance agent or broker, talk to relatives, friends, and business associates about their experiences with agents. Possibly they can recommend one with whom they've been pleased.

A good agent will be willing to put all his proposals in writing, and leave them for you to study at your convenience without pressure. He will also not object to your doing some comparison shopping elsewhere before selecting a particular policy.

Even with the guidance of a good agent or broker, there are

still many unanswered questions that the average consumer has about insurance. In an area so critical to his family's well-being, it is tragic that so many people know so little.

LIFE INSURANCE

Who Needs Life Insurance?

Is It Necessary?

A general guideline: an individual needs life insurance only if another person(s) is dependent upon him to pay for daily living expenses. Unmarrieds, childless divorce(e)s, or those with self-supporting spouses do not need this coverage.

Scare Tactics

Agents will try to convince those not in need of life insurance to buy it anyway, to avoid the possibility of being "uninsurable" at a later date. "Should you develop a heart ailment next year," they argue, "life insurance would not be available to you." Beware—this is a scare tactic without much foundation. According to the Institute of Life Insurance, 97 percent of all applicants for life insurance are accepted, including those with medical disorders. Some have to pay higher premium rates because of their classification as "extra risks," but the claim that many people eventually become "uninsurable" is erroneous.

The Remarriage Factor

When a married man buys life insurance, he would be foolish to scrimp on the amount of his coverage on the presumption that his widowed wife will eventually remarry and not have to depend on insurance for support. In fact, less than 20 percent of all widows remarry.

Two-Income Families

Families in which both husband and wife contribute to the family income should be insured to the extent of their combined incomes. For instance, if Mr. and Mrs. X each earn 50 percent of the family income, and it's clear that the family could not survive at its current standard of living without one of their incomes, then each of their lives should be insured for the amount of money the family would lose if one of them died.

Insuring Children

Do not buy life insurance for children *unless* the family breadwinners are already fully insured. Although a child's insurance policy can be bought at very low rates, remember that the child is not contributing to the family income. His or her insurance is not a high priority.

How Much Insurance?

Calculating the Amount

When trying to decide how much life insurance to buy, keep in mind that a family generally requires between 60 and 70 percent of the husband's take-home pay annually to maintain their accustomed standard of living after his death. However, the family's insurance need not cover this entire amount if the wife is agreeable to returning to work in the event of her husband's death.

Agent's Suggestion

A guideline followed by many agents is that a family man should be insured for an amount at least equal to four to five times his annual take-home income. Following this rule, a husband with an annual take-home pay of $15,000 should be insured for a minimum of $60,000 to $75,000. At present, the average American is insured for only about two times his annual take-home pay.

Factors to Consider

When calculating a family's particular life insurance needs, the day-to-day living expenses of the survivors is only one of the factors to be considered. Other factors are the money that will be needed for medical and burial costs of the deceased, as well as any large anticipated expenses, such as the cost of educating children.

Social Security Payments

Life insurance calculations should include the amount of Social Security payments the family would receive if the breadwinners were to die now. To find out what these payments would be, write on a postcard "Request for Statement of Earnings," along with your name, address, Social Security number, date of birth, and signature. Mail the card to the Social Security Administration, P.O. Box 57, Baltimore, Maryland 21203. By return mail will come a record of your income credits, from which can be determined the size of the benefits the family is entitled to. Also ask for instructions on how to determine your projected future benefits.

Changes with Age

As a person gets older, his or her life insurance needs usually decrease. Each year the person lives is an additional year during which insurance will not be called upon to support his or her family. Thus, with each passing year, each of us needs less and less protection.

What Kind of Insurance?

Term vs. Whole Life

To provide your family with a maximum amount of life insurance at the cheapest price, *term insurance* is recommended. Term coverage insures a life for a specific number of years, and its premiums rise each time coverage is renewed. Unlike *whole life insurance*, term insurance does not include a savings element called the "cash value" of the policy; it is less expensive because the policy holder does not pay additional money each month to be put into this "savings account." He pays only for protection.

Inexpensive Coverage

A young man with the large financial responsibilities of a new family can buy a substantial amount of term life insurance for a relatively small annual premium. A 35-year-old man can buy a one-year $25,000 term policy for about $100. For the same amount of protection in a whole life policy, he'd pay $500 a year.

Investing the Savings

Some insurance experts believe that the consumer will profit by buying term insurance (instead of whole life) and by investing the money saved. Joseph Belth, a professor of insurance at Indiana University, has calculated that if one is able to invest the difference in premiums at five percent (after taxes), he will have twice as much at retirement than if he were to depend solely on the cash value of a whole life policy.

Cash Value

The cash value aspect of a whole life insurance policy is a form of forced savings. Those without the self-discipline to put money aside find this a particularly attractive feature of whole life policies.

Borrowing from Yourself

The money that has accumulated in the cash value portion of a whole life policy can be borrowed. These loans are very reasonable because of their low interest rates (usually five or six percent). To obtain a loan of this kind, simply write to your insurance company, stating your policy number and the amount you want to borrow. A check is usually forthcoming within a few days, and there is no particular date by which the loan has to be repaid. The money can be used for any purpose. You will be billed for the interest as it accumulates.

Limiting Coverage

There is one significant disadvantage to borrowing on the cash value of life insurance. By so doing, the borrower decreases his life insurance protection by the amount of the loan, plus interest charges. Thus, if he has a $25,000 life insurance policy, and he dies before having paid back a $2,000 loan from the policy, his beneficiaries will not receive $25,000; they will receive $23,000 minus interest.

Variable Life

Some life insurance companies are offering the *variable life insurance* policy, a new type of coverage that is actually a form of whole life insurance. Its most distinctive feature is that the premiums paid are invested in stocks; if the stocks do well, the policy's death benefits and cash value increase. Should the stocks do poorly, the death benefit decreases, but never below a certain level. Variable insurance premiums are lower than other types of whole life insurance premiums, but are higher than term insurance premiums. Since insurance companies can in no way guarantee the returns on their stock investments, variable policies should only be taken out if some risk is willing to be assumed.

Life Insurance Contract Clauses

Beneficiary

The *beneficiary* of one's life insurance is the individual to whom the proceeds of the policy will go when the policyholder dies. If at any time the policyholder wishes to change the beneficiary named on his policy, he may do so by notifying the insurance company in writing.

Children as Beneficiaries

It is recommended that children *not* be directly named as beneficiaries. A minor may not be able to sign a legal form to release the life insurance funds, because he is not of age to enter into contracts. Money left to minors thus often causes prolonged court proceedings, and the legal expenses can sometimes actually exceed the amount of money that has been bequested. One way to avoid these legal hassles and still leave insurance to minors is to place the money in a trust fund. (Trusts are discussed in Chapter 12.)

Waiver of Premium

The buyer of life insurance should ask that the policy include a "waiver of premium" clause. This provision, which costs very little, will keep the policy in force if the policyholder becomes disabled and incapable of working. The insurer will, in effect, make the premium payments for the individual during the period of disability. When the policyholder recovers and begins making the payments again, he is in no way obligated to pay back the premiums that he did not make while ill.

Disability

Closely examine the particular "waiver of premium" clause that the life insurance agent offers. Check to see how it defines "disability." The definition should be a very broad one. Some policies define it so narrowly that it's doubtful that circumstances will ever arise under which the insurer will have to honor the clause. One policy requires that an individual be "house-confined" to take advantage of the provision. Under this stipulation, if the insured is able to be wheeled into the backyard for some sunshine, he is not considered to be disabled.

Double Indemnity

Some life insurance companies will offer to add a clause to the policy providing for "double indemnity" for accidental death. Under this stipulation, the beneficiary will receive twice the face amount of the policy if the insured dies accidentally. Although the additional cost of this clause is minimal, it's not a worthwhile investment because the insured's family will not need twice as much insurance money should he die by accident rather than by illness. Instead of spending an extra amount of money on double indemnity, it is wiser to increase the overall life insurance coverage—protecting the family regardless of the cause of the death.

Shopping for Insurance

Comparison Shopping

Don't buy life insurance impulsively; take the time to comparison shop. To understand the importance of comparison shopping, consider the following: if two insurers offer rates that vary as little as $5 per $1,000 of coverage, buying $50,000 worth of protection from the cheaper company would save you $250 a year, or $5,000 over 20 years. According to statistics compiled by the Pennsylvania Insurance Department, the price of a $10,000 whole life insurance policy for a 35-year-old male bought from Old

Republic Life is more than twice as expensive as one bought from Bankers Life of Iowa.

In 1974, a Senate antitrust subcommittee study ranked the price of whole life policies of the 198 insurance companies doing most of the nation's business. Those firms that ranked best in the cost study were Northwestern Mutual Life, Massachusetts Mutual Life, and Connecticut Mutual.

Interest Adjusted Method

When comparing life insurance costs, ask insurers for the cost of their policies as determined by the "interest adjusted method." This method is the most accurate way of comparing policies, because it not only takes into account what the premium payments will be, but it also considers the interest that could have been earned on these premiums if they had been placed in the bank rather than used to buy insurance.

Dividends

Some life insurance policies pay the insured an annual dividend—that is, an amount of money is returned to the insured if a surplus of funds exists. Dividends are not guaranteed, but policies designed to pay them do so more often than not. Although life insurance that doesn't pay dividends has lower premiums, many studies have indicated that dividend-paying policies actually cost less in the long run because their higher premium costs are usually offset by the dividend.

Company Strength

The financial strength and stability of a life insurance company should be considered before buying one of its policies. Ask your agent for a copy of the company's annual report, or check its rating in *Best's Insurance Reports,* which is available in most libraries. To be safe, a company should have the highest recommendation that *Best's* offers (called "most substantial"). Ideally, the company should be at least 20 years old, and have in excess of $500 million worth of insurance in force. Although many smaller and younger companies sell good and reliable insurance, some may still be struggling to get the kinks out of a relatively new enterprise. Newer companies also often have large initial costs, which might considerably diminish the funds left to pay dividends.

Dividend History

When evaluating the companies that pay dividends, study each company's dividend history. A company's past record is no guarantee of its future, but it does give an indication of the caliber of the firm's management, and the soundness of the company's dividend scale. If an insurer promises impressive dividends, but its history does not support that likelihood, be particularly cautious. Some companies tend to be overly optimistic about future dividend payments.

Widespread Licensing

A positive indication of a company's strength is its freedom (through licensing) to sell insurance in many states. The state insurance departments of each state provide these licenses, issuing them on the basis of an insurer's financial strength. In particular, ask an agent if the company is licensed in the states of New York, California, and Pennsylvania, which have the strictest insurance laws.

Combating Inflation

Reinvesting Dividends

Inflation can erode away an impressive life insurance program. Twenty-five thousand dollars worth of protection bought two decades ago does not seem nearly so impressive today. One way your can combat inflation is to use your annual dividends (if your policy pays them) to purchase additional insurance. Depending on the size of those dividends and your age, you will probably be able to buy from two to three percent additional whole life insurance every year, and from five to ten percent more one-year term protection.

The chart below indicates how much $50,000 worth of life insurance will be worth in terms of purchasing power in 5, 10, 15, and 20 years under varying rates of inflation.

Years into Future	Rate of Inflation		
	6%	8%	12%
Now	$50,000	$50,000	$50,000
5	36,500	33,000	26,000
10	27,000	22,000	14,000
15	20,400	14,500	7,500
20	14,500	9,500	4,000

Exchanging Policies

A Poor Transaction

It rarely makes sense to relinquish a life insurance policy you already have in favor of a new and "better" one. An acquisition cost, from which the agent's commission is drawn, will have to be paid for that new policy. The new policy will probably also have a waiting period before part or all of it goes into effect. In most states, it is illegal for an agent not to fully explain the difference between the new policy he is trying to sell and the old one he is trying to convince the customer to drop.

Inexpensive Life Insurance Sources

Savings Banks

Life insurance can be bought in saving banks in three states—New York, Connecticut, and Massachusetts. These banks offer insurance at cheaper rates than can be found almost anywhere else. Although a wide range of term and whole life policies are available, there is a limit to the amount of coverage a bank will sell—$5,000 per individual in Connecticut, $30,000 in New York, and $41,000 in Massachusetts.

Group Policies

Group life insurance can sometimes be purchased from an employer or an employee association. There are usually no medical forms to complete; all workers are automatically eligible for this protection. A disadvantage of group insurance is that when an employee leaves his job, or terminates membership in the employee association, the life insurance may terminate, too. When it is possible to continue coverage, there is usually a higher premium rate. As a rule, group insurance rarely provides for a family's entire life insurance needs; it is, however, a useful, low-cost addition to other policies.

MILITARY LIFE INSURANCE

Automatic Coverage

A Servicemen's Group Life Insurance (SGLI) policy can be written for $15,000. All members of the Armed Forces are automatically insured under the SGLI program. Premiums are deducted from their pay.

Post-Service Coverage

Regardless of his health upon leaving the service, a serviceman can switch from an SGLI group policy to an individual policy issued by any of 600 participating commercial insurance companies. This switch, however, must be made within 120 days after separation from the service.

CO Status

Any kind of a government insurance policy acquired while

in the service will automatically be voided if a soldier has subsequently sought conscientious objector (CO) status. During the Vietnam war, the American soldiers who deserted or sought release from the service via a CO exemption had their life insurance canceled.

Resolving Questions

Any questions about life insurance purchased in the service can be answered by a local Veterans Administration Office. Or if you prefer, write to the Office of Servicemen's Group Life Insurance, 212 Washington Street, Newark, New Jersey 07102. If the question is about a specific policy, be sure to include the policy number in your letter. If the policy number is unavailable, include the insured's complete name, his date of birth, and his service number.

HEALTH INSURANCE

Group Health Insurance

Group Policies

The best type of health insurance for the individual is that offered in a group plan—usually provided by an employer, a labor union, or a professional or business organization. Group policies are also frequently offered to students and alumni (and their families) by colleges and universities. Group plans are more economical than individual policies (with savings as high as 30 to 50 percent), and the benefits are usually superior. They typically cover hospital and surgical costs, physicians' expenses, and major medical fees. Group policies are sometimes advantageous when filing a claim: the collective strength of the group may stimulate the insurer to deal with the claim promptly and fairly.

Conversion

If you are a member of a group plan, check its provisions to make certain that you can convert your protection to an individual policy if you should leave the group because of retirement or change of job. Ideally, this should be possible without a delay or a lapse in coverage.

Major-Medical Insurance

Catastrophic Protection

The main concern of a subscriber to any kind of health insurance plan should be protection of himself and his family (if he has one) against catastrophic medical bills. Coverage of smaller, more manageable health costs should not be weighted as heavily. To protect against lengthy and serious illnesses, put most of your health insurance dollar into a strong major-medical plan. It will protect against the huge expenses of a long illness, usually paying the majority of hospital and physicians' bills up to a designated maximum amount.

Comprehensive Policies

Some health insurance policies combine major-medical protection with basic coverage of lesser health expenses. These plans are called "comprehensive major-medical" policies, and are usually not as costly as buying two separate insurance policies. The best of these plans are written for groups, not for individual insurance buyers, but the conscientious consumer willing to shop around can find an adequate personal policy. However, it will be expensive. In mid-1977, a 35-year-old man with a wife and two children living in Los Angeles paid $1,579 annually for Prudential's comprehensive medical/hospital policy.

The Provisions of a Health Care Policy

Maximum Benefits

Most health policies have a maximum coverage limit—from $10,000 to $300,000. Although a policy that pays maximum benefits of $25,000 is to be preferred over one that pays $15,000, that should not be the overriding factor in determining which policy is better. For example, the $25,000 policy may not cover dependents as completely as the other one does. Also, it may cover only 80 percent of one's medical costs, while the other policy may pay 85 percent. There are many ingredients that make up a policy, and although the maximum is a very important consideration, it is not the only one.

Dependent Coverage

A health insurance policy should protect the dependents of the insured as well as it protects the insured. It should cover a newborn from birth, and allow children to take out policies of their own when they have passed the age under which they are covered by the policy (Some policies don't permit this). Further, if the insured should die, or reach age 65 before his or her spouse does (and thus becomes eligible for Medicare), the spouse should be able to have the policy transferred to his or her name.

Service vs. Cash Indemnity

Whenever possible, buy health insurance that pays benefits in "services" rather than "cash indemnity." Under the "service" plan, the insurer will pay the hospital or doctor directly, often in full, for the care covered in the policy. The less desirable "cash indemnity" plan pays the insured a fixed amount of money, say $85, for each day spent in the hospital. With this money, he must pay all medical bills. If the hospital room costs $115 a day, he'll have to pay the difference between the bill and the cash indemnity out of his own pocket.

Deductible

Most health insurance policies include a deductible, which is a set amount of money that must be paid by the insured before the insurer will begin paying benefits. The amount of the deductible varies ($50, $100, $200, $500, etc.), as does the way it is paid. For instance, if the deductible is applied for "each benefit period" (that is, each year), the insured will have to pay the deductible (of, say $100) once every year. But if the deductible is applied "per illness," then the insured will have to pay an additional $100 each time a claim for a new illness is made, whenever it is made, which could eventually amount to several hundred dollars a year. Also, a single deductible should be applicable to the entire family (rather than a separate deductible for each family member). By increasing the deductible, insurance rates can significantly be reduced. For a major medical policy, raising the deductible from $500 to $1,000 can save a 35-year-old adult about 36 percent on his premium. An additional hike to a $1,500 deductible will save 19 percent over the $1,000 deductible.

Selecting Care

Find out the restrictions of the policy as to choosing a doctor or hospital. Some Blue Cross policies entitle the insured only to partial benefits when receiving care in a hospital not affiliated with Blue Cross.

Private Hospital Rooms

Rarely do even the best health insurance policies pay for more than a semiprivate room. If an individual is hospitalized and wants a private hospital room, he'll probably have to pay for it out of his own pocket.

Cancelability and Renewability

Make certain that any health insurance policy you buy is noncancelable. A noncancelable provision makes it unlawful for the company to cancel the policy unless the premiums are not paid. A cancelable policy, for which the premiums are cheaper, is risky: the company has a right to drop you as a customer as soon as you start costing them money.

In addition to being noncancelable, a health insurance policy should be guaranteed renewable. If it isn't, the company can refuse to renew the policy upon its expiration.

Companies, Policies, and Claims

Choosing a Health Insurer

As with a life insurer, make certain that any health insurance company with which you deal is licensed by the state. If you buy a policy from a company without a license, you have little recourse if that insurer fails to honor a claim. To determine if a particular company is licensed, contact the state insurance department.

Checking Complaints

Both the state insurance department and the Better Business Bureau can tell you if its files contain consumer complaints against a particular health insurance firm. If many complaints have been lodged, it is a good indication that the company may not be conducting its business in the fairest manner possible.

Completing Forms

When applying for health insurance, answer all questions honestly on the medical history portion of the application. Failure to state any ailments—past or present—leaves open the possibility of future charges by the insurance company that information has been falsified. This information can be used as a basis for denying benefits.

Reading the Policy

Examine a health insurance policy completely before buying it. If the agent refuses to give you a copy of the contract to read, find an agent who will. After buying a policy, carefully read it again when it arrives. Certain conditions are sometimes added because of the information included in your application. For instance, if you notified the insurance company that you have a long history of back ailments, the policy may limit the amount of coverage of future back problems.

Ten-Day Examination

In many states, 10 days are allotted for examination of a policy after it has been purchased. If you are displeased with the contract for any reason, it can be returned within this period, and any premiums that have already been paid will be returned.

Avoiding Duplication

If you carry more than one health insurance policy, try to avoid overlapping coverage. Many policies stipulate that the benefits to which the insured is entitled at the time of a claim can be reduced by the amount to be received from other policies. So when shopping for policies, look for those that complement rather than conflict.

Paying Health Premiums

If you're financially able, pay insurance premiums on an annual basis. When given the choice of paying premiums in monthly or quarterly installments, be aware that partial payment systems carry a surcharge of up to 18 percent a year.

Claims

Be sure to file all health insurance claims within the period specified by your policy. Some policies, for example, state that claims must be submitted within 30 days after treatment begins. Filing a claim after the designated time period grants the insurer the right to refuse to honor it.

Battling a Denial

If an insurance company denies a claim, read the policy carefully to see if its decision is justified. If you remain convinced that the claim is valid, contact a lawyer, particularly if the benefits to be gained are sizable. Even if the small print of the policy supports the decision of the insurer, you may be able to obtain at least partial benefits by suing under "the doctrine of reasonable expectations,"which provides that the small print may not void benefits which clearly seem to be promised in the large print.

Payment Delays

Although laws vary in different parts of the country, extra compensation is usually forthcoming if a health insurance company delays in paying benefits to which you are legally entitled. In Louisiana, for instance, if the insurer makes payment more than 30 days after a valid claim has been filed, the insured is entitled to a penalty fee equal to the total benefits due. In Georgia, a penalty fee of 25 percent is levied if the insurance company delays payment more than 60 days after the proper forms are submitted.

Mail-Order Health Coverage

Supplemental Protection

Mail-order health insurance should be thought of primarily

as supplemental coverage that enhances the protection of a primary health policy. Despite the unclear advertising statements of many mail-order insurers, they will admit upon questioning that the policies they offer are rarely complete enough to serve as sole health protection.

Unrealistic Promises

Dont be swayed by the alluring promises of of "$50,000 in benefits" made by mail-order firms. Look instead for the daily benefits. If the insurer pays a maximum of only $20 for each day of hospitalization, an individual would have to be hospitalized for more than seven years to collect $50,000.

Premium Hikes

Check policy stipulations about premium hikes. Most mail-order policies state that rates cannot be increased unless all policy holders in the same "class" are also given rate hikes. Find out how the insurer defines "class." Does "class" mean all the policy holders in the same age group? Or all those living in the same state? It's good to know where one stands, so disputes won't arise later.

"Dread Disease" Protection

Don't waste money on supplemental "dread disease" insurance policies that only cover such specific ailments as cancer or heart disease. Instead, use this money to strengthen your general health insurance, which should cover all ailments, including those which the special policies are designed to cover.

DISABILITY INSURANCE

Who Should Have It?

Those under 30 will more likely need disability insurance than life insurance. A young man or woman is statistically much more likely to become disabled than to die. Even at age 60, one is more than twice as likely to become disabled than to die. Disability insurance is therefore highly recommended for all those of working age.

Men vs. Women

Disability policies cost about one-third more for women than for men. These rates are based upon past statistics indicating that women claim disability more often. However, this variance in premium rate is gradually being reduced as insurance companies feel heightened pressure to eliminate sex discrimination.

Disability Policy Provisions

Noncancelable and Renewable

As with health insurance, a disability insurance policy should be noncancelable and guaranteed renewable. This assures that the insured will be able to renew the disability policy to at least age 65 without any increase in premium or reduction in benefits.

Definition of Terms

Most individual disability policies only pay benefits to those who become "totally disabled." But the definition of "totally disabled" varies among policies. Choose a policy defining it as being unable "to perform duties of his own occupation" rather than being unable "to perform duties pertaining to any gainful occupation." The former definition is more advantageous to the policyholder.

Bed-Confined

Don't buy a disability policy that stipulates that benefits will only be paid if the insured is confined to a bed. Someone well enough to leave his bed and even take short walks may still be unable to hold a job.

Elimination Period

Most disability policies have a so-called "elimination period," which is a specified number of days of disability before coverage begins. This waiting period is usually 7, 14, 30, 60, or 90 days. The longer the "elimination period," the lower the premiums. If you have a savings account that will sustain you for the initial part of your disability, buy a policy with a long waiting period. There are policies available with an elimination period of as long as a year or more, with correspondingly low premiums.

Coping with Inflation

A disability policy should be updated periodically; inflation will probably make an increase in coverage necessary from time to time. The $400-a-month disability coverage that you bought five years ago may be inadequate protection now.

One way of combating inflation is to ask the insurer if it's possible to attach a "future increase" rider to the disability policy. Often, for an addition to the premium of less than one percent, the rider grants the policy holder the right to increase benefits every few years by several hundred dollars, without having to take a new physical examination or fill out a new medical history form.

Other Disability Coverage Sources

Government Programs

In addition to one's own disability insurance policy, one may receive disability benefits from three other sources. The federal government operates a Workmen's Compensation program, which provides benefits when disabilities are caused by work-related accidents. Four states—New York, California, New Jersey, Massachusetts—sponsor their own state disability programs, covering disabilities that are not job-connected. Social Security also provides disability benefits—equal to the individual's retirement benefits—if he becomes totally disabled.

AUTOMOBILE INSURANCE

Types of Coverage

Liability Coverage

Liability protection is probably the most important part of an individual's automobile insurance. It offers protection for bodily injury and property damage to another party resulting from an accident for which the policyholder is legally responsible. Policies usually express this coverage in a series of three numbers, such as 25/50/10. These figures denote $25,000 worth of protection for another person's bodily injury, $50,000 coverage for bodily injuries of all persons in one accident, and $10,000 for property damage. Most insurance experts recommend that an individual of moderate income carry liability coverage of at least 100/300/10.

No-Fault Insurance

Even those who live in states where no-fault insurance laws have gone into effect cannot put all liability insurance worries behind them. Under no-fault the injured party in an accident receives compensation for his injuries directly from his own insurance company regardless of who was at fault for the accident. Most damage suits are prohibited in no-fault states, but lawsuits may still sometimes be instituted when injuries are very serious and expensive. Adequate personal injury liability protection is therefore essential.

Medical Coverage

Whereas liability coverage protects individuals in cars other than that of the driver who is at fault, the "medical coverage" section of an individual's automobile insurance pays the medical bills for injuries suffered by the at-fault driver and his passengers.

Medical coverage of this kind is not necessary if a driver and the passengers who ride in his car already have adequate health insurance.

Uninsured Motorist Coverage

All drivers should carry "uninsured motorist" coverage, which insures for bodily injury cost resulting from an accident caused by a driver without proper insurance. It also pays for expenses incurred when the driver's car is struck by a hit-and-run driver. Uninsured motorist coverage further insures the driver and his family when, as pedestrians, they are struck by an uninsured or hit-and-run motorist. This coverage is relatively inexpensive.

Collision Insurance

Collision insurance covers damage to one's car resulting from an accident with another vehicle or a stationary object. This insurance is usually sold with a deductible of $50 or $100, but higher deductibles are available. So if your deductible is $100, and the damage to your car is $400, you can expect to pay for the first $100 of repairs; the insurance company will pay the remaining $300. The higher the deductible, the cheaper the insurance will be; so buy collision protection with as high a deductible as you can afford. You can save 40 percent a year on collision premiums by increasing your deductible from $100 to $250; a $500 deductible will save you 55 percent.

Large Deductibles

If your collision insurance carries a deductible larger than $100, and you are involved in an automobile accident and have the damage to your own car repaired, you can take advantage of certain tax breaks when filing your income tax return the following April. The Internal Revenue Service allows the deduction of all nonreimbursed casualty losses over $100. So if your collision deductible is $250, and an accident causes damage to your car in excesss of $250, you can deduct $150 from your taxes ($250-$100=$150).

The Value of Collision Insurance

When an automobile is severely damaged or destroyed, collision insurance will only pay an amount of money equal to the current market value of the car. It's therefore not wise to buy collision insurance for cars over five years old; the insurance premiums paid out may end up being equal to any money that might be collected in the event of an accident.

Comprehensive Insurance

Comprehensive insurance is protection for a car against damages caused by fire, theft, vandalism, wind, and water. If a car is stolen, comprehensive insurance will pay for its replacement, and provide for the rental of another until it is replaced. As with collision insurance, comprehensive coverage includes a deductible. Purchase this protection with a large deductible, and consider dropping it completely when the car becomes more than five years old.

Auto Insurers

The Best Insurers

When filing a claim with an automobile insurance company, it is natural to want it handled as quickly and fairly as possible. Unfortunately, though, some insurers provide horrendous service. The only major study comparing the service offered by auto insurers was conducted and published by *Consumer Reports* in 1970. The magazine gave its highest rating to four insurance companies: State Farm Mutual Automobile Insurance Company, United Services Automobile Association, Interinsurance Exchange of the Automobile Club of Southern California, and California State Automobile Association Inter-Insurance Bureau. The insurers at the bottom of the list were the Home Insurance Company and the Allstate Insurance Company.

Car Insurance Rates

Company Differences

When Thomas D. O'Malley, Florida Insurance Commissioner, compared auto insurance rates for identical coverage in 1975, they varied considerably. O'Malley checked liability prices for a Miami adult who drives over 7500 miles a year for pleasure rather than business, has a five-year clean driving record, and buys 10/20/10 coverage. Among the rates that were charged:
  —Safeco, $112.
  —GEICO (Government Employees Insurance Company), $139.
  —Aetna Casualty and Surety Company, $147.
  —State Farm Mutual, $156.
  —Liberty Mutual Fire, $175.
  —Hartford Accident and Indemnity Company, $197.
  —Allstate Insurance Company, $224.

Factors Affecting Rates

The way a car is used will almost certainly affect insurance rates. Those who own cars that are driven long distances to and from work each day, or are used for business purposes throughout the day, will be charged higher rates because of the increased chances of accidents. By contrast, those whose vehicles are used chiefly for farming or ranching pay lower premiums because of the lower accident rates.

Accordingly, should you change your method of commutting—that is, begin to travel to work by bus rather than car—notify your auto insurance agent immediately. Your premium rates will probably drop with this substantial reduction in the use of the car.

Discounts to Women

Statistically, men are involved in more accidents than women. Therefore, some insurance companies offer discounts to women drivers. Most common is a 10 percent premium savings for women between the ages of 30 and 64 who are the sole drivers in their households.

Insuring Several Cars

Owners of more than one car should insure all vehicles with the same company. By so doing, a multicar discount—usually about 20 percent—will be awarded.

Mileage Discounts

Some insurance companies offer rate discounts of from five to ten percent to those who drive their car less than 6,500 miles a year.

"Muscle" Cars

When shopping for a new car, keep in mind that the so-called "muscle" cars cost more to insure than the smaller models. Insurers define a muscle car as one with a weight-to-horsepower ratio of 10.5 to 1 or more. Insurance for a muscle car may increase premiums by as much as 50 percent.

"Undesirable" Cars

Some insurance companies charge higher premiums for car models with histories of high repair costs bescause of unsound design. When in the market for a new car, ask your insurance agent for an up-to-date list of the models with poor records. Take this information into consideration when making an automobile purchase.

"Good Student Discount"

If one or more children in a family are drivers, a discount of as much as 20 percent on each child's share of the premium is awarded by the insurer if he or she qualifies for a "good student discount." To be eligible, a child must meet any one of the three following criteria:

(1) He must have at least a B average, (2) he must be in the top 20 percent of his school class, or (3) he must be on the dean's list at his college. Most schools will usually release a copy of the transcript of the youngster's grades, or write an appropriate letter than can be deposited with the insurance company.

Drivers' Training

Encourage teenage children to enroll in school drivers' training programs. Successful completion of such programs may reduce youngsters' premiums by 10 percent. To be eligible, though, the program must meet standards established by the National Conference on Driver Education of the National Education Association.

Distant Schooling Discounts

Youthful drivers who attend school at least 100 miles from home are usually entitled to lower rates than those who live at home. Insurance companies assume that a student living on campus drives less than normal.

Other Auto Insurance Tips

Assigned-Risk Pool

A poor driving record may make it virtually impossible for an individual to obtain automobile insurance through normal channels. In such instances, consider joining the assigned risk pool established in all states. Under the provisions that govern this pool, all insurance companies must accept a certain number of high-risk drivers. The rates for these motorists are much higher than normal, and insurers are only required to provide a minimum amount of liability coverage. Rarely will they offer collision coverage, comprehensive coverage, medical coverage, or uninsured motorist protection.

Reporting Accidents

If you are involved in an accident, be sure to report it immediately. Some insurance companies raise premiums if an accident in which the insured was a hit-and-run victim is not reported within 24 hours.

HOMEOWNERS INSURANCE

Types of Coverage

The Broad Form

Several types of homeowners insurance are available, but probably the best policy is the "Broad Form," or "Homeowners 2," which provides protection against about 99 percent of the possible mishaps to which a home may be subject. The policy covers damage caused by fire or lightning, smoke, theft, vandalism, windstorm or hail, riots, explosions, falling objects, automobiles and aircraft, the collapse of a building, breakage of glass, and failures in plumbing or electrical systems. (People who rent an apartment or a home can also insure their possessions against these misfortunes.)

Insuring Possessions

The contents of a home are normally insured for up to 50 percent of the value for which the home is covered. (If your home is insured for $50,000, its contents are covered for half of that, or $25,000.) When an insurer reimburses the homeowner for loss of personal possessions, the funds received are usually equivalent to the depreciated value of those possessions, not the amount it will cost to replace them. However, a few companies (Safeco, INA, and Kemper) sell policies covering the replacement value, but they are relatively expensive (an additional $30 a year on a $50,000 policy is typical).

Limitations

Certain types of losses have limited coverage under most homeowners policies. For instance, an insurer will normally pay no more than $500 for all the furs or jewelry stolen or destroyed; the limit on stamps or firearms is usually $500; coins are rarely covered for more than $100. To be fully insured for these items, a special endorsement—for which the insured pays extra—must be added to the regular policy.

Away-from-Home Protection

Many people are unaware that homeowners policies provide protection of personal possessions away from home, too. Most policies cover these belongings up to a value of 10 percent of the coverage of the household furnishings. So if a house is insured for $50,000 and the household possessions are covered for $25,000, the away-from-home protection equals 10 percent of $25,000—or $2,500.

Liability Coverage

Almost all homeowners policies contain personal liability protection, which provides coverage if an individual is injured in an accident on the policyholder's property. This insurance also covers accidents (except automobile accidents) that occur away from the insured's own property and that are caused by him or a member of his family. Thus, if you hit a golf ball on a public course and it strikes another person, you are protected for any injury suffered by the individual. Although most homeowners coverage automatically provides liability insurance of up to $25,000 per accident, take advantage of the opportunity to increase this protection. Coverage can be increased to $100,000 for only about $4 per year.

How Much Homeowners Insurance

Calculating the Coverage

To be safe, a house must be insured for 80 to 85 percent of its estimated cost of replacement, excluding land. If a home is insured for at least that 80 percent figure, any damage that it suffers will be covered for its full repair or replacement cost. But if the house is insured for less than 80 percent, the policyholder will receive less than the full replacement cost of any damage over $1,000. Because inflation is raising the value of homes so rapidly, reevaluate your homeowners coverage every year or two to ensure that your house is still insured for 80 to 85 percent of the current replacement cost.

Tax Valuation

When deciding how much a house is worth for insurance purposes, don't use the current tax valuation as the sole indicator. Tax valuation is frequently set at less than the actual value of the house—sometimes as much as 50 percent less. So if you rely on this figure, the consequences could be calamitous.

An Agent's Advice

If you're in doubt as to the precise amount for which to insure your home, ask an insurance agent for advice. The various insurance journals at his disposal provide charts and statistics which make calculations simple.

Inflation Guard Endorsement

To help ensure that your home is always adequately protected, ask the agent to add an "inflation guard" endorsement to the policy. This provision automatically increases coverage by one percent per quarter, or four percent per year. If the current inflation in the housing market is higher than four percent per year—which it has been during much of the 1960s and 1970s—request that the agent periodically increase your protection even more.

Reducing Homeowners Rates

Long-Term Policies

Reduce the cost of your homeowners insurance by purchasing a policy that runs for three or five years before renewal is necessary. If at all possible, cut the premiums even further by paying the entire annual premium at once, thus avoiding the finance charges that accompany monthly or quarterly payment.

Special Discounts

Ask your insurance agent about any other homeowner discounts for which you may qualify. Some insurance companies now offer premium discounts of up to 10 percent if certain types of alarm systems or fire-detection devices have been installed in the home. Discounts are also frequently available for nonsmokers and for senior citizens.

Special Types of Property Insurance

Flood Insurance

Homeowners insurance policies have always specifically excluded protection against floods (although coverage for damage caused by rain, wind, and lightning is included). But special insurance against flood damage is now available in some parts of the country. Those who live in areas prone to such disasters can buy this protection from any of 100 commercial insurance companies. This insurance, subsidized by the federal government, costs less now than when it was first introduced in 1968. In 1977, $35,000 worth of coverage cost 25 cents for every $100 of value.

Earthquake Insurance

In earthquake-prone states like California, most commercial insurance companies offer earthquake insurance. It is attached to a normal homeowners policy as a rider, at a cost of about 15 to 25 cents per $100 of valuation in California, and as little as 4 cents per $100 in New York.

Federal Crime Insurance

Those who live in high-crime areas, and are unable to buy

theft insurance because of the high-risk neighborhood, may qualify for Federal Crime Insurance. This protection now available in 14 states and the District of Columbia, can be purchased through regular insurance agents. A maximum of $10,000 of burglary and theft insurance per home is available at an annual premium averaging $60 to $80. To be eligible for this protection, all doors to the house must be secured with penetration-type, pickproof locks. Although the policy can be bought without an inspection, the locks will be checked when a claim is made. (The states in which this insurance is available are Connecticut, Delaware, Florida, Illinois, Kansas, Maryland, Massachusetts, Missouri, New Jersey, New York, Ohio, Pennsylvania, Rhode Island, and Tennessee.)

The FAIR Plan

In 26 states and the District of Columbia, another type of government-sponsored, high-risk insurance pool is available— the FAIR plan (Fair Access in Insurance Requirements). It insures a home (for up to $35,000) and its contents (up to $10,000) against fire, vandalism, explosions, storms, and damage caused by aircraft, vehicles, and riots, for an average premium of under $150 a year (with a $50 deductible). This protection can be purchased through regular commercial insurance agents in the following states: California, Connecticut, Delaware, Georgia, Illinois, Indiana, Iowa, Kansas, Kentucky, Louisiana, Maryland, Massachusetts, Michigan, Minnesota, Missouri, New Jersey, New Mexico, New York, North Carolina, Ohio, Oregon, Pennsylvania, Rhode Island, Virginia, Washington, and Wisconsin.

Preparing a Household Inventory

Room-by-Room Analysis

Prepare a room-by-room inventory of all your possessions, including a description of each item and its original cost. In addition, photograph each room, and keep these pictures and the household inventory in a safe place away from your home. If you ever have to file a claim, the information and the photos will serve as evidence that these items were indeed yours.

Filing Homeowners Claims

Help from an Agent

After a fire or theft, contact your insurance agent and request his assistance in filing a claim. This is part of his job, and he should be willing to provide the necessary help. If you've suffered a major disaster, he may be able to get an advance in funds until the claim can be processed.

Public Adjustors

If your home is seriously damaged, and the insurance company offers a settlement that seems unfair, consider hiring a public adjustor. This is particularly true for claims exceeding $5,000. The public adjustor is an expert at analyzing losses, and he will evaluate the damage and present the facts to the insurance company—for a charge of from 10 to 15 percent of the amount recovered from the insurer. Public adjustors are listed in the Yellow Pages, usually under the heading "Adjustors."

Dishonest Adjustors

When a home is struck by fire, a dishonest public adjustor may arrive at the scene. This individual typically does not work for an insurance company, although the homeowner—already shaken by the tragedy that has befallen him—may be deceived into thinking he does. This adjustor will ask the homeowner to sign a document authorizing him to act on the owner's behalf. In fact, though, the document awards the adjustor 10 to 15 percent of the money that the insurance company will eventually pay. Before affixing your signature to anything, ascertain the identity of the man presenting the document, and read the contents of the document carefully.

Amending a Claim

If after filing a claim on a homeowners policy, you then discover an oversight, contact your agent immediately. Let's say, for instance, that a week after submitting a claim for a burglary, you realize that additional valuables were taken. Contact your agent at once. If he and his company are reputable, they will process an addendum to your claim immediately. Incidentally, even if you've already received a settlement check from the insurance company, notify your agent anyway.

VACATION INSURANCE

Is It Necessary

Many types of vacation-protection insurance are on the market. But before purchasing any, check your other policies—you may already have as much coverage as you need. Life, health and accident insurance, for example, will cover you no matter where you are—at home or halfway around the world. If you have adequate hospitalization protection, there's no need to buy one of the special "travel accident policies" on the market. If your basic life insurance needs are covered, flight insurance will be unnecessary.

INSURANCE COMPLAINTS

Who Can Help

All insurance-related complaints should be filed with the state insurance commissioner. He has the power to investigate the problem and intervene on your behalf. Complaints about mail-order insurance should also be referred to the Bureau of Consumer Protection, Federal Trade Commission, Pennsylvania Avenue at 6th Street, N.W., Washington, D.C. 20580.

CHAPTER 11

Taxes

Few things in life are more distasteful than paying taxes. Yet every year, the experience becomes worse as taxes continue to rise. In 1950, the average American relinquished 12.4 percent of his income to tax collectors—federal, state, and local. By 1976, taxes were taking 20.9 percent of his income.

Each year, 83 million individual income tax returns are submitted to the Internal Revenue Service. Tax forms have become so complex that many Americans do not feel capable of preparing their own returns. Some pay several hundred dollars a year to have their forms prepared; others pay as little as $5 or $10. Tax preparation, in fact, has become a $700 million industry in the United States.

Even those individuals who prepare their own returns seek some help along the way. During the 1977 filing season, the IRS offices fielded over 18 million telephone inquiries.

The increasing complexity of income tax filing is due to the hundreds of new tax rulings that become law each year. Because tax laws change so often, preparing one's own return may lead to mistakes that will land one in front of an IRS auditor.

Essentially, an *audit* is an official examination of a tax return. The IRS audits about two million returns each year. In fiscal 1976, the IRS audited one out of every 41 taxpayers with adjusted gross incomes between $10,000 and $50,000. More than three-fourths of these audited returns were singled out by computers as containing questionable or erroneous information. Other returns are selected for audit at random.

Of all the returns audited in 1975, the IRS eventually recommended that additional taxes be paid in 71 percent of the cases. No change was suggested in 24 percent, and refunds were prescribed in the remaining five percent.

When preparing taxes, it is important to know about exemptions (an *exemption* is an amount allowed as a reduction in your gross income for a dependent, for age, or for blindness) and about deductions (a *deduction* is an allowable decrease in one's taxable income for certain expenses or losses) that one is entitled to take.

Property tax bills are often just as dismaying as income taxes. Unless one lives in a cave hidden from the rest of civilization, one is probably paying property taxes—either directly or through rent payments. When Americans were recently polled by the Advisory Commission on Intergovernmental Relations as to which tax they think is the least fair, more selected the property tax than any other.

In the United States, we pay $50 billion a year in property taxes, which are usually collected by the county or the town or city. The factors which determine how much we pay are the *assessment* of the property, and the *tax rate*. The assessment is the value of the real estate for tax purposes, as determined by the local assessor. The tax rate is set by the local government, and often can't exceed a state-imposed limitation.

Property tax appeal procedures are available to everyone, but they are used primarily by real estate investors. When a study in Boston examined 50,000 appeals over a 10-year period, individual homeowners filed only 10 percent of them, with the remainder being filed by owners of apartment houses and industrial and commercial property.

There *are* ways for taxpayers to save money on what they owe the government. But unless they are informed, and take advantage of all the various information and procedures available to them, they may end up paying more than their fair share.

INCOME TAX PREPARATION

Preparing a Return

The majority of Americans should be able to prepare their own income tax returns without professional help. The IRS contends that individuals earning less than $20,000 a year—with all this income being from salary, wages, tips, dividends, interest, or pensions—can probably make out their own returns. IRS Publication 17, *Your Federal Income Tax,* which is revised and published annually, is a very complete guide to income tax preparation, and can be obtained free by calling any local IRS office. The IRS also publishes several smaller booklets that focus on specific tax areas—like *Tax Information on Selling Your Home* (Publication 523), *Tax Information on Disasters, Casualty Losses and Thefts* (Publication 547), and *Tax Benefits for Older Americans* (Publication 554).

Answers to Questions

The Internal Revenue Service has its own Taxpayer Service Division, which answers questions about tax problems over its toll-free telephone lines. Inquiries are also answered in person at any of the 1,000 IRS offices in all parts of the United States. Depending on the time they have available, IRS employees will aid individuals in filling out tax forms. However, the information provided by IRS tax assisters cannot always be counted on to be accurate. Various studies indicate that information given by IRS assisters is wrong 20 to 25 percent of the time. Still, a government study recently showed that IRS employees make fewer mistakes than accountants and other professional tax consultants!

Deaf Taxpayers

For deaf taxpayers who own teletypewriters or TVphones, the IRS has a toll-free telephone service available to answer tax questions. The deaf can call 800-482-4732 (in Indiana 800-382-4059), any weekday from 8:30 a.m. to 6:45 p.m. EST. Teletypewriters, which type messages over the phone, sell used for from $190. TVphones, which produce messages on a TV screen, rent for about $20 a month.

Professional Assistance

If you decide to hire a professional tax consultant, inquire as to whether he is a Certified Public Accountant. If not, ask him the following questions to ascertain his qualifications for handling your taxes: Does he have at least two years of college credit, and has he successfully completed a formal tax training course? Is he in business year-round, or only during the tax season? Has he had at least two years of experience in preparing returns? Only deal with those individuals who have the most impressive credentials.

Avoiding Rip-offs

As with any other consumer-oriented service, the income tax preparation industry has its own share of frauds. To avoid being "ripped off" during tax time, heed the following advice: (1) Be wary of a tax preparer who, even before studying your particular case, guarantees you a refund. (2) Avoid preparers who insist that your refund be sent to his office. (3) Never sign a blank tax return, or a tax return prepared in pencil (which can later be changed).

CALCULATING YOUR INCOME

Sources of Income

In addition to salary, bonuses, commissions, and tips, several other sources of income must be reported on tax returns. These include: dividends exceeding $100; interest on bank deposits, bonds, notes, and tax refunds; pensions, annuities and endowments; profits from the sale of securities or real estate; rents; and alimony.

Rent Payments

If an employer pays all or part of an individual's rent, this contribution must be listed as taxable income. This often occurs when an employee is transferred to a city where rents are considerably higher, and his boss pays a portion of his rent to make the move worthwhile.

Exemptions from Income

Many types of income are *not* subject to federal income tax, and thus should not be counted as income on tax returns. They include: court-ordered child-support payments (but not alimony), a divorce settlement paid in one lump sum, inheritances, gifts, life insurance benefits, union strike-fund payments, Social Security benefits, living expenses paid by an insurance company while a home is being repaired, interest on municipal bonds, dividends not exceeding $100, and scholarships and fellowships.

SHOULD YOU ITEMIZE

Itemizing Guidelines

Each year, several million taxpayers cheat themselves out of money by claiming the standard deduction (16 percent of their adjusted gross income) instead of itemizing all deductions. An individual will probably benefit from itemizing if any of the following is applicable:

—He is a homeowner who pays interest and taxes.
—He pays alimony.
—He has suffered serious, uninsured casualty losses.
—He has large, uninsured medical and dental expenses.
—He has contributed sizable amounts of money to charity.

Itemizing Calculations

To decide definitively whether to itemize or not, take the adjusted gross income (AGI) on line 15C of the 1040 form (or line 12 of the 1040A form). Also, in separate calculations, add up all deductible items. Then use the following guidelines—

When married and filing jointly, or when you're a surviving spouse with a dependent child, itemize if:

—The AGI is under $13,125, and the total deductions exceed $2,100,

—The AGI is between $13,125 and $17,500, and the deductions exceed 16 percent of the AGI, or

—The AGI is over $17,500, and the deductions exceed $2,800.

When married and filing a separate return, itemizing should be done when:

—The AGI is under $6,562.50, and the total deductions exceed $1,050,

—The AGI is between $6,562.50 and $8,750 and the deductions exceed 16 percent of the AGI, or

—The AGI is over $8,750, and the deductions exceed $1,400.

When single, or an unmarried head of household, file an itemized return when:

—The AGI is under $10,625, and the total deductions exceed $1,700,

—The AGI is between $10,625 and $15,000, and the deductions exceed 16 percent of the AGI,

—The AGI is over $15,000, and the deductions are over $2,400.

Standard Deduction Savings

When taking the standard income tax deduction without itemizing, taxable income can be reduced if the individual qualifies for any of the various "credits" or "adjustments" on the tax books. Included are (1) contributions to the campaigns of political candidates, (2) contributions to an Individual Retirement Account or a Keogh plan, (3) alimony payments, and (4) moving expenses under certain circumstances. Many unreimbursed business expenses, such as the cost of travel and meals, may be deducted, too.

JOINT OR SEPARATE RETURNS?

Joint Return Advantages

A married couple usually saves money by filing a joint return rather than separate returns. Essentially, a joint return splits the family income down the middle, and husband and wife are each assigned half. So if the husband is the sole breadwinner in the family, and his income is $15,000, a joint return will result in a tax equal to that paid by two taxpayers, each with a $7,500 income. Because the $7,500 figure falls into a lower tax bracket, the couple will pay less taxes. If both husband and wife work, it is probably still advantageous to file a joint return, particularly if one spouse has earnings considerably higher than the other.

Separate Return Advantages

Separate returns would make sense for a married couple in cases where both husband and wife have income, and one incurs a large deductible expense during the year, such as medical bills. Let's say that the husband earns $12,000 a year, and his wife earns $8,000. She is hospitalized, and accumulates bills totaling $2,000.

By filing separate returns, the couple pays less taxes overall because their medical expenses are not based upon the $20,000 joint income, but upon the wife's lower, $8,000 income.

Itemizing

When husband and wife file separate returns, and one decides to itemize deductions, the other must itemize as well. The IRS prohibits one from itemizing while the other claims the standard deduction.

Divorcing and Remarrying

In recent years, some couples discovered that they could save on taxes by getting divorced in late December, thus capitalizing on the higher standard deduction for single people. On January 1, they would remarry, and then go through the same procedure again the following year. But in 1976, the IRS announced that it no longer would allow these "sham transactions" to save couples taxes. So although the scheme may have worked in the past, it won't in the future—if the IRS discovers what is taking place.

AN EXTRA INCOME

The Tax Bite

Have you ever wondered how much a second income in the family will amount to—after taxes? Well, let's assume that the husband earns $20,000 a year, and when his wife becomes employed, they file joint tax returns. If the wife gets a job that pays $7,500 annually, she will really only add $5,005 to the family budget after federal taxes are paid on a joint return. If she gets a $10,000 job, federal taxes will drain off enough so that she's really only adding $6,515 to the family's spendable income. Out of a $15,000-a-year job, the amount of her salary remaining after taxes will be $9,417.

DEPENDENTS

General Guidelines

Claim all of your exemptions. The IRS places no limit on the amount of dependents claimed. However, each must (1) be a close relative (such as a child or a parent), or make the taxpayer's home his principal residence for the entire year, (2) receive more than one-half of his support from the taxpayer; and (3) earn less than $750 during the year (unless he is under 19 or a full-time student, in which case his income is immaterial).

Claiming Parents

In order to claim a retired parent as a dependent, not only must the taxpayer pay half of his support for the year, but the parent cannot receive over $750 in gross income from other sources during that period. This $750 figure does not include Social Security payments, proceeds from life insurance, gifts, inheritances, or welfare payments.

Technicalities

When a taxpayer technically doesn't contribute over 50 percent of the combined support expense of both parents, he still might be able to claim one as an exemption. Let's assume, for instance, that he gives his parents $1,500 a year, and together they need $5,000 on which to live—or $2,500 each. If he gives the money to both of them, he's not entitled to an exemption because his $1,500 is less than half of their combined support money. However, if he technically designates his $1,500 for, say, only his mother, that figure is more than half of her $2,500 living expenses, and he can claim her as an exemption. If the IRS ever questions him on the matter, he should be prepared with canceled checks to prove to whom the money was directed.

Sharing Deductions

If the taxpayer is one of several offspring who contribute to a parent's support, he need not contribute over half of the total support to take his exemption. Let's say that he and his three brothers each furnish 25 percent of the support of his father. Every year, one—and only—can claim him as an exemption. To keep things fair, they may alternate so that each sibling takes advantage of the exemption once every four years. Or, if they so decide, the same brother can claim the exemption every year.

MAINTAINING RECORDS

Importance of Records

Keeping accurate records is vital to any meaningful tax planning. It is foolish to try to commit important data to memory. So maintain a written record of all income, plus any expenses which will be deductible from taxes. This record will not only be valuable when tax forms are being prepared; it will also be essential if the IRS ever audits the return.

The Method

A simple way to organize records is to keep bills, receipts, and canceled checks in folders or envelopes, categorized by tax subject (that is, one folder for medical bills, one folder for charitable contributions, etc.). In a separate ledger, keep track of day-by-day tax-deductible expenses, including major purchases (cars, jewelry) on which sizable (and deductible) sales tax has been paid.

Saving Documents

The IRS recommends that income tax records be kept for at least three full years after the April 15 filing date. Thus, all documents relating to a tax return filed on April 15, 1978 should be kept at least until April 15, 1981. If the IRS intends to audit that return, it will normally be done within 26 months of its filing. However, if a taxpayer has failed to report more than one-fourth of his income, the statute of limitations may be lengthened to six years. If the IRS ever suspects that a fraudulent tax return has been filed, no statute of limitations of that return is applicable. To be safe, keep tax records longer than the suggested three years.

Obtaining Old Returns

Copies of old tax returns that have been discarded either accidentally or intentionally can be obtained from the IRS. Fill out Form 4506 ("Request for Copy of Tax Return"), and send it to the address listed on the form. The IRS normally keeps originals for six years after the filing date.

LATE OR ERRONEOUS RETURNS

Obtaining an Extension

If an individual is unable to prepare his income tax return by April 15, a two-month extension is automatically awarded for the asking. Simply complete IRS Form 4868, and mail it in prior to April 15. On that form, an estimate must be made of what the tax will be. If the estimate is more than what has already been paid through withholding, the taxpayer must include a check for the balance. There is no late penalty for this procedure, although if one underestimates by over 10 percent, interest will be charged on the amount still due, plus a penalty fee of one-half of one percent a month until the difference is paid.

Correcting Errors

What should be done if, after filing a return, a taxpayer realizes that a mistake has been made? What can be done, for example, if he discovers that he has forgotten to claim a specific deduction, or if he has incorrectly calculated his income for the year? The best procedure is to file an amended tax return (Form

1040X). If the correcting of the mistake requires a refund, it will only be honored if filed within three years of the due date of the original return.

DEDUCTIONS

Average Deductions

The following table shows what the average taxpayer in various income brackets claims as itemized deductions. When an individual's deductions fall close to the average figure, it's not likely that he'll be questioned about them. If some of them are much higher than normal, all receipts and checks should be saved to prove the validity of the figures.

Adjusted Gross Income	Medical Expenses	Interest Paid	Contribu- tions	State & Local Taxes
$10,000-$15,000	$233	$ 931	$ 344	$1030
$15,000-$20,000	294	1097	424	1404
$20,000-$25,000	291	1208	544	1778
$25,000-$30,000	336	1360	691	2184
$30,000-$50,000	393	1686	1031	2983

Unusual Deductions

When a valid but unusual deduction is taken, prevent an audit on it by attaching to the tax return photocopies of the appropriate receipts or documents. Send copies only! Retain the originals for your own files.

Work-Related Expenses

Work Clothes

The cost of clothes, as well as the cost of cleaning or reparing them, can be deducted from income taxes if they are required on the job and cannot be used as everyday street clothes. Equipment or tools purchased for use on the job can also be deducted. This equipment must be depreciated over its useful life; if it lasts only one year, its full purchase price can be deducted on that year's taxes.

Travel Expenses

Commuting expenses are among the most difficult deductions to justify, so make sure firm basis exists on which to claim them. They must be directly attributable to the conduct of one's employment, and if the slightest doubt as to their validity exists, the IRS or the Tax Court is likely to rule against the taxpayer. For instance, an Idaho physician was called from his home to the emergency hospital 232 times during the year. Although he tried to deduct these transportation expenses, the court rejected it, saying that the costs would have never been incurred at all if the doctor had chosen to live nearer the hospital, rather than 20 miles away.

Transporting Tools

If tools must be brought to and from work, the cost of their transport can not always be deducted. Since 1976, the IRS has allowed deductions only of the amount that *exceeds* the cost of riding in the same mode of transportation without the tools. Thus, a bass player who must transport his instrument to a studio each day cannot deduct his commuting expenses, since his ride in a car, taxi, or bus will cost the same whether or not he carries the bass with him.

Home Offices

The IRS has become very selective about what it will allow as deductions for an office at home. In general, office space has to be the principal place of business to qualify for a deduction. It also has to be used *only* for business, and not also for, say, a family den.

Educational Classes

The cost of educational courses (including tuition, books, and supplies) can be deducted if the purpose in taking them is to keep abreast of developments in one's field. Also deductible is the cost of transportation to get to the school (even if it's in Paris). To support the deductions, accumulate as much evidence as possible that the courses were required by one's employer or were needed to maintain the skills required to perform the duties of one's present job.

Seeking Employment

Deduct the expenses incurred in looking for new employment in one's regular line of work—even if such employment could not be found. Until 1975, the taxpayer had to actually land the job to justify the deduction. Now, just seeking it is justification enough for the deduction.

Moving Expenses

In some cases, the cost of moving is tax-deductible. The move must have been necessary because of a new job location. As of 1977, the new job must be at least 35 miles farther away from one's former house than the old job was. Also, the taxpayer must remain a full-time employee at that new job for a minimum of 39 weeks of the 52 weeks immediately following the move. If one's employer grants a reimbursement for moving expenses, this must be reported as income; your moving expenses are then still deductible. Within limits, one can deduct the cost of househunting, temporary housing at the new location, and some costs related to the selling of the old home and the purchase of the new one. The limit on this deduction is $3,000, only $1,500 of which can be claimed for househunting trips and temporary living quarters.

Medical Deductions

Medical Travel

Among deductible medical expenses is the cost of travel to and from a doctor's office. So, too, is the cost of maintaining a dependent relative in a nursing home when the primary reason for his being there is to receive medical care.

Special Schooling

If a physically or mentally handicapped dependent is sent to a special school in order to eliminate or ease that handicap, the cost is deductible as a medical expense. This includes instruction in Braille or sign language. Also, if the cost of purchasing Braille editions of books surpasses the cost of the regular editions (which they usually do), the difference between the two prices may be deducted.

Home Improvements

Some home improvements are deductible as medical expenses. For example, if an illness requires that an air conditioner or elevator be installed in one's home, the expense incurred is deductible—but only after first subtracting any measurable increase in the value of the property as a result of this acquisition. Be prepared to prove to the IRS that such purchases are necessary for health reasons. The IRS recently refused to allow a dust-allergic individual to deduct the cost of a vacuum cleaner, claiming that the taxpayer couldn't prove the item was purchased primarily for its medical benefits.

Plastic Surgery

Costs of cosmetic surgery, even when not recommended by an individual's own physician, have been a legal medical deduction since 1976.

Casualty Losses

Catastrophic Damage

Uninsured theft and casualty losses, including those caused by fire, flood, earthquake, and hurricane, are deductible to the extent that they exceed $100. If, for example, an earthquake causes $700 damage to one's home and belongings, a $600 deduction is allowed. Remember, though, that proof of ownership of the damaged property is the burden of the taxpayer. So keep important receipts in a secure place outside the home, such as in a safe-deposit box.

Insured Losses

When some people suffer a casualty loss, particularly in an automobile accident, they decide to pay for repairs themselves rather than file an insurance claim and risk having their rates increased. However, in such cases, don't attempt to use out-of-pocket expenses as a tax deduction. A United States District Court recently ruled that if the loss is covered by insurance but a claim has not been filed, the deduction is not allowable. According to the court, IRS casualty loss provisions aren't "optional insurance coverage for those who choose to collect from Uncle Sam rather than their insurance companies."

The Year of Deductibility

Normally, casualty losses from fires, floods, storms, and earthquakes are deductible only in the year in which they occurred. However, if the loss occurs in a community that the President declares a disaster area, the loss can be claimed in either the year it actually occurred, or the previous one. So if a major flood in 1978 causes such severe damage that it will probably decrease your 1978 income, it would make sense to take the deduction on your 1977 return.

Deducting Taxes and Interest

Deductible Taxes

Several types of taxes are deductible on federal returns—including state and local income tax, property tax, general sales tax, and gasoline tax. Local utility tax is also deductible, as long as the rate is the same as the general sales tax in the same community. If the utility tax is computed at a different rate, it does not qualify as a general sales tax and is not deductible. Also, be aware that if a public utility charges a late-payment fee, it can be deducted as interest.

Interest Deductions

Interest on nearly every type of loan, including mortgages, is deductible. If you don't know how much interest you have paid on a particular loan during the year, obtain the information from the lender.

Forfeited Interest

If any interest was forfeited during the year by withdrawing money early from a time certificate savings account, deduct that interest penalty on your tax return. Although certificate accounts pay more interest than regular passbook accounts, penalties are high if money is withdrawn before the designated date. This forfeited interest can be deducted on your Form 1040.

Savings Bonds

As for United States savings bonds, one of two ways may be chosen to pay taxes on the interest earned: either report the annual interest on one's tax return each year, or wait to report all the accumulated interest in the year in which the bonds are redeemed.

Safe-Deposit Boxes

Storage of Bonds

The cost of renting a safe-deposit box used to store United States savings bonds and stocks is deductible. Most safe-deposit boxes are currently $6 to $17 per year, depending on their size.

Retirement Accounts

Keoghs and IRAs

One way to reduce current taxes is to place money in a pension plan. Under the so-called Keogh plan (named after the Congressman who initially sponsored the bill), a self-employed person can place up to $7,500 a year in a bank, a mutual fund, or other institution. That money is not taxed until the person retires and withdraws it, at which time he will probably be in a lower tax bracket. An employee of a company with no pension plan can start his own Individual Retirement Account (IRA), and make a maximum annual tax-deferred contribution of $1,500. (Further information on IRAs and Keoghs can be found in chapter XIV.)

IRA and Keogh Contributions

An individual can make contributions to an IRA as much as 45 days *after* the end of the year, and still deduct the full amount on the return. Thus, contributions could be made to an IRA until

February 14, 1978, and still be deducted on the 1977 income tax return.

Contributions to a Keogh can even be made later—up to the due date of the tax return itself. Thus, an individual could make a 1977 contribution to his Keogh plan on or before April 15, 1978.

Volunteer Work

Charity Deductions

Those who do volunteer work for a charitable organization and receive no pay in return can deduct from their taxes all commuting expenses related to such work. The cost of driving should be calculated at the rate of seven cents per mile. Sunday school teachers and scoutmasters are entitled to the same travel deduction. The cost of a special uniform, if needed, is also tax-deductible.

Personal Expenses

Alimony

Since 1977, the costs of alimony payments have been deductible as an adjustment to income instead of as an itemized deduction. Thus, it is deductible whether an individual itemizes or not. Recipients of alimony payments must include them as part of their gross.

Medical Charities

Amounts of Donations

Because contributions to charities are tax deductible, every dollar you give actually costs you less than that when your subsequent tax savings are calculated. The figures below apply to a married man who itemizes deductions on his joint tax return.

When taxable income is:	A $100 donation costs:
$12,000	$78
16,000	75
20,000	72
24,000	68
32,000	61
50,000	50

Choosing Charities

Be selective in charity giving. Some charities have such large overhead costs that they spend 50, 80, and even 90 percent of the contributions received on administrative expenses, publicity, and image-building. Reputable fund-raisers say that a well-run charity should spend no more than 25 percent of the amount it collects on administrative expenses.

Before contributing to a charity, write directly to its national office and request an itemization of how its funds are spent. Some charities will not respond to such inquiries, which in itself is a clue to their credibility.

Verifying Credibility

Local charities can be checked out with Better Business Bureaus or Chambers of Commerce. Some cities have special organizations that analyze charities. In Cleveland, one can check with the Greater Cleveland Growth Association. Government agencies in Dallas, New York City, and Los Angeles also screen philanthropic groups.

The National Information Bureau (305 E. 45th Street, New York, N.Y. 10017), a non-profit charity monitoring organization, reports on national fund-raising groups, but only to its members who pay $15 a year in tax-deductible dues. An individual who makes substantial contributions to charities might consider joining NIB in order to have access to its in-depth evaluations of individual philanthropic groups.

Board of Directors

Don't be impressed with a charity's letterhead, which may list the names of prominent personalities. Individuals who serve on the board of directors of a charity may be totally ignorant of the activities of the philanthropic organization.

Solicitations

Don't immediately respond to telephone appeals for charitable contributions—particularly from strangers who claim to be doctors or clergymen. Ask them to send relevant information through the mail. Request that the letter document what the money is needed for and how it will be spent. Door-to-door solicitations from unfamiliar organizations should also be approached cautiously. There's nothing wrong with asking the collector for an address where a contribution can be sent at a later date.

Unordered Merchandise

Refrain from donating to charities that send unordered "gift" merchandise—pens, license tags, key rings, name stickers, or similar items. First, this approach is somewhat unethical; it plays upon one's guilt feelings, making him feel he must contribute in return for the gift he has received. Second, this is an expensive fund-raising technique, costing as much as 90 percent of the funds collected. Only a small amount of the money donated actually goes to the cause to which it has been directed.

End-of-Year Tax Strategies

Medical Expenses

At the end of the year, several money-saving tax strategies can be employed. For example, medical bills received in late December should either be paid in December or January—depending on which should be most advantageous. Medical payments are deductible only when they exceed three percent of the gross income. So if paying a medical bill in December still leaves you under the three percent figure, hold off paying it until January 1, since the deduction may do you some good when filing the following year's return.

Accumulating Deductions

If you have a larger income this year than you anticipate having next year, accumulate as many deductions before December 31 as possible. Pay state and local taxes, as well as interest on debts, this year if possible. Increase contributions to charities and churches. If you own a business, buy equipment and supplies before the new year begins. (If you expect more income *next* year, reverse the process and delay accumulating deductions until January 1.)

Dating Checks

Simply because checks are dated December 31, they are not necessarily deductible in the outgoing calendar year's tax return. According to the IRS, the date of *delivery* is often the factor that determines which year the deduction can be taken. The taxpayer must be able to prove that a check was written and mailed on or before December 31. If checks are sent out close to year's end, send them by registered mail to prove when they were mailed.

Credit Card Charging

What happens if the purchase of a tax-deductible item is charged with a credit card on December 20, but the bill isn, t paid until it arrives on January 10? On which year's tax return should the deduction be claimed? According to the IRS, the deduction is applicable in the year in which you actually pay the credit card company.

INCOME AVERAGING

Savings on Taxes

If one's income is particularly large one year, taxes might be reduced by utilizing *income averaging*. Essentially, this is a way of treating peak-year income as if it were distributed over a five-year period. To determine eligibility for this technique this year, first average one's taxable income of the preceding four years (Let's say it averages out to $12,000). Then calculate 20 percent of the figure ($2,400) and add it to the average ($12,000 + $2,400 = $14,400). If one's income in the current year exceeds this new figure by more than $3,000 (that is, over $17,400 in our example), one can take advantage of income averaging.

Savings through Averaging

How much can you save through income averaging? Well, let's say that an individual makes an average of $10,000 a year, but through a sale of some property, his income jumps to $50,000 one year. By income averaging, he could save over $5,000 in taxes just in the first year.

CAPITAL GAINS TAX

Deferring House-Sale Taxes

Probably one of the most misunderstood taxes is the capital gains tax associated with the sale of a home. Basically, it is the tax due on the profit made when a house is sold. So if a house was bought 15 years ago for $24,000, and has been sold for $40,000, the profit of $16,000 is subject to taxation. This tax can be deferred by buying another house for $40,000 or more within 18 months, or building another house within 24 months. However, the tax is only *postponed* in these instances—it is *not* permanently erased. Ultimately, it must be paid, even if only after the individual dies.

Losses in House Sales

Sadly, any loss incurred in selling a house is not tax deductible. If, for example, a new airport nearby has forced a house to be sold at a lower price than was originally paid for it, the taxpayer must bear the entire loss. Under such circumstances, the best alternative is to try to rent the house for a year or two, and then sell it thereafter. This way, the loss can be legitimately considered a business loss (since the home is then technically "rental property"), and can thus be deducted on your income tax forms.

Senior Citizens Tax Break

If a taxpayer or his spouse is 65 years of age or older, and a profit is made on the sale of their house, at least part of the tax on that profit will be expunged. If the house is sold for a net price of $35,000 or less, the tax on the profit will be completely canceled. If the house is sold for over $35,000, a portion of the profit is not taxable. To be eligible for this tax benefit, an owner must have resided in the house for a minimum of five of the eight years immediately preceding the sale.

Maintaining Records

Keep all records pertaining to every house ever owned. These documents should include information on the buying and selling of the houses, and whatever capital improvements were made. When the time comes to calculate the capital gains owed—even if it is many years into the future—these records will prove invaluable.

ADJUSTING YOUR WITHHOLDING

Increasing Withholding

If a taxpayer believes that he will owe money to the IRS at the end of the taxable year, and wonders where that money will come from, he can guarantee that he will have it by increasing the amount of tax withheld from his weekly paychecks. By claiming zero dependents, he will have less take-home money each week, but at year's end, he may actually be entitled to a refund. Keep in mind, however, that by increasing the amount of taxes withheld, he is allowing the Treasury to use his money interest-free for several months. Ideally, he should claim the proper number of dependents and have the discipline to put the extra money into a savings account until it is needed—thus earning interest for *him*, not for the government.

Obtaining Forms

When leaving a job, ask the employer for a tax withholding statement. By law, he has to provide it within 30 days after an employee's departure. An employer who prefers to wait until the end of the year to send it can make matters difficult for his worker, particularly if the individual has changed addresses in the interim.

TAX AUDITS

Who Is Audited?

A high-income taxpayer has a greater chance of being audited than someone with a lower income. About eight percent of the nation's physicians are audited each year; less than one percent of those in low-income groups are audited. Those with incomes exceeding $100,000 annually can count on being audited every single year. Those whose tax payments fluctuate considerably from year to year, or whose deductions vary widely from the norm (for example, one's reported sales tax suddenly doubles, or the amount of one's charitable gifts triples) are likely candidates for an audit as well. The same will be true if a business partner is being checked for some reason.

Notification of Audit

If one's tax return is going to be audited, he will probably be notified by mail within four to six months after filing. The IRS will allow two to three weeks to prepare for the audit. Remember that an entire return will rarely be audited; usually one to three items will be singled out for explanation.

Changing the Date

The date on which the government requests that a taxpayer appear at the IRS office for an audit can be rescheduled if it is inconvenient. Although audits are usually held at all hours of the business day, the best time for an appointment is first thing in the morning, so as not to be kept waiting by taxpayers scheduled earlier in the day.

Accountant's Assistance

If one's tax return has been prepared by an accountant, ask him to appear at the IRS audit to explain the entries in question. He will often do this for no extra fee, believing it to be an extension of the tax preparation itself. However, some accountants do charge for such services—often $25 an hour and up.

Failure to Appear

If an individual has an appointment for an audit, and he or his representative (an accountant) fail to show up without notifying the IRS in advance, he will automatically be billed for the amount of money in dispute.

Stay Calm

Stay calm during an audit. As long as it can be proven that the income and deductions claimed are correct, there is nothing to be concerned about. Come prepared to the audit with receipts, canceled checks, and other supporting evidence.

Inspecting Bank Accounts

If it so desires, the IRS can legally gain access to an

individual's personal checking and savings accounts. It may add up the deposits made in these accounts. If they significantly exceed the income reported, the taxpayer may be questioned about this during the audit. He may be asked to prove the source of this unreported income (was it all from tax-free gifts?).

Appeal Procedures

If not satisfied with the findings of an auditor, don't sign a waiver agreement (Form 870) stating concurrence with his ruling. An appellate system is available, beginning with the auditor's immediate supervisor, who can be seen immediately. If not pleased with his decision, request to see the "district conferee" in the nearest IRS district office. If still dissatisfied, request a meeting with the "appellate conferee" in the IRS regional office. The IRS Tax Court is also available, either after the other alternatives are exhausted, or immediately after seeing the original auditor.

TAX COURT

Using the Court

Although the normal channels of auditing appeals can be followed, the Tax Court, which is totally independent of the IRS, probably offers the best odds for a ruling in the taxpayer's favor. Still, most of the cases that reach the Tax Court are eventually decided in favor of the IRS.

Ninety-Day Letter

If a taxpayer wants his dispute heard before the Tax Court, he must ask the IRS to issue him a "90-day letter," also known as a "statutory notice of deficiency." With this notice in hand, he can request a court hearing, but he must do it within 90 days after the notice has been issued.

Legal Assistance

It is advisable to be accompanied by a lawyer in Tax Court. However, if one's disagreement with the IRS involves $1,500 or less, the matter could be handled without one by requesting a hearing in the small cases section of the court. The docketing fee for small cases is $10.

Out-of-Court Settlements

To ease the caseload of the Tax Court, most small cases scheduled to be heard are settled out of court. If the IRS offers to settle a case in last-minute negotiations, agree to do so unless convinced there's absolutely no way the IRS can win the case when it reaches the judge. Eighty percent of all cases headed for the Tax Court never get there; instead, the IRS agrees to accept, on the average, about 55 percent of the taxes it had originally said were owed.

Small-Case Disadvantages

Be aware of the drawbacks of small-case sessions. First, no appeal is allowed; thus, the judge's decision is final. Also, the judge's ruling does not have to be based on precedent. So if in a previous and similar case, a judge ruled in favor of the taxpayer, he does not necessarily have to rule that same way in subsequent cases.

PROPERTY TAXES

Pay On Time

Pay property taxes on time so as to avoid the penalties levied for late payment. In some states, a small discount on taxes can be obtained by paying them in advance.

Tax Sales

Anyone very delinquent in paying property taxes may face a tax sale of his house, in which his home is actually put up for public sale to the highest bidder. In most states, the tax sale can be prevented by paying the overdue amount at any time until the sale occurs. Even after the sale has taken place, the property can sometimes be recovered upon payment of due taxes, plus a penalty and the cost of conducting the sale. The time period in which one can redeem his property varies from state to state.

Appealing Property Taxes

It is possible to protest a property tax assessment, and sometimes have it reduced. To do so, first visit the local assessor's office, and find your property on the assessment rolls. Then compare your assessment with that of similar property (similar lot size, similar type and size of house) in the same area. If your assessment is higher than neighboring property, formally apply for a reduction in assessment on the form provided by the assessor's office. Don't miss the deadline for filing appeals.

Preparing for Appeals

When making an appeal, be sure to prepare your case well. Write down the assessed valuation of at least five houses similar to yours that have not been taxed as heavily. Take photographs of any problems in your house (such as structural failures) that have reduced the value of the property.

Turning to the Courts

If a local appeals board rejects your request for a reduction of the assessment, you have the option to go to court to try to force the action you want. However, experts say that the expensive lawsuit process is usually more costly than anything that might be saved by a reassessment. Besides hiring a lawyer and paying court costs, an expert witness—an appraiser—who could support your case would also have to be hired. In the overwhelming majority of instances, it's foolish to take your crusade into court.

Exemptions

In some locales, certain property tax exemptions are available. People over 65 (or 62 in some states), widows, war veterans, and the blind are frequently able to obtain discounts on property taxes, often reducing tax bills by as much as 50 to 100 percent. The type and scope of these exemptions vary from city to city, as well as from state to state, so contact the local assessor to determine what, if any, exemptions may be applicable.

CHAPTER 12

Legal Matters

"The first thing we do, let's kill all the lawyers," wrote Shakespeare in *King Henry VI*.

Although few people would approve of such drastic action, many would be quite satisfied never to have anything to do with attorneys. Legal fees are often high for even the simplest of legal procedures. And the Watergate scandal of the mid-1970s, in which so many lawyers were convicted of crimes, only added to the negative sentiments about lawyers.

But lawyers are a necessity in this society. The United States has more laws than any other nation in the world. Yet most of us know little about our legal rights, and even less about how to ensure that we are not being legally abused.

Thus, the lawyer. He is a professional who may be able to quickly solve and settle matters that have been troubling clients for months. And even though his fees are sometimes high, his advice may in the long run save us much money.

A good family lawyer is in some ways as important as a good family doctor, but most people do not seek legal advice until they need it—or more accurately, until *after* they need it. By the time a lawyer is contacted, a fraudulent contract may already have been signed, or a plot of worthless land purchased. Too often, practicing do-it-yourself law creates more problems than it solves.

Even a simple and relatively inexpensive matter like a will is ignored by many people. A will, of course, is a most important document, yet only half of all the adults in the United States have one. About a third of the existing wills will eventually be disputed in court because they were poorly composed—often in longhand by the individual himself.

By definition, a will is a legal document that provides for the distribution of a person's property upon his death. True, many people put off—sometimes forever—the preparation of a will. Some simply refuse to face the reality that they will die someday. And by declining to have an attorney draw up a will, they may place their survivors in legal and financial dilemmas that can take years to resolve.

Another personal legal matter of concern to many people is the enormous rise in personal bankruptcies in the United States. Technically, bankruptcy is available to anyone who cannot pay his debts. Until recently, though, the social stigma that has accompanied it kept the number of bankrupts each year comparatively low. That is no longer the case. About 245,000 Americans now go into court each year to publicly declare that they cannot meet their financial obligations. Among their ranks have been professional athletes, movie stars, and even a member of the Du Pont family! The leading causes of bankruptcy today are expensive illnesses and divorces. Regardless of the causes, bankruptcy is another area that calls for lawyers.

SELECTING AND USING A LAWYER
When Is a Lawyer Needed?
Common Legal Tasks

There are certain times when a lawyer's services are indispensable. Among them are (1) when drawing up a will, (2) when buying a home, (3) when entering into a partnership contract, (4) when you are a defendant in a lawsuit, (5) when filing for divorce, (6) when adopting a child, and (7) when investing in a business or in real estate.

Lawyers Not Needed

For some legal matters, the services of a lawyer are unnecessary. If an individual is entitled to unemployment insurance payments or Social Security benefits which he hasn't been receiving, the government has its own officials who may be able to resolve the matter to his satisfaction. If he is having problems with the Internal Revenue Service, and has a good accountant, it's unlikely that a lawyer will be needed. If he has a claim against a merchant or another private party, he can go to small claims court and settle the issue without an attorney.

It's possible to do without a lawyer when deciding to legally change a name. All that's required is that you fill out certain papers, which will petition the court for the change and explain the reasons for the request. The paperwork is relatively simple, and if you have questions, the county court clerk can probably answer them. A lawyer would charge $50 to $250 for handling a name change.

A Specialist or a Generalist?
One Function or Many

Many lawyers specialize in particular fields. There are criminal lawyers, tax lawyers, personal injury lawyers, civil liberties lawyers, bankruptcy lawyers, patent lawyers, divorce lawyers, and corporation lawyers. For most of your legal needs, though, find one who handles a wide array of matters—that is, a "general practitioner" who can assist with contracts, real estate deals, insurance settlements, wills, and dozens of other common legal affairs.

Finding the Lawyer

The Bar Association

When in need of a lawyer—if relatives or friends cannot recommend one—call the local bar association. Every association has its own referral program, and will recommend two or three attorneys who can provide the legal service required. You can find out something about the backgrounds of these lawyers by looking in *The Martindale-Hubbell Lawyer's Dictionary*, available in most libraries. It lists every lawyer in the nation, his age, what law school he attended, how long he's been practicing, his specialties, and the type of clients he has. It will also indicate his financial standing, and how he is rated by his fellow attorneys.

Making an Appointment

Call the lawyer at the top of your list, request an interview, and explain why you are in need of legal services. Some lawyers will not charge for an initial consultation in their office; others will charge $15 to $20. At this meeting, explain thoroughly the legal predicament in which you find yourself. He may suggest several approaches to the situation, giving an indication of his own expertise.

Fees

Settling on a Fee

During a first meeting with an attorney, ask him what he will charge for handling the case. Don't be reluctant to negotiate the fee. Tell him frankly what your income is, and if the fee he has quoted will put a real strain on your budget, let him know. When a fee has finally been agreed upon, get it in writing.

Fee Variations

Lawyers' fees vary considerably for similar tasks, depending on the client's income bracket, and the amount of work involved. For instance, in a contested divorce involving a family with an income under $10,000, the husband's lawyer and the wife's lawyer will each charge a minimum of $300 to $600. If the family income is in the $10,000 to $20,000 range, their fees will jump from $600 to

$2,500 each. In the $20,000 to $50,000 bracket, fees may start at $2,000, and skyrocket to as much as $8,000 each.

Paying in Advance

On some occasions, a lawyer will request that part of the fee be paid in advance. This is common in cases where the lawyer fears that he may end up with nothing. When a client is filing for bankruptcy, for example, the lawyer may want some money in advance, since the client may be penniless at the completion of the proceedings. Likewise, in a criminal case where the client could possibly be jailed, a portion of the fee may be requested at the beginning.

Installments

If an individual's legal fees are going to be large, he should ask the attorney if he can pay the bill in installments. Some bar associations now approve of lawyers having their clients sign promissory notes. These notes are then turned over to a bank, which makes arrangements with the client for his debt to be paid off in monthly installments.

Legal Services for the Poor

Legal Aid Society

When a person is in need of legal services but cannot afford to hire a lawyer, he should contact the Legal Aid Society, which has more than 500 offices in the United States. To qualify for this free assistance: (1) he can't own property, stocks, or bonds; (2) he can't have more than a small amount of money in a savings account; and (3) his weekly salary must be relatively low. Legal Aid will not handle divorce or criminal cases.

Other Legal Assistance

Other sources of legal help include the Neighborhood Legal Service, which assists the poor in legal matters, and has more than 1,000 offices nationwide. Also find out if your labor union has a staff attorney who its members can consult free of charge for a certain number of hours per year.

Wave Project

For simple, uncontested divorce cases, contact agencies like the Wave Project, which has offices throughout California. For $65, it will assist individuals in filling out the necessary divorce papers. Similar divorce services also exist in New York State (where the program is called Divorce Yourself), Texas, and Washington.

Dealing with Lawyers

Be Honest

Be completely honest with your attorney. When you're involved in a lawsuit with another party, tell your lawyer everything you possibly can to help him prepare the case. Don't mention only the points in your favor, but also what your adversary's story is likely to be. In order to represent your interests best, the attorney should know all sides of the issues and all relevant details, no matter how trivial they might seem. Remember that everything you tell to a lawyer is strictly confidential.

Prepare in Advance

Before meeting with a lawyer for any reason, make certain you are well-prepared. Collect and organize the documents that will be referred to. Some lawyers charge by the hour, so the less time taken to discuss matters, the lower the bill will be.

Case Referrals

Occasionally, after a lawyer has undertaken a case, he refers his client to a second lawyer. Should this happen to you, carefully question the reasons behind the action. Is the second attorney desperately in need of clients, and has he offered the first lawyer a fee for your case—and will this fee be added to your bill? Except in very unusual circumstances, the procedure followed by most ethical attorneys is to refer a case to other lawyers only *before* accepting the case as his own.

Complaining About an Attorney

Lodging a Complaint

If you are unhappy about the service received from an attorney, talk it over with him. If the differences cannot be resolved, file a formal complaint with the local bar association. In too many cases, bar associations move very slowly in dealing with complaints, or in disciplining their members. But in some cities, the associations are more conscientious.

Also complain to the bar association if you feel you've been overcharged. The association has a table of recommended fees for various services; if you've been charged much more than the suggested fee, lodge a formal complaint with the association's grievance committee.

Financial Compensation

Some bar associations have created a special fund to reimburse people for lost money or property caused by the unscrupulous actions of attorneys. Many lawyers also carry professional liability insurance which may provide clients with money when the attorney has been negligent.

PROVIDING FOR SURVIVORS

Who Needs a Will

Importance for Everyone

Every adult—whether rich or poor, male or female, old or young, married or single—should have a will. Without one, settling an estate is considerably more complex, expensive, and time-consuming, and may involve prolonged proceedings in probate court. In the absence of a will, assets are disposed of according to the formula fixed by state law. The court chooses those who will administer the distribution of the estate.

Husband and Wife

Both partners in a marriage should have wills. Even though wives outlive their husbands 70 percent of the time, it is sensible for every wife to have a will. Most attorneys will draw up the two wills for only slightly more than the cost of one, particularly if the second will is almost a repeat of the first.

Regardless of whether a wife owns any property at all, she should have a will. If her husband's death precedes hers, she will probably inherit some of his estate, which will eventually be redistributed upon her own death.

The mother of minor children should most definitely have a will. If she outlives her husband, but dies before the children are of legal age, only with a will can she name a guardian to care for the children. A will is the only sure way to avoid a custody battle among relatives.

Dying Without a Will

The estate of a single person who dies without a will usually goes first to his parents, and then to his brothers and sisters. When a married person dies without a will, the law in most states stipulates that the spouse gets half of the estate, with the remainder going to the children. If the children are minors, a social worker may be asked to approve the spouse as a suitable sole guardian for the property awarded them. The spouse will be required to make regular reports to the court until the children reach legal age. A court order will have to be obtained before the family house can be sold, since the children have a financial stake in it.

Preparing the Will

Who Should Do It

Unless you're a lawyer, don't try to write your own will. For a will to be accepted by the court, it must contain proper legal language, and it must be signed and witnessed a specific way. If a will has even the most trivial ambiguity, the courts will have to decide its meaning, and court costs and legal fees for so doing will be drawn from the estate. A simple will prepared by a good lawyer costs between $50 and $150.

What Should It Say

A will should specify the following: (1) The beneficiaries of all money and property. (2) The amount awarded to each beneficiary. (3) The time at which each beneficiary is to receive his share. (4) Who is to oversee the distribution of the estate.

Preparation

Assist the lawyer in drawing up your will by listing in advance all assets, including savings accounts, checking accounts, real estate, stocks and bonds, life insurance policies, annuities, automobiles, jewelry, furs, art objects, and so forth. Next to each item, write down its estimated value, a complete description of it, its serial number, and where it is located. Obtain for the lawyer the exact legal names and addresses of all beneficiaries. Then list how all possessions are to be allocated upon your death—the amount of money, the percentage of the estate, or the particular pieces of property that each beneficiary is to inherit.

Assets Inappropriate for Wills

Certain assets can't be distributed through a will. These are ones for which the beneficiaries have already been legally designated elsewhere. For instance, a life insurance policy clearly indicates who is to receive benefits upon the holder's death. So do United States savings bonds, and pension benefits. Property that is mutually owned also can't be transferred by a will (for example, if a husband and wife jointly own a house, upon the death of one of them, title immediately passes to the surviving spouse).

Bequeathing in Percentages

When a young person prepares a will, he is wise to make many of his bequests in percentages of the net value of the estate—for example, 70 percent to his wife, and 30 percent to charity. This is safer than specifying dollar amounts, which can sometimes cause unforeseen problems. Let's say, for instance, that when the will is prepared, his estate is worth $100,000, and the will stipulates $30,000 should go to charity, and the rest to his wife. If at the time of his death, the estate has diminished in value to $50,000, his wife will only receive $20,000 after the charity is given its clearly-defined share. So if he wants his wife or other beneficiaries to receive a specific percentage of the estate, he should spell it out clearly in the will.

Disinheriting Relatives

Most relatives, including children, can be disinherited in a will. In most states, however, a wife or husband cannot be disinherited. A surviving spouse is usually entitled to at least one-third of an estate. If a will leaves a spouse less than that, the court will probably award it to him or her anyway.

The Executor

Carefully choose an executor (the person who carries out the terms of the will). He should be named in the will, and he is responsible for admitting the will to probate (presenting it to the court for verification), preparing an inventory of assets, paying debts with the money in the estate, collecting money due, submitting a final accounting to the court, and carrying out the ultimate distribution of the estate.

The executor should be a responsible friend or relative, your lawyer, banker, or spouse. Under normal circumstances, a spouse can best serve as executor; he or she will probably have access to an attorney to help with details. However, if the estate is complex, an attorney or a banker should handle everything. When this executor function is delegated to a bank, it will charge for performing the service—usually 2 to 4 percent of the value of the estate.

Information for Executor

In addition to a will, prepare a document called a "letter of last instructions." The letter, addressed to the executor, will be opened and read upon your death. It should include the following information: where the will is located; where other valuable papers (house deeds, life insurance policies, stocks and bonds) have been stored; location of all safe-deposit boxes (and keys); the names and addresses of all business associates and financial advisors; and funeral instructions. (Desires for your own funeral should not be included in the will itself: by the time the will is located and read, you may already have been buried.)

Updating a Will

When Is a Will Outdated?

A will becomes outdated when a major change occurs in one's life. Marriage or divorce, the deaths of beneficiaries or witnesses, the birth of a child, the purchase or sale of real estate, the acquisition of interest in a business or of new assets in general—they all render a will obsolete.

A Codicil

The simplest way to alter a will is to have a lawyer attach a codicil (a document that contains additions or amendments to a will). Never cross out obsolete provisions on the original will and and write or type in the new conditions. A codicil must be prepared with the same care as the original will, and must be signed, dated, and witnessed like the will itself. Over the years, a lawyer may add as many codicils as you so wish. However, once they become cumbersome, request that an entire new will be prepared.

Moving to a New State

Upon moving to another state, it's wise to have a new will drawn up. Even though all states recognize wills legally prepared in other states, some stipulations in the will may be voided if they run counter to the existing laws of the state to which you have moved. It is also true that if an individual moves his residence to a state other than that in which his will was prepared, and if his will describes him as a resident of that state where he formerly lived, both states may try to impose a death tax on his estate.

Where to Keep the Will

Banker or Lawyer

The original of a will should be kept in a safe place—with a bank or with the lawyer who drew it up. The trust department of a bank, which cares for wills as a regular service, is probably the best choice because it would completely eliminate the possibililty of problems arising due to the unavailability at the time of your death of the lawyer who drew up the will (His death may precede yours, or he may be out of town when you die).

Avoid Safe-Deposit Boxes

If the original of a will is placed in a safe-deposit box, the executor may have difficulty gaining access to it right away. The law requires that a bank seal a safe-deposit box upon the death of the renter—even if a spouse is its co-holder. Some married couples sidestep this quandary by keeping the husband's will in the wife's safe-deposit box, and vice versa. But should they both die together in an accident, the same access problem will exist for their heirs.

ESTATE TAXES

Legal Exemption

Until 1976, the first $60,000 of an estate was exempt from federal taxation. But in 1977, federal law replaced the exemption with a tax "credit" of $30,000, which is equivalent to an exemption of $120,660. By 1981, this credit will increase to $47,000, which is equivalent to a $175,625 exemption. Thus, by 1981, estates of up to $175,625 will be totally exempt from federal taxation.

Gifts Before Death

One of the best ways to reduce estate tax is to give away some of your assets while you're alive. Once they no longer belong to you, they won't be taxed as part of your estate. In any single year, and for as many years as desired, you can give as much as $3,000 per person to as many people as you wish. But any amount in excess of $3,000 per person per year must be reported to the government on a gift tax return. After a total of thirty thousand tax free dollars has been given away, all subsequent gifts are subject to taxation.

Before giving away any assets during your lifetime, consider the following two problems that may arise: (1) Once the gifts have been disbursed, will you have funds enough to provide for personal needs for the rest of your life? (2) Are you giving money to minors or other persons unable to properly manage these assets? (This latter problem can usually be solved by establishing a trust fund.)

Spouse Tax Breaks

Special tax breaks are provided for that portion of an estate left to a surviving spouse. According to law, up to one-half of an estate may be left to a spouse without being subject to federal estate taxes. So let's assume that a husband dies, leaving his entire $90,000 estate to his wife. The first $60,000 of that estate is exempt from federal estate taxes as a marital deduction. The remaining $30,000 would ordinarily be taxed, except that it, too, is exempt under the provisions mentioned above.

Trusts

Establishing a Trust

If you wish to leave money to a brother, sister, or spouse—or anyone who you are afraid will be unable to manage the money properly if it is granted in one lump sum—create a trust that will be activated upon your death. The money left will be placed in this trust, and the recipient will receive part of it each month until his or her death. At that time, the money remaining in the trust will go to whomever you designate in your will.

Multi-Purposes

Trusts can be established in much the same way for many other purposes—to educate a minor child, or to provide funds for a specific charity.

Trustee

To oversee a trust, you must appoint a trustee. The trustee may be an individual, the trust department of a bank, or a trust company. Fees are charged for this service by a bank or trust company, but they are usually no higher than one percent of the trust's assets per year.

SMALL CLAIMS COURT

Settling Minor Disputes

If a consumer has a complaint with a merchant which cannot be settled amicably, he has the option of taking the dispute to small claims court. These limited-jurisdiction courts concern themselves with such matters as disputes over accidents, clothing lost or ruined by cleaners, contract hassles, squabbles between landlords and tenants, and damage caused by movers.

Where Is It?

To locate the small claims court in your community, call the local bar association, or write the Small Claims Study Group, Quincy House, Room 1, Cambridge, Massachusetts 02138.

How It Works

Although regulations vary from one jurisdiction to another, small claims courts usually handle only disputes involving less than $500 (although the limit in a few states is a high as $3,500). Anyone 18 years old and over can file suit in these courts. During the proceedings, the plaintiff and the defendant will state their cases and present evidence (bills, receipts, etc.) before the judge. Should the plaintiff win, the defendant will not only be ordered to pay him the money owed, but also pay *all* court costs.

Legal Representation

Although legal counsel is rarely retained by plaintiffs in small claims cases, in all but six states representation by a lawyer is permissible. The exceptions are California, Michigan, Oregon, Washington, Nevada, and Idaho.

Filing the Lawsuit

To file a small claims suit, fill out the appropriate forms at the Office of the Clerk of the court. On the forms, list precisely the name of the person, business, or corporation being sued. To find out the legal name of a store, check the business records in the county clerk's office. Return the completed forms to the small claims clerk, pay a filing fee of from $3 to $15, and a court date will usually be assigned at that time.

In preparing for a small claims court appearance, remember that any witness may be subpoenaed—such as a passerby who saw a traffic accident. The court clerk will issue these subpoenas, which will order the court appearance of the individual(s) you name.

Inability to Appear

If because of unforeseen circumstances, you are unable to appear in court on the date for which your case has been assigned, request a postponement. The court will not accept telephone requests; either send a registered letter, or ask a friend to appear on the date of the trial to explain your absence.

If the party being sued does not appear in court on the scheduled date, the judge will nevertheless ask you to present your case. He will then usually rule in your favor by default.

Appeals

The verdict of a small claims court may be appealed in most states. Should you appeal to a higher court, it would be wise to retain an attorney, since the proceedings become more complicated as one moves along the appeal process.

Further Action

Should you win a small claims court case, there is no guarantee that the party being sued will voluntarily comply with the wishes of the court (for example, by paying the money owed). A Consumers Union study in 1970 revealed that in 62 cases in which the plaintiff won, 12 of the judgments were never collected. It may be necessary to ask that the local sheriff or marshal collect the money for you (a percentage of the money will be forfeited for this service). The marshal can also seize the defendant's property to satisfy the debt. Or you can request that the court place a lien on the defendant's bank account, or attempt to have his wages attached.

PERSONAL BANKRUPTCY

An Ultimate Solution

Removing Debts

Those who are continuously in financial debt and can find no way of extricating themselves from the situation are prime candidates for bankruptcy. An individual who suspects that he might fall into this category should calculate what his take-home pay will be over the next three years; if it's unlikely that this income will enable him to pay off all debts and to live a life of reasonable comfort, bankruptcy may be advisable.

According to one study, the average personal bankrupt had debts totaling nine percent more than his gross annual income. So if an individual makes $12,000 a year, bankruptcy may be valid if he has $13,080 in debts.

Continuing Responsibilities

Contrary to popular belief, declaring bankruptcy doesn't relieve all debt responsibilities. The bankrupt is still required by law to pay both federal and state taxes that have come due in the three years prior to his declaration of bankruptcy. He must also pay alimony and child support, debts resulting from intentionally malicious acts, debts acquired through deceit or fraud, fines for criminal acts and traffic violations, and debts owed on a house or car.

How to Do It

(1) A lawyer can handle the bankruptcy for you (for $250 or more), but you can probably do it yourself, if you're not in business for yourself and your assets aren't large. To declare bankruptcy, first file the proper bankruptcy petition forms with the U.S. District Court nearest you. These forms, which cost about $4, can be purchased in any legal stationery store. On the forms, list all debts and assets. (Don't leave out any assets, including the money in your wallet; omissions can result in criminal prosecution.) Also submit information about occupation, income, and copies of recent tax returns. A filing fee of $50 is charged, but this fee may usually be paid in monthly installments.

(2) By the time a bankruptcy hearing in District Court is

held, usually a few weeks after the filing of the proper papers, all creditors will have to be notified. In the period before a hearing is held, the court can appoint a *receiver* or *conservator* for your property, who assumes control over your assets during this interim time. When the hearing is eventually held, creditors may be present to question you. The judge makes certain all papers are in order, and he may ask why you've chosen to file bankruptcy. The entire hearing usually lasts no longer than 15 or 20 minutes, and the ruling is almost always in the favor of the individual filing for bankruptcy. When the bankruptcy is officially ruled, the court distributes all assets among the creditors, according to a formula required by law.

(3) About 60 days after the hearing is held, the bankruptcy court will issue a "discharge in bankruptcy," which will forever erase all nonexempt debts. The court can also issue an order preventing old creditors from demanding payment of outstanding debts, if they are continuing to bother you for money.

What Can a Bankrupt Keep?

Depending on the state, the bankrupt is permitted to retain certain possessions after declaring bankruptcy. In most states, these exemptions include a share of his earnings from the 30 to 60 days preceding bankruptcy, a portion of the equity in his home, all clothes, some furniture, part of his savings in a savings and loan association or a credit union, life insurance if his spouse or a dependent relative is the beneficiary, and some of the tools of his trade.

Under federal law, an individual's declaration of bankruptcy does not deprive him of Social Security payments, veterans benefits, Railroad Employees Retirement benefits, or Federal Civil Service retirement benefits.

To ensure that bankruptcy is as advantageous to him as possible, the potential bankrupt should change many of his nonexempt assets into exempt ones before filing. For example, money could be withdrawn from the bank and used to purchase life insurance, making a spouse or child the beneficiary. Although this may seem devious, it is quite legal and is common practice.

Maintaining Favorable Credit

It is possible to maintain a good credit standing with at least some creditors while filing for bankruptcy. Let's say, for instance, that you owe money on ten credit cards, and would like to keep at least one of them after declaring bankruptcy. Accumulate the money to pay off this one account prior to going into bankruptcy court. If this account is clear, it would not be listed among your creditors; thus, the court would not notify it of your filing, and your good credit there would remain intact.

After the Bankruptcy Becomes Final

Maintain Financial Stability

Anyone who has declared bankruptcy should promise himself never to fall into the same financial dilemma again. Should he slip back into debt, he will be truly helpless: bankruptcy cannot be declared more than once in six years.

Re-establishing Credit

Because a record of bankruptcy remains on one's credit history for 14 years, re-establishing a good credit rating after bankruptcy is not easy. Many banks and stores will simply refuse bankrupts who apply for loans or credit. The best way out of this dilemma is to apply for a small loan from a bank, and ask a relative or close friend to be a cosigner. Repay the loan quickly, and the lender will probably be disposed to make future loans without requiring a cosigner.

AN ALTERNATIVE TO BANKRUPTCY

Wage Earner's Plan

Before making the final decision to declare bankruptcy, consider using Chapter 13 of the Federal Bankruptcy Law instead. Also known as the "wage earner's plan," it is an alternative to bankruptcy. Under its provisions, one may request that the court intervene in his debt problems, and set up a program in which he will systematically pay creditors all or part of what he owes over a fixed time period, usually from 12 to 36 months. To effect this plan, at least half of an individual's creditors must agree to it; the debtor must also agree to turn over his weekly paycheck to the court for distribution. Many creditors will settle for less than the entire debt owed them, or will cease adding interest or late charges to the balance due. Unlike bankruptcy, Chapter 13 proceedings do not require that any assets be forfeited, and one's credit rating is less tarnished.

How Does It Work?

The average Chapter 13 plan covers $3,000 worth of debts, but for anyone owing more than $1,000, it is a route to consider. To set a Chapter 13 plan in motion, there are $30 in initial court fees. Thereafter, 5 to 10 percent of the amount of the consolidated debts will be levied to defray the costs of operating the program. Of course, if the services of a lawyer are engaged, that will be an additional expense—from $100 to $400—which can usually be paid in monthly installments.

Generally, a Chapter 13 proceeding cuts monthly bills by 50 percent. Unless an individual is in very desperate financial straits, he should choose Chapter 13 over a declaration of bankruptcy. Chapter 13 leaves much less of a lasting stigma against his credit rating.

CONSUMER COMPLAINTS

The Better Business Bureau

In case of suspected fraud or cheating, notify the local Better Business Bureau immediately. Although the BBB rarely brings any legal action against businesses, it will formally notify them of a complaint, and ask for an explanation. Some businesses, in order to keep their good standing with the BBB, settle disputes quickly so as to avoid complaints becoming a part of their permanent file.

The Media

Many newspapers and radio and television stations have their own consumer complaint staffs, who will attempt to use their influence in the community to settle disputes with local businesses. Under such titles as Action Line, Consumer Corner, or Call for Action, these programs have effectively pressured merchants to settle altercations with customers.

Letters and Copies

When complaining by letter to a business, make several photocopies of the document and send them where additional pressure can be applied. This might mean sending copies to presidents of companies (when dealing with their agents), government agencies that would be interested in the case, and local, state, and federal legislators.

Lawsuits

When one has been cheated by a merchant or a company, the ultimate legal recourse is to sue for fraud. Unfortunately, the cost of the litigation may exceed the amount of the suit. Filing a suit against a merchant for an amount in excess of the small claims court limit may cost more than the amount the plaintiff might be awarded. In such cases, proceed against the merchant in other ways, including (1) complaining to state or local consumer agencies, (2) bringing a class action suit (see below), or (3) taking him into small claims court, suing for the maximum amount of money that the court allows, and just forgetting about the rest of the money owed.

Class Action Suits

A group of individual consumers may bring legal action against a company which has sold them merchandise or services using deceitful practices. The suit, called a "class action," allows these individuals to share the legal costs. So if you find that you are just one of many people who have been sold, say, an expensive typewriter illegally, join with the other consumers in a joint lawsuit. If the legal expenses of bringing the case to trial amount to $1,500, and there are 15 individuals involved in the suit, each will only have to pay $100 in litigation costs.

CONTRACTS AND GUARANTEES

Read Before Signing

Contracts are legally enforceable agreements between two or more parties, in which each consents to fulfill specified obligations. Before signing a contract, read and reread it thoroughly. Make sure that everything is carefully articulated, and that nothing is left to interpretation. Never sign a contract if any part is unclear, even if it's a single sentence. Also, always keep a copy of the agreement for future reference.

Altering a Contract

After a contract has been signed, it cannot be altered or voided without the consent of all parties involved. The Truth in Lending law, however, provides for a "cooling-off" period of three business days for a contract involving a credit transaction in which one's home is used as collateral. At any time during these three days, the agreement can be voided. A similar three-day cooling-off period exists for a contract signed with a door-to-door salesman that involves more than $25.

The Small Print of Guarantees

Read the small print of all guarantees. Too often, the small print takes away what the large print appears to promise. Determine, for example, if the entire product is guaranteed, or only its parts (Is the entire television set under guarantee, or only the picture tube?). Does the guarantee include only materials, or also labor? And where will the guarantee be honored? Can the product be taken to a local service center, or must it be mailed halfway around the world?

PERSONAL RECORDS

Safe-Deposit Box

What to Place There

Over the years, each of us collects many documents and papers of special value. Some should be kept in a safe-deposit box; others can be kept at home. Because of the need for greater security, the following items should be placed in a safe-deposit box: birth and death certificates, adoption papers, marriage license, citizenship papers, deeds to property, records of mortgage payments, stock and bond certificates, installment sales contracts, titles and bills of sale for automobiles, and military service records. A copy of one's will may be kept in the safe-deposit box, provided that a bank or lawyer has the original.

The safe-deposit box should also include an inventory of all your household items. This list will be very useful when filing an insurance claim if your home is ever burglarized or damaged by fire. This inventory should state the value of each item, when it was purchased, and its serial number (if applicable). Take photographs as further proof of ownership, and make these pictures part of the inventory.

Are Contents Insured?

Read through your homeowners insurance policy to ascertain whether the contents of your safe-deposit box are covered, and for how much. Also, study the agreement you have signed with the institution from which the box is being rented. Is the liability of the institution limited in any way?

Most homeowners insurance policies provide only minimal coverage of the contents of a safe-deposit box. In 1977, only one insurance company (Aetna Life & Casualty) was promoting a separate policy for safe-deposit box insurance—at a premium of 50 cents per $1,000 of coverage per year (with a minimum premium of $5).

What to Keep Elsewhere

Stock Certificates

Some people prefer to leave stock and bond certificates with their brokers rather than in their safe-deposit boxes. (Brokers often charge for this service.) Either way is fine, but definitely do not keep them in the house. If they are lost or destroyed, replacing them is costly and time-consuming. Not only does the replacement process take several months, but a fee of about four percent of the market value of the stocks or bonds will be charged for the replacement.

Documents for Home Storage

All records kept at home should be stored in a central location, where they are easy to locate and difficult to lose. These items include: bankbooks, copies of income tax returns, canceled checks, life insurance policies, passports, diplomas, records of pension plans, family medical histories (including records of inoculations), a list of credit cards and their numbers, and appliance and equipment records.

Record-Keeping

Canceled Checks and Check Stubs

Canceled checks and check stubs make record-keeping easy. By paying for most purchases by check and by keeping detailed check stubs, you'll have a continuing record of expenditures. On each stub, write the name of the recipient of each check, the dollar amount, and important details about the purchase—such as "bicycle for Michael," "school clothes for kids," "2nd install- ment of life insurance payment," or *Newsweek* subscription— through November 1979."

Keep canceled checks for at least a year (although checks for tax-deductible items should be kept longer to justify deductions). Once checks have been discarded, should you need a copy of one of them, your bank can provide it. Banks keep records of all checks on microfilm, and can make a photocopy of a particular check upon request.

Maintain a Record Book

The simplest way to keep track of personal papers is to maintain a record book noting the location of all important papers and documents. Such record books are available in stationary stores, or make one using a looseleaf notebook. Whatever is used, make photocopies of this log, letting each of your adult children have one, so they'll know where to find important papers in case of an emergency. Also keep a photocopy at your office or at some other location away from home.

Among other things, a record book should note the follow- ing: locations of certificates of birth, death, marriage, divorce, and naturalization; location of your Social Security card and its number; the names and addresses of the banks where accounts are held, with the account numbers; the serial numbers, issue dates, and denominations of United States bonds; insurance policies, including a notation of the names and addresses of the companies involved; credit cards, including the names and addresses of the issuing companies; and a household inventory of personal possessions.

CHAPTER 13

Travel and Recreation for Less Expense

Tens of millions of Americans travel as tourists every year. Tourism has in fact become so large an enterprise—$70 billion in 1976—that three states—Florida, Hawaii, and Nevada—consider it their principal industry.

The travel agent is crucial to the travel business, at least from the consumer's point of view. His or her expertise (or lack of it) often determines whether his customers' trips are pleasurable. A good travel agent is more than a ticket seller—he or she knows something about the cities to which his clients are going and how to get them there comfortably and inexpensively.

Airplane travel has become so commonplace in the United States that the Wright brothers would probably never believe what has happened since their first ascent near Kitty Hawk, North Carolina. In a typical week, 3½ million passengers fly on America's commercial airlines.

Train travel is in the midst of a resurgence. Almost all intermediate distance and long-distance passenger trains are now owned by Amtrak, the semi-public corporation formed to revitalize the stagnating American passenger train system. Amtrak now operates coast-to-coast, and connects more than 450 cities.

Cruise ships are another popular mode of travel. About 220 cruise ships are in service today, about 50 of them out of American ports. They sail to virtually every coastal country and every continent, including Antarctica.

There are many inexpensive motels and hotels for tourists throughout the country. It is also possible to live in someone else's house on vacation, while they live in yours.

Over 16,000 campgrounds are available in the United States and Canada, and a total of over half a million individual campsites. With their tents and sleeping bags securely stashed in their recreational vehicles, Americans are discovering that "roughing it" can be both fun and economical. Some campgrounds can be used for free; others charge just $1 to $4 per day.

And eating in restaurants can cost three times as much as buying groceries and cooking them at the campgrounds.

Of course, traveling is rarely a trouble-free experience. For instance, some three million passengers on domestic airlines in 1976 were inconvenienced by lost, stolen, or damaged luggage. And the problems seem to be getting worse. No wonder that many people are choosing to stay closer to home—bicycling, motorcycling, sailing, or engaging in any of dozens of recreational activities.

TRAVEL
Travel Agents

Using Their Services
Travel agents can offer invaluable assistance in planning a vacation. They can help in the selection of itineraries and air routes, and can make all reservations. Agents usually receive their fees not from their clients, but from commissions paid by the airlines and hotels whose services the clients will be using.

Selecting an Agent
Travel agents are not licensed, so some research will be necessary to determine the competence of a particular agent. Call the local Better Business Bureau, which maintains a complaint file on agents. Check whether the agent belongs to the American Society of Travel Agents, a trade association which maintains a standard of ethics for its members.

Travel Information
Every state has a tourist bureau that publishes an array of free brochures and maps of places worth visiting within its borders. Travel agents usually have many of these, but the complete package can be obtained by writing a letter or postcard to the State Tourist Bureau, in care of the capital of the state to be visited. Ask in particular for information about free activities in that state—including recreational areas, art galleries, museums, and concerts.

Agent Alternatives
If you travel a lot, it may be economical for you to join a club called Travel Masters rather than using an agent. Travel Masters charges a $10 membership fee, and in return it will make all your worldwide airline, hotel, and car-rental reservations. Twice a year, it returns to you at least 50 percent of the commissions it received from the hotels and car rental agencies (It is not allowed to make rebates on airline fares). Generally, being a member of Travel Masters will be worthwhile if you spend over $200 annually on hotel rooms, or over $150 on rental cars each year.

Write Travel Masters, 140 County Road, Tenafly, New Jersey 07670.

Commercial Air Travel

Special Fares

Special fares of all kinds are available to air travelers. Most commercial air carriers offer a variety of discount fares, including night coach, excursion, Discover America, Freedom, family, children's, take-the-wife along, ITX, and APEX. Night coach discounts, for example, are available on planes that depart after 9 p.m., and are usually 20 percent cheaper than standard coach fares. For 7- to 30-day excursion fares, tickets must be purchased at least two weeks before departure. These excursion fares are 15 percent cheaper than standard coach fares, except for children under age 12, who pay 50 percent less.

Avoiding the Crowds

Whenever possible, avoid air travel from Christmas through New Year's, Washington's birthday weekend, and mid-June through Labor Day. Generally, Saturdays are a good day for avoiding the airport crunch. A lunchtime flight is preferable to a morning or evening flight, when businessmen do their traveling.

ITX Fares

Most major commercial airlines now offer "individual tour packages," also called ITX. These plans offer travelers discounts of 25 percent on air fares if they agree to spend a minimum of $65 for on-ground accommodations arranged by the airline, including two nights at a hotel, and either meals, sightseeing, or car rental.

APEX Fares

One of the cheapest ways to fly to Europe on a regularly-scheduled flight of a commercial carrier is via the Advance Purchase Excursion (APEX) fare, which offers savings of 43 percent. APEX requires (1) that reservations be made at least two months before departure, (2) that tickets be paid in full within a week after reservations are made, and (3) that the European visit lasts a minimum of 22 days and a maximum of 45 days. Cancellations or changes in reservations before departure carry with them a penalty fee of $50 or 10 percent of the fare, whichever is more. APEX is only a bargain for those absolutely certain of their dates of departure and return.

Icelandic Discounts

Before committing oneself to a flight to Europe, contact Icelandic Airlines. Icelandic, which never joined the fare-regulating agency, the International Air Transport Association (IATA), charges less than the fixed IATA fares. Depending on the time of year and the time of day, flights cost from 15 to 44 percent less than IATA-approved flights. En route to Europe, all Icelandic flights stop in Reykjavik, the capital of Iceland, and then proceed only to Luxembourg on the European continent. Those who don't mind beginning their European tours in Luxembourg can save money by flying Icelandic.

Fare Confusion

Because of the many and often-confusing special discount fares available, it's not uncommon for agents to mischarge travelers for airline tickets. In 1972, *Consumer Reports'* investigators bought 31 tickets, and were overcharged for 20—at an average overcharge of $12. So take precautions to avoid overcharges. Telephone at least two travel agents and the airline itself for price quotes. If the three quotes aren't identical, ask the airline representative why.

Luggage Problems

If a suitcase is lost or damaged in transit, notify the airline immediately. The airline representative normally will present an official loss or damage form; if he doesn't, request one and fill it out immediately. If the representative asks for the baggage claim ticket, show it but don't relinquish it to anyone until either the bag has been found and is in your possession, or adequate compensation has been made.

Luggage Insurance

Airlines are responsible for up to $750 per bag of lost or damaged luggage. When traveling with luggage whose contents are worth over $750, buy additional insurance from the airline when checking in for the flight. The cost of the extra protection is about 10 cents per $100 worth of insurance, usually up to a limit of $1,500.

Overbooking

When a passenger has a confirmed reservation on a flight, and because the airline has overbooked, he is "bumped" from the flight, the carrier must meet certain responsibilities. Primarily, it must immediately arrange for him to get to his destination as soon as possible. If it is able to get him there no later than two hours after the originally scheduled arrival time, the airline is not liable in any way for the delay and inconvenience. But if he arrives at his destination after the two-hour time limit, the airline must reimburse him the full cost of the ticket, up to a maximum of $200.

Flight Delays

When a flight is delayed more than four hours, the airline is obligated to provide passengers with meals during normal eating hours, plus hotel accommodations during normal sleeping hours. It is also responsible for bearing the expense of cab or bus fares to and from the hotel.

Complaints

Complaints about fares or service provided by airlines are abundant: about 15,000 people file complaints every year with the Civil Aeronautics Board. To file a complaint, write the Office of Consumer Advocate, Civil Aeronautics Board, Washington, D.C. 20428.

Charter Air Travel

Travel Clubs

Travel clubs, a relatively new phenomenon, offer travel packages to members at substantially reduced rates. They arrange charter flights to destinations as diverse as London, Paris, Rome, Copenhagen, Madrid, Zurich, Honolulu, Mexico City, Tokyo, and Tahiti. Hotel provisions, at reduced rates, are often part of the travel package. Discounts at restaurants in destination cities are also sometimes arranged, as are special tours of the cities. Usually these clubs issue monthly newsletters, providing information about upcoming flights and tours far in advance. Some allow payment of travel costs to be extended over a 12-month or 24-month period. Membership fees for these travel clubs average about $20 to $30 a year

OTC's

The "one-stop inclusive tour charter," or OTC, allows people who aren't members of travel clubs to take advantage of considerable savings. Your travel agent probably knows about inexpensive OTC plans in which you can participate. Under the OTC provisions, tickets must be purchased at least 15 days in advance for North American travel, and 30 days in advance for travel to other continents. The OTC plans include hotel reservations and are for minimum stays of four days in North America, and seven days elsewhere.

ABC's

"Advanced booking charters" have only been available since late 1976, but are already attracting a large share of the charter travel. They do not include any land accommodations; the arrangement includes only air travel. Bookings must be made a month ahead, and occasionally 45 days in advance for European destinations. The traveler must stay in Europe for a seven-day minimum, but there is no time requirement for domestic sojourns.

A New York to Athens ABC charter flight cost $499 in 1977; Los Angeles to Hong Kong cost $699. New York to Paris flights cost $329, and New York to Madrid, $339. Some ABC's (like those offered by Nationwide Leisure) provide first class travel for an extra $100—New York to London first class was $389, compared to a commercial flight first-class fare of $1,312.

The Risks of Charters

Although sizable cost reductions are available with charter flights, they also involve risks. Tours can be canceled—often at the last minute—if not enough people sign up. Also, if after paying for the flight, a ticket holder becomes ill and is not able to make the trip, he sometimes must forfeit the entire cost of the ticket. (The amount forfeited is usually based on how soon before departure the cancellation is made.) To protect oneself against having to forfeit a charter fare because of illness, buy a very inexpensive insurance policy designed for this purpose.

Agent's Advice

Arrange charter flights and tours through an experienced travel agent. He will know which tour operators have the best records regarding cancellations of flights. He should also be able to advise as to which tours give the best accommodations for the money.

Commercial Charters

Many charters are booked onto commercial carriers, including TWA, Pan American, and United. Other charter tour operators have their own jets. These special charter-operated planes are often not as comfortable as commercial planes—the rows of seats are frequently closer together, providing two or three less inches of leg room, and a reduced number of stewardesses aboard a charter flight means slower service.

Train Travel

Amtrak Reservations

Except during holiday periods, when travel volume is particularly heavy, Amtrak reservations can be obtained just a few days prior to intended departure dates. Sleeping compartments, however, should be reserved as far in advance as possible.

Rail Pass

Amtrak offers a U.S.A. Rail Pass, which permits unlimited coach travel for all of its own trains (except Metroliners), and all Southern Railways passenger trains. In 1977, the Rail Pass cost $165 for 14 days of travel, $220 for 21 days, and $275 for 30 days. (By comparison, the round-trip Los Angeles-New York fare was $322.)

Special Fares

Amtrak offers various special fares for certain routes at certain times of the week. These include the runs between New York and Florida, Chicago and Florida, Chicago and Minneapolis, New York and Washington, D.C., New Orleans and El Paso, and Seattle and Portland.

European Train Travel

Europe's passenger railroad service is flourishing. One of the best ways to tour the Continent is to buy a Eurailpass, which must be purchased before leaving the United States. These passes are available for two-week or three-week periods, or one-month, two-month, or three-month time spans. Buy the pass which best fits your own needs. A Eurailpass entitles the holder to unlimited first-class riding privileges on Europe's trains. (In summer 1977, a 15-day Eurailpass cost $170, a one-month pass cost $260, and a three-month pass cost $420.)

Night Traveling in Europe

When riding the trains in Europe, travel at night whenever possible. Not only are the trains less crowded during the nighttime hours, but beds for sleeping are usually available at no additional cost.

Eurailpass Fringe Benefits

Eurailpass is useful for more than train travel. It can be used for trips aboard steamers owned by various rail companies (German Federal Railroad and Austrian Railways), and entitles the holder to some free bus transportation. When purchasing a Eurailpass from a travel agent in the United States, ask him for an up-to-date list of the various transportation facilities covered. If he doesn't have such a list, write to Eurailpass, c/o French National Railroad, 610 Fifth Avenue, New York, New York 10020.

Bus Travel

Reservations

For intercity or interstate bus trips, a reservation is usually not a necessity. Even during the months of busiest travel, most bus companies have alternate buses on standby, in case the primary bus becomes filled to capacity.

Special Bus Rates

Many of the major bus lines offer special rates that allow for considerable sightseeing inexpensively. Greyhound has its Ameripass, and Trailways has its Eagle Pass, which allow unlimited travel over a designated period of time. In 1977, both bus lines charged $99 for nine days of unlimited travel, $165 for 15 days, $250 for 30 days, and $350 for 60 days.

Cruises

Bargain Prices

Steamship cruises are expensive, but keep in mind that a single fare includes transportation, sleeping quarters, food, and entertainment. Cruise rates tend to be lowest during the month of December, before Christmas. Lower-deck accommodations are less expensive, as are rooms farther away from midship.

Cruise Considerations

When selecting a cruise, be sure you clearly have the answers to the following questions:
—What is the length of the cruise, and the date of departure?
—What will it cost, and in what ports will it stop?
—What type of cabins are available?
—What is the crew-to-passenger ratio? A 3-to-5 crew-to-passenger ratio is a good figure to use as a guideline.
—Is it possible for you to fly one way and cruise back, if you desire?

Health Care for Travelers

Inoculations

When traveling out of the country and inoculations need to be taken beforehand, take them well before the planned departure date. Adverse reactions are not uncommon, and sufficient time for any necessary recuperation should be allotted.

Foreign Doctors

For information on how to find health care when traveling abroad, obtain a free list of English-speaking foreign doctors from the International Association for Medical Assistance to Travelers, 350 Fifth Avenue, New York, New York 10001. Physicians in 500 cities in 116 countries are included on the list, all of whom have agreed to charge no more than $15 for an office visit, and $20 for a hotel or house call. Without this type of guidance, the traveler often finds himself paying exorbitant fees for overseas health care.

Inexpensive Accommodations

Club Accommodations

Travelers have found that by joining organizations like the International Vacation Club, they have been able to cut motel costs by 50 percent. This club has made arrangements with over 300 hotels and motels in the United States and in foreign countries (including some Holiday Inns and Ramada Inns) to offer its members two nights of accommodations for the price of one. For an annual $25 family membership fee, the club supplies its members with a directory of participating motels and hotels. It is located at 17070 Collins Avenue, North Miami Beach, Florida 33160.

Budget Motels

There are over 1,000 budget motels across the country which, while usually lacking such luxuries as swimming pools and color televisions, are clean, comfortable and inexpensive places to stay. To keep their low rates, many of theses motels do not accept credit cards. The major nationwide chains that fall into the budget-motel category include the Day Inns of America, Imperial 400 National, and Motel 6. Others that are just as economical, but are only regional, are the Downtowner/ Rowntowner Motor Inns, Econo-Travel Motor Hotels, L-K Motel Enterprises, Regal 8 Inns, and Scottish Inns of America.

Youth Hostels

Also inexpensive are the more than 150 youth hostels across the United States. Despite what many people think, it is not only the young who can take advantage of these accommodations. For a fee of $10 (or $5 if you're under 18) one can become a member of American Youth Hostels. Members are entitled to stay in the youth hostels in the United States. The cost per night for these accommodations is between $2 and $5, and stays are limited to a maximum of three nights.

Hostel Regulations

Most hostels have rules that must be adhered to. Alcoholic beverages are usually not allowed on the premises, and smoking is permitted only in designated areas. Although beds are provided, linens are not. Lights are usually turned off at 11 P.M. Men and women usually sleep in separate dorms, although family rooms are available in some hostels. For further information, contact American Youth Hostels, National Campus, Delaplane, Virginia 22025.

Swapping Condominiums

If you own a resort condominium, but would like a change of scenery on your next vacation, consider swapping your condominium for one in a different location for a few weeks. For $12, a brief description of your condominium will be listed in the *Home Exchange Directory* (350 Broadway, New York, New York 10013). Also contact Resort Condominiums International (5638 Professional Circle, Indianapolis, Indiana 46241), which for an annual membership fee of $36 allows you to swap your condo for two weeks a year with any other one in its listings that's available.

Swapping Homes

Swapping homes is as simple as swapping condominiums. All you must do is find a family living in a place you would like to visit, and who would like to spend some time in your area. Several agencies specialize in home swapping. Among them is Vacation Exchange Club, which for a reasonable fee will list your home in its *Home Exchange Directory* (mentioned above), and which will provide you with a copy of the directory which lists those homes that are available for swapping. Other home exchange services include Holiday Home Exchange Bureau (P.O. Box 555, Grants, New Mexico 87020), Adventures-in-Living (P.O. Box 278, Winnetka, Illinois 60093), and Homex Directory Ltd. (P.O. Box 27, London NW6 4HE, England). They all list homes in the United States and throughout the world.

Tipping

Waiters

Waiters and waitresses are tipped an average of 15 percent of the total bill. In elegant restaurants, tips average 20 percent.

Bellhops

The bellhop in a luxury hotel who carries baggage to and from rooms is customarily tipped $1 for a minimal amount of luggage, and more for a larger amount.

Room Service

If room service delivers a meal to your hotel room, a tip of about $1 is appropriate for the waiter who has carried up the food. If he stays and actually serves the food, he should be tipped as a normal waiter—that is, about 15 percent of the price of the meal.

Chambermaids

It is customary to leave—in a sealed envelope marked "Chambermaid"—about 50 cents per day for the hotel maid, particularly if your stay has been for several nights.

Cabana Boys

The cabana boy who brings the towels and beach chairs at a beach resort should be tipped about 50 cents a day for each family member he serves—but no more than $1 per day is necessary.

Taxi Drivers

Taxi drivers should receive a tip of approximately 15 percent of the fare. The hotel doorman who summons the cab should receive a tip, too, of from 25 to 50 cents. Drivers of airport shuttle buses should not be tipped.

Porters

At an airport, the porter who helps you with your luggage should be tipped about 50 cents for a single small suitcase, $1 for two suitcases, and $2 if you have many pieces of luggage.

European Custom

In most parts of Europe, tips are usually included in the bill; additional tipping is generally unnecessary. This applies to hotels as well as restaurants. However, if a waiter has been extemely good, an additional tip of between five and ten percent of the total bill is appropriate.

Traveling with Money

Traveler's Checks

When traveling, carry traveler's checks rather than large amounts of cash. Most traveler's check companies (American Express, Bank of America, Citibank) charge fees of up to one percent of the face value of the checks bought—that is, for $100 worth of traveler's checks, a service fee of $1 is charged. Many savings and loans institutions, however, now issue traveler's checks with no service charge for their patrons. Barclays Bank International also issues traveler's checks without charge.

Besides the safety value, there's an additional advantage to carrying traveler's checks instead of cash. Most European banks will offer better exchange rates for traveler's checks than for cash, simply because these checks are easier and less expensive to process.

Pre-trip Conversion

Travelers to foreign countries may find it convenient to

exchange a little money into foreign currency before leaving the United States. Either a foreign money broker or some banks will be happy to cooperate. But keep in mind that there is often a limit on the amount of foreign currency that can be brought into a country. Check with a travel agent on the current limitations.

Before Returning

Before returning to the United States from a foreign country, either spend or exchange the foreign currency in your possession. Many United States banks won't exchange foreign currency because of the expense, and foreign money brokers may exchange it for less than the going rate.

Luggage

Molded vs. Soft-Sided

When buying suitcases, choose from either molded or soft-sided styles. Molded cases, with rigid shells made of nylon, fiberglass, or thermoplastic, can be treated roughly without much risk of damage, and are easy to clean. Soft-sided suitcases are made of more flexible material—leather, canvas, or olefin—and can easily be stored because of their collapsibility. They weigh less than molded bags, and because of their pliability, new items can easily be "stuffed in."

Skids

Suitcase "skids" (on which the suitcase rests when perched upright) should be riveted tightly to the suitcase frame. The skids will be less likely to fall off, and the suitcase will remain protected from wear.

Handles

When shopping for new luggage, inspect the handles carefully. They should be securely fastened to each suitcase, and preferably, steel cords (or heavy plastic ones) should run through them for extra strength.

Guarantees

Although luggage manufacturers rarely provide warranties on the materials and workmanship of their products, retailers sometimes offer guarantees of their own, particularly if they have repair facilities on their premises. All such guarantees should be in writing.

What to Pack

Most travelers pack suitcases full of unnecessary clothes. To avoid having to lug heavy bags, select only clothes that are appropriate for the climate and the activities to be encountered. Select one or two basic color schemes, and mix-and-match clothes to create various "looks." Bring only items that are easy to care for. Limit the number of heavy items like shoes.

How to Pack

Proper packing eliminates wrinkling of clothes (and will reduce the necessity for dry cleaning services). Pack the bottom layer of the suitcase with clothing that can be folded flat—such as blouses, shirts, dresses, pants, and jackets. Alternate the direction of these clothes so as to evenly distribute the bulk. Heavier items—shoes and toiletries—should be placed on top, with such small, miscellaneous items as underwear and socks tucked into available spaces. Upon arrival at the hotel, unpack everything immediately, and hang up dresses and suits in the closets provided.

Special Packing Items

Glass and other fragile items should not be packed in a suitcase. If they break during a flight, the airline is not liable for them: its insurance does not cover such wares.

RECREATION

Camping

Equipment

When preparing for a first camping experience, buy as little equipment as possible. From this trip, you will discover if camping is indeed an enjoyable form of recreation, and you will learn what types of equipment will best fit your needs. In most areas of the country, there are places to rent all kinds of camping apparatus—from tents to sleeping bags. Many items useful on camping trips can be found in the home—such as old pots and pans, paper plates and cups, a picnic jug, a cooler, and a flashlight.

RV Camping

Camping in a recreational vehicle can be a money-saving experience—unless, of course, that vehicle is an expensive, elaborate motor home, in which case it will take years to recoup the investment. One alternative is to rent an RV (recreational vehicle). In fact, about 35 percent of all the RV's driven on vacation trips are rented. Rentals are frequently listed in newspaper classified sections, as well as in the Yellow Pages under "Motor Homes—Renting & Leasing."

Combining RV's and Flying

For extra-long trips, consider flying to your destination point and renting an RV upon arrival. All arrangements can be made in advance through a national agency, such as Motor Homes Rental Associates, which can be called toll-free at (800) 487-4781.

RV Parking

About 15,000 sites in the United States are designed specifically for the parking of RV's. Many have running water and electrical outlets. Some charge fees ranging from $3 to $15 a night.

Special Outdoor Programs

Golden Eagle Passport

A Golden Eagle Passport card, issued by the United States government, allows the driver of a car and his passengers access to nearly all of the facilities of the National Park Service. These cards are available—for an annual $10 fee—at all national parks and most national forests and post offices. People 62 years of age and older can obtain the cards free of charge.

Outings of All Kinds

Many national groups sponsor their own wilderness and camping outings, usually at nominal costs. The Sierra Club (1050 Mills Tower, 220 Bush Street, San Francisco, California 94104) organizes hiking, backpacking, and horseback riding excursions. So does the Wilderness Society (4260 Evans Avenue, Denver, Colorado 80222). The National Audubon Society (950 Third Avenue, New York, N.Y. 10022) has 60 natural sanctuaries throughout the country, and they are available for camping and picnicking. The Audubon sites charge $3 per day (tax deductible) for adults, and children under 12 go free.

Rafting

Rafting has become an increasingly popular recreational activity on dozens of North American rivers. More than 100 commercial rafting companies sponsor rafting trips ranging from a few hours to 17 days, with prices from $10 to $750 per person. For information on commercial rafting trips, contact: The National Park Service, Department of the Interior, Washington, D.C. 20240; the U.S. Forest Service, Department of Agriculture, Washington, D.C. 20250; or the Western River Guides' Association, 994 Denver Street, Salt Lake City, Utah 84111.

Houseboating

Does renting a houseboat and floating it down a river like the Mississippi sound appealing? Well, many people are doing it, and considering that most rented houseboats sleep eight people, the cost—when split among three families—is not particularly high. One can float along the upper Mississippi for a week, on a houseboat equipped with furniture, beds, carpets, sundecks and even a stereo, for under $500. Houseboats are available for rent along most major inland waterways. For more information on where to rent one, pick up a copy of *Family Houseboating* magazine, 23945 Craftsman Road, Calabasas, California 91302.

Sailing

Purchasing Sailboats

Buying a sailboat can be an expensive venture. Small sailboats, designed for only a few hours of sailing at a time, cost from $1,000 (for an ultralight 14-foot model) to over $4,000 for boats designed to hold three people. Cruisers, which range from 21 to 26 feet in length and sleep up to five people, range in price from $4,500 to $10,000. To these costs should be added the prices of other necessary items: An outboard motor ($500 to $1,000), a boat trailer (as much as $1,700), and such safety equipment as anchors and fire extinguishers (as much as $500).

Used Boats

Used boats can often be found for bargain prices—but shop carefully. Closely examine a boat with a fiberglass hull to determine if the craft has any structural damage. A wooden boat is more difficult to inspect. In fact, it's best to have an experienced marine surveyor check the boat, looking for dry rot and other problems. He will charge from $100 to $150 to inspect a small boat.

Learning to Sail

Before sailing on his or her own, the beginner should enroll in a brief course on how to use and enjoy a boat. Most courses last from two to five days, and cost from $95 to $200 per person. Family rates are also available, at discounts of up to 50 percent per family member.

Skiing

Ski Lessons

New skiers suffer 55 percent of all the injuries on the slopes, although they represent just 21 percent of all skiers. Most experts say that a minimum of five lessons is essential for the beginning skier.

Ski Boots

Don't wear the ski boots of a friend, unless he or she has a foot size identical to yours. Boots that are too tight impede circulation, which makes one vulnerable to frostbite. By contrast, boots that are too large limit the skier's control and maneuverability.

Time to Buy

The best month to purchase ski equipment is March. More bargains are available then than at any other time of the year.

Cross-Country Skiing

Cross-country skiing (or ski touring) is gaining more popularity each winter. Unlike downhill skiing, it is usually done on level ground, and is comparable to walking with skis. Neither many lessons nor much equipment is needed to participate safely.

Cross-Country Clubs

Cross-country skiing clubs are forming throughout the nation, and any good ski shop will gladly make referrals. Another source of referrals is the *Ski Touring Guide,* which can be purchased for $2 from the Ski Touring Council, West Hill Road, Troy, Vermont 05868.

Fishing Tackle

Surf Fishing Rods

When shopping for surf fishing tackle, be certain to check features like the cranking action of a rod.

It should move smoothly, and the line retrieval should be at least 25 to 30 inches per crank turn. With the rod itself, the longer it is, the greater the casting potential. Also, the ferrules (the joints that connect the rod sections) should be secure. There should be at least four guides on an average-sized (nine-foot) rod, and at least five on a longer rod.

In the surf fishing category, *Consumer Reports* has consistently given high marks to rods manufactured by Browning, Penn, South Bend, and Sears.

Fly Fishing Rods

When buying a fly fishing rod for the first time, start out with a medium-priced, level line until you are comfortable with this more difficult type of fishing. When you become proficient and at ease with this sport, then you can move up to a double-tapered model, which costs about three times as much.

Consider a more expensive rod initially only if the store owner offers you the right to return it. You can only really judge how it feels by casting it. More than with surf fishing tackle, a personal test is extremely important with fly fishing rods.

Some of the best buys in fly fishing rods are manufactured by Browning, Garcia, Orvis, and Phillipson.

Binoculars

How Expensive

There's no need to buy the most expensive pair of binoculars for non-professional, recreational purposes. Using binoculars at football games or concerts requires no more than an inexpensive pair. A good, adequate pair should cost no more than $130; some can be bought for as little as $70.

Judging Quality

When shopping for a pair of binoculars, take the one you're considering to a nearby window, preferably on the second floor where you can see for long distances. Test it for the following features.

—Is it easy to focus, or does it take more than the few seconds it should require?

—Are the eyecups comfortable?

—Does it come with a cover to protect the lenses from scratching?

—Is it lightweight?

—Are you satisfied with its power?

Brands

There are many manufacturers of good quality binoculars. However, pay particular attention to the following brand names, renowned for their excellent, reasonably-priced models: Bushnell, Tasco, Binolux, Fujica, Kalimar, Mayflower, and Yashica.

Playground Sets

Selecting a Set

Backyard playground sets are rising in price (well over $100 for an elaborate set), but quality is often uneven unless you choose carefully. With slides, swings, and other similar equipment, you get what you pay for. Although some sets may seem like bargains, they may start rusting almost immediately, and will soon be bent out of shape after heavy use. Be sure to choose a sturdy, durable set.

Safety

To minimize bumps, bruises, and broken bones, keep these safety tips in mind when shopping for playground equipment:

—The swing seats should be made of plastic, to reduce injury if they strike a child.

—All screws and bolts that could scratch or cut should be covered with a plastic cap.

—Ladder rungs should have ridged or embossed surfaces to prevent slipping.

—Trapeze rings should be more than 10 inches in diameter, or less than five. Any size in between could trap a child's head if he should slip it through the ring.

Bicycling

Selecting a Bicycle

Occasional bike riders need not invest in an expensive 10-speed bike. Instead, consider buying a "touring bicycle"—a three-speed model which will be perfectly adequate but will cost as much as $50 less than a good 10-speed model. When in the market for a 10-speed bicycle, count on spending well over $100 for a good-quality machine.

The Proper Size

A bicycle must be bought to "fit the body." The perfect bike frame will measure 9 to 10 inches less than the rider's inseam (from crotch to floor in stocking feet). Thus, when the rider straddles a closed-frame model (a men's bike), the horizontal top tube should be about an inch below the crotch when his feet are flat on the pavement.

Used Bicycles

Used bicycles in good condition are often advertised in the newspaper classified pages. Save 25 to 50 percent by purchasing a used bicycle.

Tire Inflation

Always keep bicycle tires inflated to the proper level. Correct tire pressure is indicated by raised letters on the tire itself. Periodically check the tires for bald spots.

Night Riding

When riding at dusk or at night, be sure the bicycle lights

and reflectors are functioning. Headlights should be visible from 500 feet away, and reflectors from 600.

Cleaning

A bicycle should be thoroughly cleaned at least once a year, and more often when used year-round. To clean, wipe the bike with a damp cloth, and remove mud from the wheels, chain, and frame. Then lubricate the chain with a thin coat of household oil. To keep the paint protected, apply a coat of car wax to the fenders.

Wheel Alignment

Periodically turn the bike upside down, and spin the wheels. If they wobble, they need to be aligned. At the same time, tighten and/or adjust all loose parts.

Locks

The best type of bicycle lock is a thick aircraft-type cable (at least 7/16" thick) or a heavy chain that is case-hardened, coupled with a lock with a hardened shackle. Buy a cable or chain with a plastic wrapper to prevent scratching up the bike itself. The lock should have a shackle ⅜" in diameter. The cost of both lock and chain will be between $10 and $15.

Insurance

It's wise to insure one's bicycle. Some homeowners policies cover bicycles, but if those policies have $100 deductibles, little or no reimbursement may be forthcoming if the bike is stolen. It is possible to have a clause attached to the policy, insuring the bike for its full worth. Inexpensive bicycle insurance is also available through many bike shops. The policies are offered by the National Bicycle Dealers Association. For more information, write directly to the association at 29025 Euclid Avenue, Wickliffe, Ohio 44092.

Motorcycling

Motorcycle Sizes

Small motorcycles (55cc models) are usually adequate for local recreational trips. A bigger motorcycle, though, is needed by those who frequently carry passengers or who must often negotiate hills. Medium-sized motorcycles (250 to 350cc) will fill almost all needs.

Operating Costs

The operating costs of a motorcycle are half that of an

automobile. And small motorcycles are more economical than their larger counterparts. Lightweight cycles with engines under 100cc usually get more than 100 miles per gallon. By comparison, a heavy 600cc bike will get roughly 50 miles per gallon.

Safety

Fatal motorcycle accidents occur more frequently per mile driven than fatal auto crashes. When buying a new motorcycle, take it to a vacant lot or some other area away from cars and people, and become familiar with the machine. An emergency situation is not the time to learn how to brake or how to use the clutch properly.

CB Radios

Cost and Performance

The Citizens Band two-way radio has become a popular recreational item. It can be installed almost anywhere—at home or work, in a car or boat. A basic CB set is available for as little as $150 to $175. But to talk over distances greater than 150 miles, an antenna will be needed.

There are 40 CB radio channels that have been made available by the FCC, two of which are not for public use. Channel 9 is for emergency calls. Channel 11 is for establishing communication, but once contact has been made, the operator must switch to another channel. While driving, keep the CB tuned to channels 10 or 19; these are the frequencies used by truckers, who keep each other informed of various road hazards and speed traps.

Licenses

Although licenses are needed to operate CB radios, they are simple to obtain. Just fill out an application available at any CB retailer, and mail it to the Federal Communications Commission, Gettysburg, Pennsylvania 17325. No fee is required; application processing takes from 2½ to 3 months. Operating a CB set without a license can result in a fine of up to $10,000.

Books and Book Collecting

What's Valuable

Most people enjoy recreational reading, and some like holding onto the books they've read, particularly if they have some monetary worth. Books of particular value these days include Americana items at least a century old, like state, county, and local histories, almanacs, and atlases. Other valuable books are scarce editions by various 20th-century authors—like Steinbeck, Hemingway, Faulkner, and O'Neill.

The Book's Condition

The better a book's condition, the more it is worth. A book soiled or damaged may not have any value to collectors, even though it might have been worth a lot were it in mint condition. Also, if a book is part of a set (like an encyclopedia), it will have only limited value unless all volumes are intact.

Pinpointing Value

To determine what value a book may have, consult a reference source called *American Book-Prices Current* at the public library. This volume, issued annually, lists how much books have sold for at auction recently (The first edition of *Canterbury Tales* is worth $200,000; an 1827 edition of Poe's *Tamerlane and other Poems* is priced at $100,000).

For additional information on collecting books, read: *The New Gold in Your Attic,* by Van Allen Bradley (Arco); and *The Book Collector's Handbook of Values,* also by Van Allen Bradley (G.P. Putnam's Sons).

Golfing

The Traveling Golfer

Those who vacation frequently and are lovers of golf can join Golf Card International (1625 Foothill Drive, P.O. Box 8339, Salt Lake City, Utah 84108). An annual membership fee of $35 entitles one to play up to two rounds a year at each of the 150 courses in the United States, Mexico, and the Bahamas that have a working relationship with the organization.

Vacationing at Home

Inexpensive Fun

Family fun does not have to be expensive. Free or low-cost entertainment and recreation are available in every community. Local newspapers often list community attractions and events that cost little or nothing. Libraries and chambers of commerce can also usually provide such information.

Swimming

For organized recreational and competitive swimming, consider turning to the Amateur Athletic Union's Masters Swimming Programs. These programs, operating in cities in all parts of the country, are open to everyone over the age of 25. More information about the program can be obtained from June Krauser, 2308 N.E. 19th Avenue, Fort Lauderdale, Florida 33305.

Summer Camps

Specialty Camps

Parents who have children interested in attending summer camps have more to choose from than ever before. In addition to the conventional camps that offer everything from swimming to hiking to horseback riding, there are specialty camps catering to specific sports (baseball, football, gymnastics), to specific arts (music, dance, drama), or to a particular need (weight reducing). First-time campers and younger children generally enjoy the all-purpose camps most, which provide exposure to a wide variety of activities.

Visiting a Camp

Before parent and child decide on a particular summer camp, they should personally visit it. Meet the camp director, and ask him about his qualifications and experience. The ideal director will have at least two years of administrative experience, and will have completed relevant training programs. Ask, too, about the qualifications of the counselors. They should be at least 18 or 19 years old. In overnight camps, no camp counselor should be responsible for more than eight children. In day camps, the ratio of campers to counselors should be no higher than ten to one. Make sure that this ratio includes only counselors, not other camp employees.

Camp Location and Facilities

When choosing a camp, be sure that it is safely removed from highways and local industry. Camp buildings should be well constructed and cared for. If sleeping facilities are not all on ground level, check for adequate fire escapes. Swimming areas should be roped off, and lifesaving equipment should be visible nearby. Eating facilities should be sanitary and the meals well planned. Check that camp medical facilities are adequate, and that a registered nurse is always in residence and a doctor always on call.

Additional Camp Information

For the names of camps in your area, write to the Advisory Council for Camps, 400 Madison Avenue, New York, N.Y. 10017. Or read *Parents Guide to Accredited Camps,* published by the American Camping Association, Bradford Woods, Martinsville, Indiana 46151 (cost—$2.40).

CHAPTER 14

Retirement

There are now more than 27 million retired Americans—and their ranks are growing each year. Most of them probably wish they had prepared a little (or a lot) better for retirement.

Not surprisingly, to the typical individual in his twenties, thirties, and even forties, retirement is of small concern. After all, he has a family to feed, clothing to buy, mortgage payments to make, and college educations to finance. Everyday living is difficult enough; retirement seems too distant to even think about. Not true: it is never too early to begin planning for retirement.

About 25 percent of all elderly Americans live in poverty. And that percentage is growing. For many of these poor senior citizens, their tragic financial plight is beyond their control; but for others, some forethought could have prevented the sad situation in which they find themselves.

Retirement should be of greater concern to us than it was to our ancestors. Improved diets and medical advances have extended our expected life spans. This, coupled with the trend toward earlier retirement, leads most of us to expect many more retirement years than our fathers did. According to U.S. government statistics, a man of age 65 can anticipate living an average of 15.9 additional years. A woman of 65 can expect another 19.11 years of life.

During the retirement years, the typical American's income is about half what he was earning while working. Fortunately for them, most retirees have already paid for their homes, the college educations of their children, and their life insurance policies. Also, their clothing expenses are reduced, their medical care costs are usually less (thanks largely to Medicare), and there are various senior citizen tax breaks of which they can take advantage. Even food costs are likely to be lower, since the daily caloric requirement of the elderly is less than that of the young.

There are many steps people can take in their younger years to make their retirement as pleasant as possible. They should learn, for example, exactly where they stand—in terms of future benefits—with Social Security. Since 1935, the government has been paying retirement benefits to Americans under the Social Security Act. But unfortunately, the benefits which are paid are never enough to fully support a retired individual adequately.

The Medicare program, also designed for senior citizens, is essentially a federal health insurance plan for persons 65 and older. During fiscal 1977, the cost of the program was $22 billion. Even so, 12 million elderly people carry some additional private health insurance. A government study shows that Medicare alone pays only about 72 percent of all hospital costs for individuals 65 and over, and even less—54 percent—of their doctor's bills.

Certainly retirement is not something to be left until you're there—that is, unless you're willing to risk making those later years your most miserable ones.

RETIREMENT LIVING EXPENSES

How Much to Live

According to experts, for retirees to maintain the lifestyle they enjoyed while working, their income must be 60 to 70 percent of what it was while working. If the retired person is very thrifty, he might get by on 50 percent. However, these figures should only serve as guides. They will vary according to where one lives, conditions of health, and the prevailing rate of inflation.

Estimating Retirement Expenses

When approaching retirement age, it would be a good idea to chart expenses for several months to obtain a complete picture of how you spend your money. Because during retirement you'll probably be living on less income, try to determine how expenses can be reduced. In fact, it might be interesting to try living for a month on the income you can expect upon retirement.

Sources of Retirement Income

Part-Time Work

Many people continue working part-time once they reach retirement age. For some, it's a way of remaining active. For others, the added income eases any existing strain on their budgets. The retiree's income, however, should not be so large as to necessitate forfeiture of all or part of his Social Security benefits (See the section of Social Security later in this chapter).

Typical Retirement Income

Want to compare your own probable sources of post-retirement income with those of other Americans? Examine the following statistics. The figures below show that the typical retirement budget draws upon not just one or two sources for income, but several. As is evident, these percentages (provided by the Social Security Administration) indicate that work is the largest source of income in the budget of the average American 65 and over:

Earnings from work............................30%
Social Security..................................26%
Earnings on investments
    and savings 25%
Miscellaneous public pensions 6%
Private pensions 5%
Veterans benefits................................3%
Public assistance................................3%
Other sources...................................2%

INVESTING FOR THE FUTURE

Secure Investments

Money that is depended on for retirement should be placed in an insured savings account, or invested in top-quality blue-chip stocks, or some other secure place. It is foolish to speculate with the money that is being set aside to provide the necessities of later life.

How Much Can Be Accumulated

No later than the middle years, begin accumulating money for retirement. The following chart indicates the amount of capital that can be saved by age 65 if regular deposits are made in a savings account paying 5¼ percent interest, compounded daily:

Present Age	$50 monthly	$100 monthly	$200 monthly
45	$21,277.28	$42,554.56	$85,109.12
50	13,720.40	27,440.80	54,881.60
55	7,908.30	15,816.60	31,633.20
60	3,438.12	6,876.24	13,752.48

How long will savings last once regular withdrawals are made from it? Here are some examples: If you have $35,000 in a savings account earning seven percent annual interest, and you withdraw $5,000 a year, the money will last 17 years. If you withdraw only $2,800 a year, the money will last 30 years. Now, let's assume, you are only able to earn six percent interest, and your savings account totals $50,000. If you withdraw $5,000 a year, the money will last 15 years; but by decreasing withdrawals to $3,500 a year, the money will last 33 years.

Company Pension Plans

Analyzing Benefits

If the company an individual works for sponsors a pension or profit-sharing plan that will provide retirement benefits, he should find out now how much he can expect to receive. Will it pay a specified percentage of the salary earned before retirement? Will a lump sum payment be received, or monthly checks? Upon his death, whether before or after retirement, will his spouse receive any benefits?

Past Employment

Even when an individual has changed jobs frequently during his working life, he might still be entitled to partial pensions from the various companies for whom he has worked. When leaving a job, he should find out exactly how that firm's pension plan reads. It may provide for a single lump-sum payment upon termination of employment, or it may stipulate that monthly payments will be awarded upon retirement.

The Keogh Plan

Plan for the Self-Employed

The Keogh Plan, established by an act of Congress and named after the legislator who proposed it, allows self-employed persons to create their own retirement plan, with accompanying income tax benefits. The plan allows an individual to place as much as 15 percent of his income, but no more than $7,500 per year, in a retirement fund. No matter how low his income, the individual may deposit at least $750 in the fund per year.

Who Qualifies?

According to the Keogh Plan's provisions, an individual is considered "self-employed" and thus eligible for the program if he is compensated for personal services. Generally, if the individual files schedules C or F with his income tax return, or pays self-employment Social Security tax, he qualifies for the plan. Self-employed individuals include small businessmen, physicians, dentists, lawyers, grocers, accountants, actors, writers, artists, farmers, gardeners, architects, and ministers.

Moonlighting

If one is self-employed on only a part-time basis, in addition to holding a full-time job as an employee of someone else, he may still set up a Keogh Plan with the income received from his moonlighting. This is the case even if his regular job already provides a pension plan. So if he is a part-time free-lance writer, or an after-hours accountant, he can establish a Keogh Plan with his extra earnings.

How Much

The following chart illustrates how $3,750 deposited each year into a Keogh Plan will grow in a savings account that annually earns 7½ percent compounded interest.

After		
	5 years	$ 23,612.76
	10 years	57,967.79
	15 years	107,952.09
	20 years	180,676.00
	25 years	286,484.52

Individual Retirement Accounts

IRA Eligibility

Those employed by companies that do not sponsor pension plans can establish an Individual Retirement Account (IRA) of their own. A person can deposit $1,500 or 15 percent of his salary (whichever is less) annually into a personal IRA account. Working couples may maintain separate IRA's; thus, they can jointly set aside a maximum of $3,000 per year.

Transfering Funds into IRA

If an individual is a member of a company-sponsored pension plan, and the company terminates the plan, or if the individual finds employment elsewhere, he can take the lump-sum pension benefit to which he's entitled and deposit it into an IRA. If this IRA is established within 60 days of receiving the money, no taxes on the funds will be due until retirement.

How Much

The chart below shows how much can be accumulated in an IRA if $1,500 is contributed each year, and earns a compounded interest rate of 7.5 percent annually:

After		
	5 years	$ 9,425
	10 years	23,090
	15 years	42,904
	20 years	71,633
	25 years	113,289

Common Features of Keoghs and IRA's

Deductible Contributions

Contributions to both Keogh Plans and IRA's are fully

deductible from the gross income figure for federal income tax purposes. These deductions can be made even if deductions are not itemized.

Establishing the Program

The simplest way to establish a Keogh Plan or an IRA is to place one's money in a standardized program offered by a bank, savings and loan, or a mutual fund, or to buy Government Retirement Bonds. In all of these programs, the paperwork is minimal. There are other ways to establish a personal retirement plan (trusts, for example), but all personalized plans must receive IRS approval. For details on setting up more individualized programs, contact the IRS.

Where to Invest

When deciding where to place retirement funds, consider the service charges involved. Most banks and savings and loan institutions charge only a nominal $5 to $10 custodial fee. Mutual funds will usually charge a much larger seven to nine percent sales commission. By contrast, retirement bonds can be purchased with no added charge.

Government Retirement Bonds are designed specifically for personal pension plans. They currently pay six percent interest compounded every six months, are available in $50, $100, and $500 denominations, and can be purchased from Federal Reserve Banks, the U.S. Treasury, and many savings institutions.

Switching Investment Sites

A Keogh Plan or IRA may be switched from one type of investment program to another—for example, from a savings account to a mutual fund. But after one change has been made, future changes can be made only once every three years.

Tax Deferments

No income tax is paid on the money accumulating in a Keogh Plan or IRA as long as it remains in the fund. At age 59½ or thereafter, the individual may withdraw the money in one lump sum, or can elect to receive partial payments from the plan at various intervals over the years. These amounts are taxed in the year or years they are withdrawn. Because withdrawal will likely occur after retirement, and because the tax bracket of a retiree is usually lower than it was when he made the contributions, less taxes will be paid.

Early Withdrawal

Money can be withdrawn early from a Keogh Plan or an

IRA, but a penalty is imposed for anything removed from the account before age 59½. Both ordinary income tax and a federal penalty tax equal to 10 percent of the amount withdrawn must be paid on all monies taken out before age 59½.

Non-Penalty Withdrawals

Under federal law, an individual can gain access to the funds in a Keogh or an IRA before age 59½ *without* penalty if he becomes permanently disabled. Also, at the time of death (regardless of age), the money in his account is paid to the named beneficiary. It will be subject to estate tax, but not income tax.

Annuities

Lifetime Benefits

One way to provide a regular income upon retirement is to buy a *straight life annuity*, which is sold by insurance companies and which guarantees a fixed amount of income to the buyer each month for the duration of his life. For a lump sum premium of about $12,000, a man of 65 can buy a straight life annuity that will pay him $100 a month until his death—whether that is one month or 50 or more years hence. However, upon his death, his survivors receive nothing. (Because a woman's life expectancy is higher, she will pay more for the same $100-a-month straight life annuity—probably about $13,000 at age 65.)

Installment Annuities

Some people prefer to buy *installment annuities*, which usually cost slightly more than straight life annuities, but which guarantee a minimum number of payments—that is, a payment every month for 10 years. Under this plan, the individual receives monthly payments for the duration of his life; if he dies within 10 years after purchasing the annuity, his survivors receive the payments for the remainder of the guaranteed time period.

Drawback

A major drawback of the annuities program is that the amount received each month remains constant, with no adjustment for cost-of-living increases. Because of inflation, the $100 a month received at age 70 will be worth less than the $100 received at age 65. To circumvent this problem, buy a *cost-of-living annuity* from an insurance agent. This kind of annuity, which costs more than a regular annuity, adds three percent to the payments each year.

When to Avoid Annuities

People in poor health should not buy annuities for themselves, particularly ones that do not provide for payments to dependents in case of death. Actually, many insurance companies will not sell an annuity to an individual in ill health—and not because doing so would be less than profitable. These insurers are well aware that a sale under such circumstances might someday result in a lawsuit, based on the premise that the annuity was not in the best interest of the buyer.

Even individuals in good health should not purchase annuities if they seek a substantial return on their investment. Although annuities can provide a secure lifetime income, better growth can be achieved on one's money invested elsewhere.

SOCIAL SECURITY BENEFITS
Receiving Funds
Applying for Benefits

To collect Social Security benefits, an application must be filed. Remember that the government in no way reminds us when we are entitled to these benefits. Contact the local Social Security office for the proper forms as early as three months prior to retirement. It normally takes three to six weeks for the Social Security Administration to process all necessary papers.

Meeting Basic Needs

Although Social Security benefits are intended to be adequate to maintain a minimal standard of living, most recipients find that this money does not even provide for the basics— housing, food, and clothing. So despite the fact that Social Security benefits rise periodically with increases in the cost of living, most retirees find that they must rely on other sources of income as well.

Calculating Benefits

The amount of Social Security benefits paid to an individual is calculated via a formula that, among other things, averages his total wages subject to Social Security taxes during a specific time period. He will obtain maximum benefits if he earned the maximum amount subject to Social Security taxes during the entire period in which his earnings are averaged. To determine what your retirement benefits will be, contact the local Social Security office, which will supply you with a booklet, *Estimating Your Social Security Retirement Check*. This booklet will explain the way to calculate the amount of benefits you can expect.

Should You Retire Early?

Reduced Monthly Checks

An individual can choose to retire at age 62 rather than 65, and begin collecting Social Security retirement benefits then. But by doing so, his monthly checks will not equal the amount that would be received beginning at age 65; it will be 80 percent of that amount. If he retires at age 63, the benefits will rise to 86.67 percent of the full amount he'd be entitled to at 65. And if he retires at 64, he'll receive 93.33 percent.

Is Early Retirement Sensible?

Does it pay to retire at age 62 instead of 65, in terms of the Social Security benefits received? Estimates are that if an individual retires with full benefits at age 65, he would have to reach age 77 to be paid the same amount of money that he would receive by retiring at age 62. Thus, if you live beyond age 77, it would be advantageous from a monetary point of view to retire at 65. Of course, none of us can predict our life span. But even if we could, we must also consider other factors like the pleasure that might be received from three additional years of retirement. Even if an individual somehow knew he would live to be 100, he still might decide to retire at age 62 to enjoy three more years of retirement.

Should You Retire Late?

The Right to Delay Benefits

If there's no mandatory retirement age of 65 at your place of work, or if you can find full-time after-65 employment elsewhere, you can continue working and postpone drawing your Social Security benefits. The right to eventually claim benefits is not forfeited by delaying retirement.

If you postpone retirement until after age 65, you'll be rewarded with slightly higher Social Security benefits when you begin drawing them. Benefits will be one-twelfth of one percent higher for every month after 65 that retirement is delayed—or one percent higher per year. Thus, if an individual retires at age 68, he will receive benefits three percent higher than he would have obtained had he retired at 65.

Working and Social Security

Reduced Benefits

Once a retiree begins receiving Social Security benefits, he is allowed to acquire any amount of money from sources other than work (such as investments) without losing any benefits.

However, if he works part-time, and the earnings from that job exceed a certain amount, his Social Security benefits will decrease. The maximum amount of money that can be earned from working—while still allowing the full Social Security income to be retained—is clearly defined by law. Before reaching age 72, an individual is permitted to earn up to $2,760 annually without forfeiting any of his Social Security benefits. Above $2,760, $1 of Social Security funds is forfeited for every $2 earned working.

After 72

If an individual is still working at age 72, he is entitled to receive *full* Social Security benefits, no matter how much he earns on the job. Benefits will no longer be reduced in any way because of employment.

Benefits for Spouses

Amount of Benefits

A wife is entitled to a Social Security check equal to 50 percent of her husband's when she reaches 65—or she can receive a lower benefit if she chooses to take it at age 62. So if both husband and wife are 65, and the husband's benefits amount to $320 a month, the wife will receive an additional $160 in benefits of her own.

Divorcees or Widows

A divorced woman is eligible for Social Security retirement benefits based on her former husband's earnings—if their marriage lasted a minimum of 20 years. A widow is entitled to benefits, too, beginning as early as age 60 if she desires. She will receive 71½ percent of her late husband's basic benefit if she begins drawing the money at age 60, 82½ percent if she starts at age 62, and 100 percent at age 65 (provided neither he nor she ever drew benefits before).

Dual Benefits

If an individual is entitled to dual benefits, he (or she) can't receive both. For instance, if a wife is eligible for Social Security payments based on her own work record as well as her husband's, she can obtain only one—normally whichever is higher.

Receiving Your Checks

Protecting Against Theft

Particularly in high-crime communities, the theft of Social

Security checks from mailboxes is increasing. Some recipients have been robbed after cashing their checks. To alleviate these problems, the Social Security Administration can now mail checks directly to banks or savings and loans, which immediately deposit them in the appropriate accounts. The individual needs only to withdraw funds as he requires them, and thus can avoid carrying large amounts of cash. To arrange for checks to be handled this way, fill out the proper forms available at a bank or savings and loan.

MEDICARE

Who Qualifies?

Nearly everyone age 65 or older, retired or not, qualifies for the Medicare program of the Social Security Administration. It is a two-part program: Part A provides hospital insurance to all those in the program; Part B is a voluntary medical insurance plan.

Part A of Medicare

Coverage

Part A covers the following hospital costs: a semiprivate room, operating room expenses, X-rays, regular nursing services (including intensive care), and the use of such devices as wheelchairs and braces.

Medicare benefits under Part A extend to general hospitals, to tuberculosis hospitals, and Christian Science sanatoriums. Care in psychiatric hospitals is covered, too, although for a maximum of 190 days in a lifetime.

Uncovered Expenses

Don't expect Part A to cover *all* hospital expenses. A private telephone, television, or radio must be paid for by the patient. Private nurses' and doctors' services also are not covered. Neither is a private hospital room, unless the doctor considers it to be "medically necessary."

Deductible

Be aware that Part A requires payment of a $104 deductible per illness (or benefit period). It will pay all covered expenses over that amount in full—up to a maximum of 60 days. If a hospital stay lasts more than 60 days, the patient is required to begin paying part of the bill. From the 61st through the 90th day, he must pay $26 a day; Medicare will pay the balance. After that, there is a "Lifetime Reserve" from which the patient can draw, for a maximum of 60 additional days. When using this Lifetime Reserve, the patient's share of the charges will rise to $52 a day.

Nursing Homes

If the patient enters a skilled nursing home or convalescent hospital after being discharged from the hospital, Part A will pay most of his expenses for 100 days in the facility. It will cover the entire cost of the first 20 days there. During the next 80 days, he is required to pay $13 per day; Medicare pays the remainder.

Part B of Medicare

Voluntary Protection

Part B of Medicare—which pays doctors' fees and other bills for medical services (see below)—is completely voluntary. To take advantage of it, an individual must enroll in the program and pay monthly premiums of $7.20 a month (There are no premiums for Part A).

Prompt Enrollment

If an individual intends to join Part B, he shouldn't procrastinate. Those who wait more than one year after reaching age 65 to enroll in the program are charged a 10 percent higher premium. Those who haven't applied for the coverage by age 68 are no longer eligible to obtain the insurance.

Coverage

Part B provides coverage at a lower premium cost than is available in the commercial insurance marketplace. For that reason, everyone should seriously consider signing up for it. Part B covers medical and surgical bills, whether one is treated by a doctor in a hospital, a clinic, a doctor's office, or a nursing home. It also pays for various outpatient and supplementary services and supplies, including ambulances, emergency room care, diagnostic tests, surgical dressings and splints, pacemakers, and artificial limbs and eyes.

Extra Expenses

With Part B, be prepared to pay some expenses out-of-pocket, aside from the $7.20 a month premium. Each calendar year, a $60 deductible must be paid. Thereafter, Medicare pays 80 percent of all covered expenses; the patient pays the remaining 20 percent. So, for instance, if in a single year, your covered medical bills total $1,000, you will pay the initial $60 deductible, Medicare will pay $752 (80 percent) of the remainder, and you will be responsible for paying the balance of $188 (20 percent).

Uncovered Costs

Keep in mind that various types of medical care are *not* covered by Part B. These include drugs administered to oneself, even if prescribed by a doctor. Also not covered are routine physical exams; routine dental care; examination for and purchase of eyeglasses, hearing aids and false teeth; and cosmetic surgery.

General Medicare Tips

Billing Procedure

Ask your personal physician if he bills Medicare directly (for services covered by Part B), or if he sends the bill to his patients. Under the former arrangement, Medicare mails payment to the doctor; under the latter, the patient pays the doctor and is reimbursed by Medicare. It is to the patient's advantage if the doctor bills Medicare directly. First, it eliminates the patient having to come up with the funds to pay the doctor in full, while waiting to recoup the money from Medicare. And second, when a doctor bills the patient, he may charge whatever fee he chooses, which is often higher than the maximum that Medicare will reimburse the patient.

Correcting Errors

Both computers and people make mistakes. If you think Medicare hasn't paid out all the benefits to which you're entitled, file an appeal. You can fill out the proper forms at the local Social Security office, and if you want quick action, send a copy of the appeal to your Congressman, who will stamp it "C.I." (Congressional Inquiry) and forward it to the Social Security appeal board. The appeal will probably be handled more swiftly that way.

Supplemental Medical Insurance

What to Look For

Because Medicare does not provide complete coverage, most elderly Americans are continually looking for ways to pay their out-of-pocket expenses. Those who don't have a savings account to fall back on often seek supplemental commercial insurance coverage. When shopping for this extra coverage, look for a policy that covers the following:

—The initial deductibles of Parts A and B—$104 and $60, respectively.

—The $26 per day that must be paid in Part A for the 61st through 90th day of a hospital stay, and the $52 a day thereafter

—The 20 percent of all bills for which the patient is responsible in Part B.

—Exclusions of Parts A and B, such as out-of-hospital prescription drugs, private-duty nurses, routine physical examinations, etc.

Continuing Present Coverage

Before reaching age 65, check with the health insurance carrier at your place of employment to see if your current coverage can be altered after retirement to fill in the Medicare loopholes. If the same policy can be continued, you will avoid having to undergo a new waiting period that's stipulated in most commercial policies. The protection provided by a converted policy of this kind is usually better than anything available on the open market.

Wrap-Around Policies

If the insurance policy that protected you during your working years cannot be converted, look for other types of coverage to supplement Medicare. Seek a so-called "wrap-around" policy—a plan offered by Blue Cross, Blue Shield, and several commercial insurers, including Continental Casualty, Mutual of Omaha, Physicians Mutual, and Colonial Penn Franklin. The cost of these policies is $15 to $20 per month beginning at age 65.

Other Sources of Coverage

Supplemental Medicare policies are also offered by several senior citizens organizations, including the American Association of Retired Persons (1909 K Street, N.W., Washington, D.C. 20049), the National Council of Senior Citizens, Inc. (1511 K Street, N.W., Washington, D.C. 20005), and Senior Advocates International, Inc. (801 Ernston Road, South Amboy, New Jersey 08879). These same organizations sponsor mail-order drug programs, which usually sell prescription drugs cheaper than they can be bought in most pharmacies.

Avoid Duplication

Avoid buying a supplemental commercial policy that merely duplicates Medicare coverage, or provides protection against highly unlikely eventualities. One mail-order policy recently on the market was advertised as a Medicare supplemental policy "paying up to $50,000." However, the only benefits that the policy offered during the initial 60 days of hospitalization were three pints of blood, if needed. More substantial benefits began only after the 60th consecutive day of hospitalization. Inasmuch as less than one-half of one percent of all elderly Americans are ever hospitalized for over 60 consecutive days, this kind of policy is essentially worthless for most people.

TAX BREAKS

Special Provisions

Take advantage of the various tax breaks available to senior citizens:

(1) Anyone 65 or older on the last day of the tax year can claim an extra exemption of $750 on his income tax return. This is in addition to the personal exemption of $750. Thus, a married couple who are both 65 or older can claim a total of four exemptions on their joint return.

(2) Anyone 65 or older, a United States citizen, unmarried, and with a gross income of under $3,100 does not have to file a tax return. A married couple (both partners 65 or older) need not file a joint return if their combined gross income is under $4,900. If only one partner has reached age 65, a tax return need only be filed if the couple's combined gross income is at least $4,150. (Anyone not required to file a return, who has had income tax withheld from his pay, should file anyway to get a refund on the tax withheld.)

(3) Social Security benefits are *not* taxable. Thus, if an individual has received Social Security benefits of $1,500 during the year, and also has income of $3,200 from wages and interest, tax is due only on the $3,200.

(4) Anyone past age 65 who sells a house can exclude from taxable income the entire profit from the sale—if the price is $35,000 or less. If the house is sold for more than $35,000, at least part of the profit is tax exempt, with the amount of the tax determined on a sliding scale.

(5) A retiree who is past age 65 may qualify for up to a 15 percent tax credit on that portion of his retirement income acquired from pensions, annuities, interest, dividends, and rents. To be eligible, he must have earned more than $600 in each of any 10 calendar years prior to the current one. Calculating this credit can be an involved process; an accountant or the local IRS office should be contacted for full instructions on eligibility and the proper method of computation.

Added Tax Information

For additional information about taxes in the retirement years, ask the local office of the Internal Revenue Service for a free copy of publication 554, *Tax Benefits for Older Americans.* The request may be made by telephone.

FINDING RETIREMENT BARGAINS

Special Services

Anyone approaching retirement age should begin looking for and asking about discounts frequently available to older people (or ask your State Commission on the Aging if it has a publication listing these discounts). Price reductions are often offered by public transportation systems, various movie theaters, concert halls, museums, and some stores. Banks frequently provide special services for senior citizens. In some cases, these discounts are available at age 65; in others, individuals are eligible as early as age 60.

RETIREMENT COMMUNITIES

Caution Necessary

Retirement communities have been developed in many parts of the country. Although these villages have proved desirable for individuals wishing to avoid inactive, lonely lives, take precautions to ensure that this dream existence doesn't become a nightmare. Developers sometimes fail to provide promised facilities, such as a recreation room, a swimming pool, or shuffleboard courts. Monthly maintenance costs, for which all residents are responsible, often rise far beyond what was projected. To be safe, only move into a retirement community that has all its recreational facilities completed, and says in writing precisely how much maintenance costs can be increased over the years.

Security

An important advantage of living in a retirement community is that security is usually good. There are regular patrols, particularly at night, by a private police force, and security guards are often located around the clock at the entrance to developments. Another advantage of these communities is that many of them provide all gardening and snow removal services for their residents.

APPENDICES

OFFICIAL STATE CONSUMER OFFICES

Alabama

Consumer Protection Officer
Office of the Governor
138 Adams Avenue
Montgomery, Alabama 36104
Tel.: (205) 269-7477
Toll free: 1-800-392-5658

Alaska

Office of Attorney General
Pouch "K"
State Capitol
Juneau, Alaska 99801
Tel.: (907) 586-5391

Arizona

Office of Attorney General
159 State Capitol Building
Phoenix, Arizona 85007
Tel.: (602) 271-5579

Arkansas

Consumer Protection Division
Office of Attorney General
Justice Building
Little Rock, Arkansas 72201
Tel.: (501) 376-3871

California

Department of Consumer Affairs
1020 N Street
Sacramento, California 95814
Tel.: (916) 445-4465

Colorado

Office of Consumer Affairs
Office of Attorney General
112 East 14th Avenue
Denver, Colorado 80203
Tel.: (303) 892-3501

Connecticut

Department of Consumer Protection
State Office Building
Hartford, Connecticut 06115
Tel.: (203) 566-4999

Delaware

Consumer Affairs Division
Department of Community Affairs and
  Economic Development
704 Delaware Avenue
Wilmington, Delaware 19801
Tel.: (302) 658-9251

District of Columbia

Consumers Retail Credit Division
D.C. Department of Economic Develop-
  ment
614 H Street, N.W., Room 306
Washington, D.C. 20001
Tel.: (202) 629-2618

Florida

Consumer Advisor to the Governor
Office of the Governor
State Capitol
Tallahassee, Florida 32304
Tel.: (904) 222-1900

Georgia

Assistant Attorney General for
  Deceptive Practices
Office of Attorney General
132 State Judicial Building
Atlanta, Georgia 30334
Tel.: (404) 656-3346

Hawaii

Director of Consumer Protection
Office of the Governor
250 S. King Street
602 Kamamalu Building
Honolulu, Hawaii 96811
Tel.: (808) 531-5995

Idaho

Deputy Attorney General for
  Consumer Protection
Office of Attorney General
State Capitol
Boise, Idaho 83702
Tel.: (208) 384-2400

Illinois

Consumer Fraud Section
Office of Attorney General
134 N. La Salle Street
Chicago, Illinois 60602
Tel.: (312) 641-1988

Indiana

Consumer Protection Division
Office of Attorney General
215 State House
Indianapolis, Indiana 46204
Tel.: (317) 633-5512

Iowa

Consumer Protection Division
Iowa Department of Justice
220 East 13th Court
Des Moines, Iowa 50319
Tel.: (515) 281-5926

Kansas

Consumer Protection Division
Office of Attorney General
State Capitol
Topeka, Kansas 66612
Tel.: (913) 296-3751

Kentucky

Consumer Protection Division
Office of Attorney General
309 Shelby Street
Frankfort, Kentucky 40601
Tel.: (502) 564-6607
Toll free: 1-800-372-2960

Louisiana

Consumer Protection Division
Office of the Governor
P.O. Box 44091
State Capitol
Baton Rouge, Louisiana 70804
Tel.: (504) 389-2525

Maine

Consumer Protection Division
Office of the Attorney General
State House
Augusta, Maine 04330
Tel.: (207) 289-3716

Maryland

Protection Division
Office of Attorney General
One South Calvert Street
Baltimore, Maryland 21202
Tel.: (301) 383-3713

Massachusetts

Executive Office of Consumer Affairs
State Office Building
100 Cambridge Street
Boston, Massachusetts 02202
Tel.: (617) 727-7755

Michigan

Consumer Protection and
  Antitrust Division
Office of Attorney General
Law Building
Lansing, Michigan 48902
Tel.: (517) 373-1152

Minnesota

Assistant Attorney General
  for Consumer Protection
Office of Attorney General
102 State Capitol
St. Paul, Minnesota 55155
Tel.: (612) 296-3353

Mississippi

Consumer Protection Division
Office of Attorney General
State Capitol
Jackson, Mississippi 39201
Tel.: (601) 354-7134

Missouri

Consumer Protection Division
Office of Attorney General
Supreme Court Building
Jefferson City, Missouri 65101
Tel.: (314) 751-3555

Montana

Department of Business Regulation
805 North Main Street
Helena, Montana 59601
Tel.: (406) 449-3163

Nebraska

Assistant Attorney General for
  Consumer Protection & Antitrust
Office of Attorney General
State Capitol
Lincoln, Nebraska 68509
Tel.: (402) 471-2211

Nevada

Deputy Attorney General for
  Consumer Affairs
Office of Attorney General
Supreme Court Building
Carson City, Nevada 89701
Tel.: (702) 882-7401

New Hampshire

Consumer Protection Division
Office of Attorney General
State House Annex
Concord, New Hampshire 03301
Tel.: (603) 271-3641

New Jersey

Deputy Attorney General for
  Consumer Protection
Office of Attorney General
State Office Building
1100 Raymond Building
Newark, New Jersey 07102
Tel.: (201) 648-2478

New Mexico

Consumer Protective Division
Office of Attorney General
Supreme Court Building
Box 2246
Santa Fe, New Mexico 87501
Tel.: (505) 827-5237

New York

Consumer Protection Board
Office of the Governor
Twin Towers Office Building
99 Washington Avenue
Albany, New York 12210
Tel.: (518) 474-3516

North Carolina

Consumer Protection Division
Office of Attorney General
Box 629
Justice Building
Raleigh, North Carolina 27602
Tel.: (919) 829-7741

North Dakota

Consumer Fraud Division
State Capitol
Bismarck, North Dakota 58501
Tel.: (701) 224-2217

Ohio

Consumer Frauds and Crimes Section
Office of Attorney General
State House Annex
Columbus, Ohio 43215
Tel.: (614) 469-4986

Oklahoma

Consumer Protection
Office of Attorney General
112 State Capitol
Oklahoma City, Oklahoma 73105
Tel.: (405) 521-3205

Oregon

Consumer Protection Division
Office of Attorney General
555 State Office Building
Portland, Oregon 97201

Pennsylvania

Bureau of Consumer Protection
Department of Justice
25 South Third Street
Harrisburg, Pennsylvania 17101
Tel.: (717) 787-3919

Rhode Island

Consumer Affairs
Office of Attorney General
Providence County Court House
Providence, Rhode Island 02903
Tel.: (401) 831-6850

South Carolina

Office of Consumer Affairs
Governor's Office
State House
Columbia, South Carolina 29201
Tel.: (803) 758-3261

South Dakota

Commissioner of Consumer Affairs
Office of Attorney General
State Capitol
Pierre, South Dakota 57501
Tel.: (605) 224-3215

Tennessee

Consumer Protection
Office of Attorney General
Supreme Court Building
Nashville, Tennessee 37219
Tel.: (615) 741-2041

Texas

Antitrust and Consumer Protection
    Division
Office of Attorney General
P.O. Box 12548
Capitol Station
Austin, Texas 78711
Tel.: (512) 475-3288

Utah

Consumer Protection
Office of Attorney General
State Capitol
Salt Lake City, Utah 84114
Tel.: (801) 328-5261

Vermont

Consumer Protection Bureau
Box 981
Burlington, Vermont 05401
Tel.: (802) 864-0111

Virginia

Special Assistant to Governor on
    Minority Groups and Consumer Affairs
Office of the Governor
Richmond, Virginia 23219
Tel.: (804) 770-2211

Washington

Consumer Protection and Antitrust
    Division
Office of Attorney General
1266 Dexter Horton Building
Seattle, Washington 98104
Tel.: (206) 464-7744

West Virginia

Office of Attorney General
State Capitol
Charleston, West Virginia 25305
Tel.: (304) 348-3377

Wisconsin
Consumer Affairs Coordinator
Department of Justice
State Capitol
Madison, Wisconsin 53702
Tel.: (608) 266-7340

Wyoming
Office of Attorney General
210 Capitol Building
Cheyenne, Wyoming 82001
Tel.: (307) 777-7384

Index

Air conditioners, home, 110-111
    cost, 111
    repairs, 123-124
    selecting, 110
Air travel, 269, 271-274
    bargain fares, 271-272
    charter, 273-274
    complaints, 273
    luggage, 272
Amtrak, 274-275
Annuities, 297-298
Apartments
    federal rent assistance, 82
    landlords, 83, 84
    leases, 82-83
    renting vs. buying, 64-65
    shopping for, 81-82
Appliances, 99-112
    See also specific items
    gas vs. electricity, 100
    operating costs, 99-100
    repairs, 101, 121-123
    shopping tips, 99-101
Aspirin, 39-40
Assets, 1-2
    defined, 1
Assigned-risk pool, automobile insurance, 220
Audit, income tax, 227, 244-246
Automobile infant seats, 95
Automobile insurance, 200, 216-220
    accident reporting, 220
    assigned-risk pool, 220
    collision coverage, 217
    comprehensive, 218
    deductible, 217
    "good student" discount, 219-220
    insurance companies, 218
    liability coverage, 216
    medical coverage, 216
    no-fault, 216
    rates, 218-220

    uninsured motorist coverage, 217
Automobiles, 131-153
    batteries, 152-153
    diesel, 133-134
    financing, 131, 138-139
    gas, 134-135, 148-149
    leasing, 142-144
    negotiating the purchase, 135-137
    new car buying, 132-139
    operating costs, 131
    renting, 144-145
    repairs, 131-132, 145-148
    sales frauds, 137
    second car, buying, 132-133
    selling your own, 145
    sizes, 133
    used, 131, 140-142

Baby foods, buying, 10, 26
Baby furniture, buying, 94-95
Bacon, 19
Bakeries, 13
Bankruptcy, 250, 261-262
    chapter XIII, 263
    cost of, 261
Banks, 156-162, 189-190
    checking accounts, 156, 162-164
    commercial banks, 156
    loans, 189-190
    Mexican banks, 161-162
    mutual savings banks, 156
Batteries, 15-16
Beds and mattresses, buying, 90, 93-95
Beef, buying, 15, 17-18
    See also Meat, buying
    fat content, 17
    freezer use and, 18
    grades, 17
    labels and, 17
Beneficiary clause, life insurance, 204
Better Business Bureau, 264

Bicycling, 286-287
    insurance, 287
Bills, budget keeping and, 4
Binoculars, 285
Blouses, buying, 56
Bonds, investing in, 155, 171-174
    corporate bonds, 172-174
    general obligation bonds, 155
    municipal bonds, 155, 174
    revenue bonds, 155
    treasury bonds, 172
    United States savings bonds, 171-172
Books, collecting, 288-289
Bread, buying, 23
Brokers
    real estate, 65, 85-86
    stock, 164-166
Budget, family, 1-9
    assets and liabilities, 1-2
    debts, 6
    defining goals, 2-3
    emergency funds, 5
    everyday expenses, 4-5, 8
    family involvement, 8
    fixed expenses, 4
    impulse buying, 7
    income estimating, 3
    reducing expenses, 6, 7
    spending patterns, 5-6
    spending priorities, 6
    unnecessary purchases, 6-7
    unpaid bills, 5
Burglary prevention, 120-121
Bus travel, 275-276
Butcher shops, 13
Butter, buying, 22

Camping, 269, 281-282
Candy shops, 13
Capital gains tax, 243-244
Carpeting, buying, 95-99
    costs, 97-98
    choosing fibers, 95-97
    labels, 97
    life expectancy, 98
    rugs, 98-99
CB radios, 288
Cereals, breakfast, buying, 24
Certificates of deposit (CD's), 159-160
Chapter 13 ("wage earner's plan"), 263
Charities, 240-242

Checking accounts, 156, 162-164
    cost of, 162
    interest-paying accounts, 164
    overdraft protection, 162-163
    regular, 162
    special, 162
    stopping payment, 163
Cheese, buying, 16, 22
Childbearing expenses, 42-43
Children's clothes, buying, 57-58
    shoes, 57-58
Chili, buying, 16
Chiropractors, 44-45
Christmas clubs, 161
Cigarettes See Smoking
Cleaning of clothes, 58-61
Clinics, medical, 33
Closing costs of home mortgages, 63-64, 76
Clothing, buying, 48-62
    See also specific items
    care and maintenance of, 58-61
    garment life, 60
    wardrobe planning, 49, 55
Codicils, wills and, 257
Coffee, buying, 25-26
Coins, gold, investing in, 177-178
Collision automobile insurance, 217
Commercial banks, 156
    interest paid by, 156
Common stock, 155
Comprehensive automobile insurance, 218
Condominiums, 77-79
    advantages and disadvantages, 77-78
    maintenance fees, 78
    resale potential, 78-79
    rip-offs, 78
    swapping for vacations, 278
Consumer protection, 264-265
    class action suits, 265
    complaints, 264-265
    state consumer offices, 307-310
Contract(s), 265
Contractors, home improvement, 114-116
    and frauds, 115-116
Convenience foods, cost of, 24-25
Cooperatives, food, 26-27
Corporate bonds, 172-174
    interest paid on, 173
    ratings, 172-173

Coupons, food, 15, 16
Credit, 180-188, 196-197
    advantages and disadvantages, 181-182
    cash vs. credit, 181
    creditworthiness, 183-184
    how much, 184
    sources of, 184-185
Credit bureaus, 196
Credit cards, 180-182, 185-188
    applying for, 186
    cash advance, 186
    disputes, 187
    interest rates, 186
    liability and, 188
    types of, 180, 185-188
Credit rating, 183-184, 196-197
Credit unions, 157-158, 188-189
    life insurance, 157-158
    loans, 188-189
    savings in, 157
Cribs, buying, 90, 94-95
Cruises, 269, 276

Dairies, shopping at, 13
Dating of food, 15, 26
Debts, 6, 197-198
    adjusting payment schedules, 197
    budgeting and, 6
    collection agencies, 197
    debt consolidation loans, 197-198
    financial counseling, 198
Deductibles
    automobile insurance, 217
    health insurance, 211
Deductions, income tax, 227, 235-237
Dental care, 40-41
Diamonds, investing in, 178
Disability insurance, 200, 214-216
    elimination period, 215
    "future increase" rider, 215
    need for, 214
    state programs, 216
Dishwashers, buying, 106-107
Dividends, life insurance, 206-207
"Double indemnity" clause, life insurance, 205
Dresses, buying, 56
Drugs (medications), 30, 37-40
    advertisements for, 39-40
    aspirin, 39
    generic, 37-38
    mail-order sales, 38

over-the-counter, 38-40
saving on, 37-40
Dryers, buying, 106

Education
    cost of, 195
    income tax deduction for, 236
    loans and, 193-195
Eggs, buying, 21-22
Electric skillets, buying, 112
Elimination period, disability insurance, 215
Emergency funds, budget-keeping and, 5
Energy, saving on, 124-129
Escrow accounts, 73-74
Estate taxes, 258
Eurailpass, 275
Everyday expenses, budgeting and, 4-5, 8
Executor, wills and, 256
Exemptions, income tax, 227, 232-233
Eye care, 41-42

FAIR insurance plan, 224
Fat content, meat, 17
    hamburger, 18
Federal Crime Insurance, 224
Federal Deposit Insurance Corporation, 157
Federal Housing Administration mortgages, 75-76
Federal Savings and Loan Insurance Corporation, 157
FHA Mortgages, 75-76
Financing, automobiles, 131, 138-139
Fish, buying, 20-21
Fishing tackle, buying, 284-285
Fixed expenses, budgeting and, 4
Food, buying, 10-29
    comparison shopping, 13
    costs, 10, 13, 14
    coupons, 15, 16
    eating out and, 28-29
    food labels, 15-16
    frozen foods, 13
    freshness dating, 14, 26
    house brands, 16
    impulse buying, 12
    shopping lists, 10, 12
    typical buying patterns, 11-12
    unit pricing, 14
    Universal Product Code System, 14
    where to shop, 13

Food co-ops, 26-27
Frankfurters, buying, 18-19
Freezers, buying, 103
Freshness dating, food, 15
Frozen foods, 13, 25
Fruits and vegetables, buying, 22-23
Furniture, buying, 90-95
    deceitful selling practices, 90
    for babies, 90, 94-95
    quality, 91
    sales, 91
    unfinished, 92
    upholstered, 92-93
    wood, 91-92

Garage door openers, 121
Gardening, 11, 27-28
Gasoline, automobile, saving on, 134-135, 148-149
Gems, precious, investing in, 178-179
General obligation bonds, 155
Goals, defining for a budget, 2-3
Gold, investing in, 156, 177-178
    coins, 177-178
Golden Eagle Passport, 282
Golf, 289
Greyhound Bus, travel on, 276
Guaranteed (Student) Loan Program, 194
Guarantees, product, 265

Ham, buying, 15, 19
Hamburger, buying, 18-19
    fat content, 18
Health care, 30-47
    blood, donating, 36-37
    childbearing expenses, 42-43
    chiropractors, 44-45
    clinics, 33
    community health resources, 34
    costs, 35-36
    dental care, 40-41
    drugs and medications, 30, 37-40
    eye care, 41-42
    Health Maintenance Organizations (HMO's), 43-44
    hearing problems, 40
    hospitals, 30, 31, 34-36
    income tax deductions, 237
    Medicaid, 33-34
    nursing homes, 30-31, 46-47
    physicians and, 30, 31-34

Health insurance, 43-44, 199-200, 209-214
    cancelability, 211-212
    claims, 213
    deductible, 211
    disability, 214-216
    group, 209
    Health Maintenance Organizations (HMO's), 43-44
    mail-order, 213-214
    major medical, 209-210
    Medicare, 301-305
    renewability, 211-212
    service vs. cash indemnity, 211
    shopping for, 212-213
Health Maintenance Organizations (HMO's), 43-44
Hearing aids, 40
Hearing problems, 40
"Holder in due course," 192
Home improvements, 113-121
    contractors, 113, 114-116
    costs, 113
    do-it-yourself, 118-121, 122, 123
    frauds, 113, 115-116
Home office, tax deduction for, 236
Home Owners Warranty, 67
Homeowners insurance, 200, 221-225
    amount of coverage, 222-223
    broad form, 221
    claims, 224-225
    covering possessions, 221
    crime, 223-224
    earthquake, 223
    FAIR plan, 224
    flood, 223
    "inflation guard" endorsement, 222-223
    inventory, 224
    liability, 222
    rates, 223
Home Protection Program, 69-70
Hospital care and services, 30, 31, 34-36
    accreditation of hospitals, 34
    admission, 35
    choosing, 34
    nursing care, 35
    saving on, 34-36
    tests, diagnostic, 34-35
Hostels, 277-278
Hot dogs, buying, 18-19
Hotels, 269, 277
House brands, food, 16

House moving, 89
Houseboating, 283
Houses, buying and selling, 63-81, 84-89
    See also Housing
Housing, 63-89
    building a home, 70-71
    buying vs. renting, 64-65
    capital gains tax, 243-244
    closing costs, 63-64, 76
    homebuyer complaints, 65-66
    inspecting a house, 69, 77
    legal matters, 76-77
    mortgages, 63, 71-77
    new houses vs. old, 66-68
    selling a house, 84
    shopping for homes, 65-66
    swapping homes for vacations, 278
    warranties, 67, 69-70

Income averaging, 243
Income tax(es), 227-247
    accountants and preparers, 229
    alimony and, 240
    audits, 227, 244-246
    charities and, 240
    deductions, 227, 230-231, 235-237
    end-of-year strategies, 242
    errors, 234-235
    exemptions, 227, 232-233
    income averaging, 243
    income reporting, 229-230
    joint vs. separate returns, 231-232
    late filing, 234
    medical care deductions, 237
    publications, 228
    record keeping and, 233-234
    retirement accounts and, 239-240
    retirement, advantages during, 305-306
    tax court, 246-247
Individual Retirement Account (IRA), 239-240, 295-297
Installment loans, 181, 191-193
Insurance, 199-226
    See also specific kinds
    agents and brokers, 200
    complaints, 226
Interest rates, bank, 156, 158-160
    certificates of deposit, 159-160
    computing, 158
    grace days, 159
International Vacation Club, 277

Investment clubs, 160-161

Keogh Plan, 239-240, 294-297

Lamb, buying, 19
Land, investing in, 176-177
    See also Real estate
Landlords, 83-84
Lawyers, 249, 250
    choosing, 250-251
    complaints against, 253-254
    fees, 251-252
    need for, 250
Leases, apartment, 82-83
Leasing, automobile, 142-144
Legal Aid Society, 252
Legal matters, 249-263
    See also Lawyers; Small Claims Court; Wills
    class action suits, 265
Liabilities, net worth and, 1-2
Liability insurance
    automobile, 216
    homeowners, 222
Life insurance, 1, 74, 188, 199, 201-209
    amount required, 202
    beneficiary, 204
    budgeting and, 1
    dividends, 206-207
    double indemnity clause, 205
    exchanging policies, 207-208
    group policies, 208
    loans on, 188
    military, 208
    mortgage insurance, 74
    need for, 201-202
    savings bank, 208
    shopping for, 205-207
    Social Security and, 202
    term, 203
    variable, 204
    waiver of premium clause, 205
    whole life, 203-204
Liquor, saving on, 29
Load and no-load mutual funds, 170
Loans, 181, 188-196
    banks, 189-190
    credit unions, 188-189
    debt consolidation, 197-198
    education, 193-195
    installment, 181, 191-193
    life insurance, 188
    mortgages, 191

passbook loans, 189
savings and loan associations, 189-190
"sharks", 195-196
small loan companies, 190-191
Locks, burglary prevention and, 120-121
Luggage, buying, 280-281
Luncheon meats, buying, 19-20

Mail-order health insurance, 213-214
Major medical health insurance, 209-210
Margarine, buying, 22
Margin, investing in stocks on, 168-169
Meat, buying, 17-20
    bacon, 19
    fat content, 17
    freezer use and, 18
    grades, 17
    ham, 19
    hamburger, 18
    hot dogs, 18
    labels and, 17
    lamb, 19
    luncheon meats, 19-20
    veal, 19
Medicaid, 33-34
Medical care and services
    See Health care; Health insurance;
    Physicians
Medicare, 301-305
    deductibles, 301-302
    errors, 303
    nursing homes and, 302
    Part A, 301-302
    Part B, 302-303
    supplementing, 303
Men's clothes, buying, 52-55
Microwave ovens, buying, 91, 104-105
    disadvantages of, 104
Military life insurance, 208
Milk, buying, 21
Mobile homes, 79-81
    building codes, 79-80
    depreciation, 80
    parks, 81
    shipping, 81
    types, 79
Mortgages, home, 68, 71-77
    calculating payments, 73
    defined, 63
    escrow accounts, 73-74

FHA, 75-76
foreclosure, 74
life insurance, 74
paying off, 76-77
rates, 71
shopping for, 71-72
tax benefits, 71
Veterans Administration, 76
variable interest, 74-75
Motels, 269, 277
Motorcycling, 287-288
Moving (movers), 86-89
    best time, 86
    costs, 87
    estimates, 86
    house moving, 89
    income tax deduction for, 236-237
    insurance, 88
    packing, 88
    performance record of companies, 87
    self-moving, 89
    tipping movers, 89
Municipal bonds, 155, 174
    general obligation, 155
    revenue, 155
    tax exemptions, 174
Mutual funds, 155, 169-171
    load funds, 170
    "muni" funds, 170
    no-load funds, 170
    types of, 169-170

National Audubon Society, 282
National Direct Student Loans, 194
National Park Service, 282
Negotiable Order of Withdrawal accounts, 164
Neighborhood Legal Service, 252
Net worth, 1
No-fault automobile insurance, 216
No-load and load mutual funds, 170
Nursing homes, 30-31, 46-47
    shopping for, 46-47
    Medicare, 302

Orange juice, buying, 16, 24-25
Ovens See Ranges

Painters, hiring, 119
Paints, 118-119
Pension plans, 294
    budgeting and, 1

Physicians, 30, 31-34
  choosing, 31-32
  complaints against, 33
  office visits and house calls, 33
Playground equipment, buying, 285-286
Postage stamps, investing in, 179
Poultry, buying, 16, 20
Preferred stock, 155
Property taxes, 228, 247-248
  appeal procedures, 228, 247-248
  assessment, 228
  exemptions, 248
  rates, 228
Protein value of foods, 18, 19, 20

Rafting, 282
Raincoats, buying, 55
Ranges, 103-104
  gas vs. electric, 104
  self-cleaning, 103-104
  shopping advice, 103
Rating, credit, 183-184, 196-197
Real estate, investing in, 155-156, 174-177
  advantages, 174-175
  guidelines for, 175-176
  raw land, 176-177
Realtors, 65, 85-86
Record-keeping, 267-268
  and taxes, 233-234
Recreation, 269-270, 281-290
  bicycling, 286-287
  camping, 269, 281-282
  fishing, 284-285
  golf, 289
  houseboating, 283
  motorcycling, 287-288
  national parks, 282
  rafting, 282
  sailing, 283
  skiing, 283-284
  swimming, 289-290
Recreational vehicles, and camping, 281-282
Refrigerators, 101-102
  choosing the size of, 101
  costs, 102
  guarantee, 102
  when to buy, 101
Renting, automobile, 144-145
Repairs and repairmen
  air conditioner, 123-124

appliances, 101, 121-123
automobiles, 131-132, 145-148
television, 123
Restaurants, eating in, 28-29
Retirement, 291-306
  annuities, 297-298
  discounts during, 306
  income, sources of, 292
  Individual Retirement Account, 239-240, 295-297
  investing for, 293
  Keogh Plan, 239-240, 294-297
  living expenses, 292
  Medicare, 301-305
  pension plans, 294
  retirement communities, 306
  Social Security, 202, 291-292, 298-301
  tax advantages, 305-306
Revenue bonds, 155
Rugs, 98-99

Safe-deposit boxes, 239, 257-258, 266-267
Sailing, 283
Salary, increases in, 4
Sales on food, 14-15
Savings, 3, 154, 156-162
  budget-keeping, 3
  investment clubs, 160
  savings accounts, 154, 156-162, 293
  where to keep your money, 156-158
Savings accounts, 154, 156-162, 293
  certificates of deposit, 159-160
  Christmas clubs, 161
  insurance on, 157
  interest on, 154, 158-159
  regular accounts, 156
  term accounts, 156
Savings and loan associations, 156-157, 189-190
  interest paid by, 156
  loans from, 189-190
Savings bank life insurance, 208
Savings bonds, United States, 171-172
  interest, 171
  series E & H, 172
Servicemen's Group Life Insurance, 208-209
Sewing machines, buying, 111
Shoes, buying, 48, 54-55, 57-58
  caring for, 59
Shopping lists, 10, 12

Sierra Club, 282
Skiing, 283-284
Small claims court, 259-261
Small loan companies, 190-191
Smoking, stopping, 45-46
Social Security, 291-292, 298-301
    benefits, calculating, 298-300
    spouse benefits, 300
Soft drinks, 25
Soups, buying, 25
Spending, 5-6, 7, 8
    cutting, 6, 7
    patterns, 5-6
    priorities, 6
Stamps, postage, investing in, 179
State consumer offices, 307-310
Stereos, buying, 108-110
Stocks, 154-155, 164-169
    brokers, 155, 164-166
    certificates, 169, 267
    choosing a stock, 166-169
    common, 155
    discount brokerage houses, 165-166
    margin, buying on, 168-169
    Monthly Investment Plan, 168
    mutual funds and, 155
    preferred, 155
Strollers, baby, buying, 95
Suits (clothing), men's, 53-54
Summer camps, 290
Sunglasses, 61-62
Surgery, 36
    unneccessary, 36
Sweaters, buying, 56
Swimming, recreation and, 289-290
Swimming pools, 113, 116-117

Tax court, 246-247
Taxes, 227-248
    See also Capital gains tax; Estate
    tax, Income tax; Property tax
Telephone bills, cutting 129-130
Television sets, buying, 107-108
    color vs. black-and-white, 107
    life expectancy, 108
    repairs, 123
    trade-ins, 108
Term life insurance, 203
Ties, buying, 55
Tipping, 278-279
Tires, 150-152
    buying, 150-151
    caring for, 151-152

Trailways Bus, travel on, 276
Train travel, 269, 274-275
    European trains, 275
Travel, 269-281
    airline, 269, 271-274
    bus, 275-276
    cruises, 269
    foreign currency, 279-280
    health during, 276, 277
    hotels and motels, 269, 277-278
    insurance, 225-226, 272
    luggage, 280-281
    swapping homes and condominiums, 278
    tipping, 278-279
    train, 269, 274-275
    travel agents, 270
    traveler's checks, 279
Travel agents, 270
Travel Masters, 270-271
Traveler's checks, 279
Treasury bills, 172
Treasury bonds, 172
Trusts, 259

Uninsured motorist insurance, 217
Unit-pricing, supermarket, 14
United Student Aid Fund, 194-195
Universal Product Code System, 14
Upholstered furniture, 92-93

Vacation insurance, 225-226
Vacuum cleaners, buying, 111-112
Variable interest mortgages, 74-75
Variable life insurance, 204
Veal, buying, 19
Vegetable gardens, 11, 27-28
Vegetables and fruits, buying, 22-23
Veterans Administration mortgages, 76

"Waiver of premium" clause, life insurance, 205
Wallpapering, 119-120
Warranties
    appliances, 102
    house, 67, 69-70
Washing machines, buying, 105-106
Water heaters, buying, 112
Wave Project, 252
Waterbeds, buying, 94
Western River Guides' Association, 282
Whole life insurance, 203-204
Wilderness Society, 282

Wills, 249, 254-258
  codicil, 257
  executor, 256
Women's clothing, buying, 55-56

Wood furniture, buying, 91-92
Workmen's Compensation disability
  program, 216